INDIAN TRANSNATIONALISM ONLINE

Studies in Migration and Diaspora

Series Editor:
Anne J. Kershen, Queen Mary, University of London, UK

Studies in Migration and Diaspora is a series designed to showcase the interdisciplinary and multidisciplinary nature of research in this important field. Volumes in the series cover local, national and global issues and engage with both historical and contemporary events. The books will appeal to scholars, students and all those engaged in the study of migration and diaspora. Amongst the topics covered are minority ethnic relations, transnational movements and the cultural, social and political implications of moving from 'over there', to 'over here'.

Also in the series:

Inhabiting Borders, Routes Home
Youth, Gender, Asylum
Ala Sirriyeh
ISBN 978-1-4094-4495-4

Second-Generation Transnationalism and Roots Migration
Cross-Border Lives
Susanne Wessendorf
ISBN 978-1-4094-4015-4

Cultures in Refuge
Seeking Sanctuary in Modern Australia
Edited by Anna Hayes and Robert Mason
ISBN 978-1-4094-3475-7

Whiteness and Postcolonialism in the Nordic Region
Exceptionalism, Migrant Others and National Identities
Edited by Kristín Loftsdóttir and Lars Jensen
ISBN 978-1-4094-4481-7

European Identity and Culture
Narratives of Transnational Belonging
Edited by Rebecca Friedman and Markus Thiel
ISBN 978-1-4094-3714-7

Indian Transnationalism Online
New Perspectives on Diaspora

Edited by

AJAYA KUMAR SAHOO
University of Hyderabad, India

JOHANNES G. DE KRUIJF
Utrecht University, the Netherlands

Routledge
Taylor & Francis Group

LONDON AND NEW YORK

First published 2014 by Ashgate Publishing

2 Park Square, Milton Park, Abingdon, Oxon OX14 4RN
711 Third Avenue, New York, NY 10017, USA

Routledge is an imprint of the Taylor & Francis Group, an informa business

First issued in paperback 2016

British Library Cataloguing in Publication Data
A catalogue record for this book is available from the British Library.

The Library of Congress has cataloged the printed edition as follows:
Indian transnationalism online : new perspectives on diaspora / edited by Ajaya Kumar Sahoo and Johannes G. de Kruijf.
    pages cm.—(Studies in migration and diaspora)
Includes bibliographical references and index.
ISBN 978-1-4724-1913-2 (hardback)
1. East Indian diaspora. 2. East Indians—Foreign
countries--Ethnic identity. 3. Transnationalism. 4. Internet and immigrants. 5. Internet—
Social aspects. I. Sahoo, Ajaya Kumar, editor of compilation. II. Kruijf, Johannes G. de, editor of compilation.
DS432.5.I447 2014
304.80954—dc23
                                                                    2013029922

ISBN 978-1-4724-1913-2 (hbk)
ISBN 978-1-138-25561-6 (pbk)

Contents

SECTION I: IDENTITY

SECTION II: POWER

List of Figures and Table

Figures

Table

Notes on Contributors

Emilia Bachrach is a doctoral candidate in the Department of Asian Studies at the University of Texas-Austin where she studies Hindi and Gujarati literature and religion in India. Emilia's dissertation, tentatively titled 'The Living Tradition of Hagiography in the Vallabh Sect of Contemporary Gujarat', discusses the ways in which members of the Vallabh Sampraday ritually read and interpret pre-modern hagiographic literature as a way to negotiate between ideals inherited in the past and everyday life in the present. Emilia holds an MTS degree in South Asian Religions from Harvard Divinity School and a BA in Religious Studies from Smith College.

Urmila Goel is a researcher in social and cultural anthropology based in Berlin (Germany). She is currently working on a virtual ethnography of the internet portal *Indernet*, linking internet studies with migration studies, critical racism theory, postcolonial theory and gender studies, and is interested in particular in methodical challenges of virtual ethnographies. She conducts her ethnographic research mainly among people marked as Indian in German-speaking countries. Besides working on the *Indernet* she has conducted research projects on questions of migration history, citizenship, and religion as well as gender and sexuality, and has co-edited two books on migration from South Asia to Germany. She is the author of *Economists, Entrepreneurs and the Pursuit of Economics* (1998).

Sumana Kasturi is a Ph.D. Research Scholar at the Department of Communication, Sarojin Naidu School of Arts & Communication, University of Hyderabad, India, and Resident Director of the American Institute for Foreign Study (AIFS), Hyderabad.

Johannes G. de Kruijf is Assistant Professor in the Department of Cultural Anthropology at Utrecht University, the Netherlands. His research interests include migration, diaspora, ethnicity, and multiculturalism. He is the author of *Guyana Junction: Globalisation, Localisation, and the Production of East Indianness* (2006).

Vinay Lal has been teaching History and Asian American Studies at the University of California, Los Angeles since 1993. Vinay writes widely on Indian history, the popular and public culture of India (especially cinema), the Indian diaspora, global politics, contemporary American politics, and the politics of knowledge systems. His books include *The History of History: Politics and Scholarship in Modern*

India (2003; new edition, 2005); *Of Cricket, Guinness and Gandhi: Essays on Indian History and Culture* (2003); *Introducing Hinduism* (2005; translations into Spanish, Finnish, and Korean; new edition published as *Introducing Hinduism: A Graphic Guide*, 2010); and *The Other Indians: A Political and Cultural History of South Asians in America* (2008).

Ananda Mitra is Professor in the Department of Communication, Wake Forest University, North Carolina, USA. His research focuses on the role of new digital technologies in shaping everyday life practices that range from the use of computers in teaching to the way in which the marginalised can gain a voice through the use of the Internet. His publications include: *Alien Technology: Television and Popular Culture in India* (1999), *Coping with Modern Mysteries* (2012), *Needs Assessment* (2012), a 12-volume series called *Digital Life*, and numerous articles in peer-reviewed journals.

Usha Raman is Associate Professor and Head, Department of Communication, Sarojin Naidu School of Arts & Communication, University of Hyderabad, India. Her research has been in the fields of cultural studies of science, science and health communication, clinician-patient communication, children's media, and the impact of new technologies on communication within and between different communities. She is the author of *Writing for the Media* (2009).

Mirian Santos Ribeiro de Oliveira was awarded her Ph.D. in Sociology in 2012 from Universidade de São Paulo. She is currently a Researcher at the Asian Studies Lab, Universidade de São Paulo. Her study on emigration and Indian (trans) national identities included field research in India from December 2010 to May 2011. Her thesis, *The Nation and its Emigrants: Analysis of Contemporary Hindu Nationalist Discourse on the 'Hindu community abroad'* (Portuguese) (2012), is currently under review for publication.

Ajaya Kumar Sahoo is Assistant Professor and Director of the Centre for Study of Indian Diaspora at the University of Hyderabad. His research interests include migration, diaspora, transnationalism and ageing. Some of his recent publications include: *Diaspora and Identity: Perspectives on South Asian Diaspora*, co-edited with Gabriel Sheffer (2013); *Indian Diaspora and Transnationalism*, co-edited with M. Baas and T. Faist (2012); and *Transnational Migrations: The Indian Diaspora*, co-edited with W. Safran and B. V. Lal (2009).

Ashish Saxena presently teaches at the Department of Sociology, Central University of Allahabad, India. His areas of research interest include development studies, subaltern and community studies in India; especially J&K and U.P. states (INDIA). He has contributed articles to journals such as *ICFAI Journal of International Relations*, *The Radical Humanist*, and *Journal of Security & Society*.

Heinz Scheifinger is a Lecturer in Sociology-Anthropology at the Universiti Brunei Darussalam, Brunei. His research focuses upon contemporary Hinduism, particularly the intersection of this religious tradition and the Internet, and his publications in this area include (2008) 'Hinduism and Cyberspace' in *Religion* 38 (3): 233–249, (2010) 'Internet Threats to Hindu Authority: *Puja* Ordering Websites and the *Kalighat* Temple' in *Asian Journal of Social Science* 38 (4): 636–656, and (2012) 'Hinduism and Hyper-Reality' in Possamai, A. (ed.), *Handbook of Hyper-Real Religions*.

Emily Skop is an Associate Professor of Geography in the Department of Geography and Environment Studies at the University of Colorado, Colorado Springs, USA. Her interests include international migration processes and the social and spatial constructions of racial/ethnic/gender identities in a variety of contexts. Dr Skop's accomplishments include a recent book, *The Immigration and Settlement of Asian Indians*, which includes 16 peer-reviewed book chapters and 18 peer-reviewed research articles, including ten in top journals in geography, as well as one in the flagship migration journal: *International Migration Review*.

Indian Transnationalism Online

Transnationalism is not a new phenomenon. Migrants have been maintaining linkages between spatial locations for centuries; from the Vikings in the ninth and tenth centuries to Italian migrants to Britain in the late nineteenth and early twentieth centuries. More recently, immigrants from the Indian subcontinent have established binary existences across, rather than within, continents – a condition facilitated by the arrival of telephones (land and mobile), videos and long-haul flights. However, the coming of the internet and its transformation into a user rather than a reader system revolutionized the world of the transnational and wrought re-evaluations of self-identity and the exercise of power in the virtual universe. With contributions from academics from a variety of disciplines, this book explores the way in which Indians in the Diaspora, and at home, have incorporated modern technology into the age-old experience of migration, settlement and the movement between *desh* (homeland) and *videsh* (another country).

The majority of the chapters in this volume focus on the various aspects of reflexive self-identity that the internet encourages and enables, but also questions. For example, one author asks just what is an 'Indian transnational'; is the term defining nationality or ethnicity? Another writer proposes that for female Indian bloggers on the internet, their virtual identity is not presented as what they are offline but rather what they would like to be perceived as online. In virtual space the choices are endless, particularly in that third space – one a contributor defines as being between 'the lived in' and the 'distant remembered'. As in the real world so in that of the internet, self-identity is not static but is a variable which is reconstructed in accordance with changes in lifestyle. For example, second generation Indian migrants in Germany created an *indernet*, a space for 'exploring and developing their Indian identity'. However, as these young people became more integrated into mainstream society their usage of the *indernet* grew less as the perception of their immigrant identity modified.

Studies of transnationalism tend to focus on those who migrate and the ways in which, in their new places of settlement, they put in place the linkages that facilitate their becoming transnationals. However, what this volume shows us is that the role of the internet in transnationalism is not one which stems solely from the *videsh*. It is a tool used by some religious sects in the *desh* to maintain – and spread – religious connectivity through the diaspora, ensuring in this way that the local becomes global. In a similar way, the internet has facilitated the virtual globalization of Hindu nationalism and raised the issue of the concept of citizenship in the global/virtual arena.

There is no doubting the impact of the world wide web on the Indian Diaspora and, indeed, diasporic communities generally. The internet ensures the retention of connectivity between home and away and the opportunity for constant self re-evaluation and positioning. This book demonstrates the versatility of the system and of the variety of those it serves. It also highlights the fact that it is a structure which may not be open to all, either due to cost or lack of technique. The implications of this on those who are excluded from the internet, and of the negative role of an internet used for corrupt purposes, are the unspoken questions that emerge from a reading of this book. It is a book which, though devoted to one specific group of diasporics, urges the reader to apply its theories and message to others, and by so doing enhance our understanding not only of transnationalism in the early decades of the twenty-first century, but also of the consequences of the arrival of technology in a centuries-old tradition.

Anne J. Kershen
Queen Mary University of London
Summer 2013

Acknowledgements

This volume has its origins in the International Seminar 'Indian Transnationalism Online: Ethnographic Explorations' held at the University of Hyderabad on the 26th and 27th March 2012. The seminar was jointly organised by the Centre for Study of Indian Diaspora, University of Hyderabad and the Department of Cultural Anthropology, Utrecht University. Over 20 eminent scholars from India and the Indian diaspora – working in the interdisciplinary field of Indian diaspora and transnationalism – participated in this seminar. We would like to thank all the participants for responding to the call for papers and participating in the seminar.

We would like to acknowledge and thank all the contributors to this volume who have cooperated in sending their revised papers on time, without which this volume would not have been possible.

We would like to thank Professor Ramakrishna Ramaswamy, the Vice Chancellor; Professor E. Haribabu, the Pro Vice Chancellor; and the Dean, School of Social Sciences of the University of Hyderabad for their encouragement and support in organising the seminar. We would also like to thank all the administrative staff of the University of Hyderabad, especially the Finance Section and the Development Section for their cooperation in making this seminar successful.

Ajaya would particularly like to thank the Centre for Study of Indian Diaspora for providing an intellectual environment and necessary infrastructural support. He would also like to thank his colleague Dr. Amit Mishra for his friendly support throughout. Without the cooperation of the students (M.Phil and Ph.D. students) of the Centre, this seminar would have been difficult to organise. Special thanks go to all the students of the Centre.

Johannes would particularly like to thank the Department of Cultural Anthropology for facilitating and supporting this collaboration from a distance. In particular he would like to thank Prof. Dr. Robben and Prof. Dr. Eisenlohr for their encouragement and intellectual input. He would also like to thank Mrs. Willemse for her practical assistance and the UU Committee on Internalization for their confidence in this project.

We would like to thank the following funding agencies who supported this seminar financially: **Centre for the Study of Indian Diaspora** (UGC Area Studies Program), University of Hyderabad; **Department of Anthropology & Advisory Committee on Internationalization**, Utrecht University; **Indian Council of Social Science Research** (ICSSR), New Delhi; and the **University with Potential for Excellence** (UPE Phase II), University of Hyderabad.

Finally we would like to thank Dr. Anne J. Kershen, Series Editor of 'Studies in Migration and Diaspora'; Neil Jordan, Senior Commissioning Editor; and Dymphna Evans, Publishing Director, Social Sciences of Ashgate Publishing for their guidance and support in bringing out the volume in time.

Ajaya Kumar Sahoo
Johannes G. de Kruijf

Glossary

Adi Shankara (also Shankaracharya): Hindu philosopher and Saint (788–820 A.D.).

Advaita Vedanta: School of Hindu philosophy and practice that gives a unifying interpretation of the ancient sacred texts the *Upanishads*.

Ashirwad: Hindi word meaning blessings.

Avatar: The online representation of the user or the user's online character or alter ego.

Bhajan: Any type of devotional song, forming an important part of religious life of Hindus.

Blog: (Weblog) an online journal or informational site that consists of 'posts' (discrete entries) usually displayed in reverse chronological order (with the most recent entry first).

Blogger: A person who keeps a blog.

Blogosphere: All blogs and their interconnections imagined as a collective whole.

Cyber(netic) space: (sense of) social setting that exists only within a computer space.

Dalit: A designation for a group of people traditionally regarded as untouchables in India.

Darshan: Glance of a deity, very holy person or artefact.

Desi: This refers mainly to the people, culture and tradition of the Indian subcontinent.

Diwali or Deepavali: Festival of lights; it is a popular Hindu festival.

Ganesh: One of the best-known and most widely worshipped deities in Hinduism.

Holi: Festival of colours; it is a popular Hindu festival.

Indernet: A virtual space founded by people identifying themselves as (second generation) Indians in Germany. The term is a blend of the German word for Indian 'Inder' and Internet.

Internet (or web) portal: A website that combines information from different sources and offers it in a uniform way. It can be used to access the Internet.

Internet: The technological system of connectivity that allows numerous computers to be able to communicate with each other.

Jagadguru: Guru (teacher or master) of the World.

Kali: Also known as Kālikā in Sanskrit, Kali is the Hindu goddess associated with empowerment.

Kanchi Kamakoti Peetham (or Kanchi *math* [Hindu monastery]): Religious institution based in the south Indian city of Kanchipuram. It has numerous followers amongst Indians living in diaspora. The total number of devotees runs into the millions.

Kanchi Shankaracharya: Head of the Kanchi Kamakoti Peetham.

Kannada: An Indian language, predominantly spoken in the South Indian state of Karnataka.

Kirtan: Call-and-response chanting performed in India's *bhakti* devotional traditions.

Krishna: Literally the eighth avatar of the Vedic Supreme God Vishnu in Hinduism.

Lurkers: A member of a website or online group who does not actively participate but observes instead.

Marginalised groups: Mainly refers to the minority groups such as the Scheduled Castes (SCs), Scheduled Tribes (STs) and Other Backward Castes (OBCs) who are in the lower limit of social standing in India.

Multi-player virtual (or online) games: Online video games that allow large numbers of players to participate simultaneously.

Narbs: Narrative bits that users generate on online platforms (such as blogs). These bits together serve to build a specific identity that then is put to service in creating a presence online and participating in communities online.

Non-resident Indian: A citizen of India who holds an Indian passport and has temporarily emigrated to another country for six months or more for work, residence or any other purpose.

Person of Indian origin: A person of Indian ancestry (other than from Pakistan, Bangladesh, and some other countries) who was or whose ancestors were born in India but is not a citizen of India and is the citizen of another country.

Personal/lifestyle blogs: Weblogs that focus on the 'private' or domestic aspects of people's lives (e.g. food blogs, parenting blogs, fitness blogs, design blogs).

Prabhu: This means master or the supreme lord in Sanskrit; it refers to God.

Pravasi Bharatiya Divas: The day celebrated in India on 9 January each year to mark the contribution of the overseas Indian community to the development of India. The day commemorates the arrival of Mahatma Gandhi from South Africa on 9 January 1915.

Public blogs: Blogs that relate to matters circulating widely in the public sphere (politics, technology, consumer advocacy, business, news, health, etc.).

Sanatan Dharma: The original name of what is now popularly called Hinduism or Hindu Dharma.

Satsang: Devotional singing programme, forming an important part of the religious life of Hindus.

Shiva: A Hindu deity who is considered the Supreme God within Shaivism, one of the three most influential denominations in Hinduism.

Smarta Brahman: Member of a class that follows the Dharma Shastras – texts that emphasise that *Brahmans* are 'the class with the highest status' and are required to be 'the upholders of purity'.

Social media: Media that facilitate interactions and thus the formation and maintenance of digital networks and communities.

Social web: Websites and software developed to facilitate social interaction.

Sringeri math: A religious institution situated in south India. It belongs to the same tradition as the Kanchi math.

Thirdspace: Term used to explain the way in which migrants fashion alternative social spaces located between the two poles of 'here' and 'there'. Within these 'thirdspaces' migrants often engage in transnational activities that create new spheres of interaction.

Transduction: The constant making anew of a domain in reiterative and transformative practices. The term is used to explain the way in which technologies become bound to place. Transduction produces thirdspaces.

Transnational (Also Trans-Indian): Someone with expanded opportunities to reformulate both the self and the place that the self dwells in. These expanded opportunities are characteristic of life in the 'Digital Age'.

Untouchability: This is the social-religious practice of ostracising a minority group by segregating them from the mainstream by social custom or legal mandate.

Vedic period: The Vedic period is a period in history during which the *Vedas*, the oldest scriptures of Hinduism, were composed.

Vishwa Hindu Parishad: A Hindu organisation in India based on the ideology of Hindutva. It was founded in 1964 and its main objective is to promote a Hindu society.

VoIP (Voice over Internet Protocol): Communication protocols, technologies and transmission techniques that concern voice communications over Internet Protocol networks like the Internet.

Web 2.0: Refers to the development of the World Wide Web into a participation platform. It specifically concerns websites that allow users to interact, collaborate and create (so called user-generated) content (e.g. social networking sites, blogs, video sharing sites).

Webmaster: The website administrator, someone who is responsible for the maintenance of a website.

World Wide Web: A system of Internet servers that supports documents formatted in a specific markup language called HTML (HyperText Markup Language). This allows links to other documents as well as graphics, audio and video files. In this way, users can move from one document or file to another simply by clicking on hot spots.

Yatra: A religious tour or pilgrimage to a sacred site.

Introduction

Migrant Transnationalism and the Internet

Johannes G. de Kruijf

Introduction

This volume is an assessment of transnationalism in and through emerging digital spaces. It is a collection of papers that analyses the (re)formative force of the Internet in migrant circuits by means of an exploration of online manifestations of one of the world's largest, most heterogeneous and most dynamic diasporas. The book is meant to exploit the analytic potential of the Indian case and harvest insights that contribute to important debates concerning the nature of subjectivity, sociality and collectivity in contexts of unprecedented time-space compression. Although the authors univocally reject the offline/online binary, and advocate the study of transnationalism online as a multiple embedded phenomenon, they share the view that the WWW's shift from a mostly read-only and provider-generated resource to a participatory web shaped by user-generated content has profound implications for especially day-to-day migrant transnationalism and justifies a focus on the Internet. In only two decades, virtual spaces took shape that have become crucial environments for border-crossing interactions and exchanges across diasporas as well as between migrants and homelands. The versatility of these environments and their role as catalysts of reflective projects of identity and community explain the Internet's great impact on contemporary migrant transnationalism and the variegated nature of expressions and practices of transnationalism online. The chapters in this book reflect this variegated nature. They involve analyses of hegemonic as well as counter-hegemonic or subaltern projects, of religious as well as secular quests, and of collective and public as well as individual and private expressions of self-identity. An awareness of the multifaceted approach required to capture such complexity shows in the disciplinary diversity of this volume. Its composition was a collaborative effort of pioneering authors from the fields of socio-cultural anthropology, communication, geography, history, political science and sociology.

The organisation of the book is determined by two key themes; identity and power. One section is devoted to each theme. Chapters 1 to 6 explore identity and the impact of transnationalism online on, for instance, constructions of self, senses of belonging, and attachments to migrants' here and there. Chapters 7 to 9 revolve around the manifestation and contestation of power in virtual transnational spaces. Explicitly assessed in some chapters, and implicitly present in all the others, are methodological contemplations. These contemplations are inevitable and imperative in studies of a complex phenomenon that is not just changing the lifeworlds of the people we study, but also transforming the very practice of research. Ghorashi and Boersma (2009: 670) argue this requires strategic open-mindedness:

> Escobar (1994) suggests that the use of new technology – ICT and especially the Internet – has created a new dimension in the ways that social realities are being constructed and negotiated. In this respect, the virtual dimension of networks has proven to be a powerful heuristic to study this social reality (Schultze and Orlikowski 2001; Shields 2002). To study this new dimension, the use of a single methodology is not sufficient. We need to experiment with a variety of methods and combine and recombine them in order to grasp the diverse ways in which transnational social realities are negotiated within virtual space and the interactions between the virtual space and the actual or material world (Hine 2000; Panagakos and Horst 2006). Only then will we be able to grasp how rhizomatic networks function and how they are mediated through ICTs. It also casts light on the ways in which use of the Internet within transnational space enables new forms of identity constructions. (Hine 2000)

Papers in this volume indicate this strategic open-mindedness and, as a collection, show and advocate the need for a multifaceted approach to transnationalism online. As such, the book illustrates the potential of eclectic assessments of contemporary socio-cultural complexity; the relevance of combining insights gained through a variety of qualitative and quantitative quests that ranges from content-analysis and semiotics, to social network analysis and extensive (online and offline) ethnography.

In this first chapter, the present-day Indian diaspora is briefly introduced as a massive and immensely heterogeneous construction and emergent outcome of a perpetual formative process. The subsequent theoretical exploration of this formative process begins with some reflections on 'globalisation' as the presumed essence of vital changes in the conditions of contemporary migration and diaspora. The way in which globalisation, in the form of time-space alterations that complicate the reproduction of cultural forms and social formations, manifests as migrant transnationalism is discussed in the next paragraphs. After that, the book's ultimate subject of transnationalism online will be explained as a product of radical changes in migrants' instrumentarium of connectivity. These radical changes have resulted in the materialisation of space that was non-existent and is constituted in a fundamentally new fashion. Besides an outline of the volume's ten empirical chapters, it is the dissection of the reformative impact of this virtual space that the final part of this introduction revolves around.

The Indian Diaspora

The Indian diaspora is one of the largest in the world. Comprising over 25 million people scattered across the globe, it is second in size only to the Chinese diaspora.

A defining trait of the Indian diaspora is its heterogeneity. This is the consequence of the episodic history of emigration, the diversity of the migrants in terms of, for instance, their linguistic, geographic and ethno-religious profile, and great variances in skill level of India's overseas workers as well as in (interrelated) places and patterns of settlement.

An important distinction in academic categorisations of difference within the Indian diaspora concerns the division between the so-called 'old' and 'new' diaspora. As Vijay Mishra (2005: 13) suggested:

> To explore the narrative of the Indian diaspora critically, we may want to read it as two relatively autonomous archives designated by the terms 'old' and 'new'. The old (that is, early modern, classic capitalist, or, more specifically, nineteenth-century indenture) and the new (that is, late modern of late capitalist) traverse two quite different kinds of topographies. The subjects of the old [...] occupy spaces in which they interact, by and large, with other colonized peoples with whom they have a complex relationship of power and privilege, as in Fiji, South Africa, Malaysia, Mauritius, Trinidad, Guyana, and Surinam; the subject of the new are people who have entered metropolitan centres of Empire of other white settler countries such as Australia, Canadian, New Zealand, and the United States as part of a post-1960s pattern of global migration.

Traces of this binary also surface in policy-related categorisations. The Indian administrative conceptualisation of its diaspora differentiates between Person of Indian Origin (PIO) and Non-resident Indians (NRI). Members of Mishra's 'old' diaspora, along with for example those of Indian ancestry in/from East Africa, can claim a PIO status. Non-resident Indians include those Indian passport holders who have 'entered metropolitan centres of Empire' since the 1960s as well as the millions of Indian citizens now working in places like Kuwait, Bahrain, the UAE, and Saudi Arabia.

Undoubtedly, as Bose (2012: 392) states, this formalisation of a differentiated diasporic belonging narrates the effort of the Indian state to capitalise on the wealth and resources of its entire diaspora. Despite their utterly distinct biographies, recent migrants and descendants of merchants and labourers who left India several generations ago are thus considered to share an indelible connection to India as well as their status of 'mythic global Indian' (Bose 2012: 394). Inspired by Clifford (1994) Mishra, in his explanation of the 'diasporic imaginary', describes the sense of displacement as a common denominator and defining trait of diasporas. In other words, the subjectivities of members of the 'old' and 'new' Indian diaspora, albeit in many different ways, are inevitably shaped by 'the idea that against one's *desh* ("home country") the present locality is *videsh* ("another country")' (Mishra 2005: 16). This, Mishra acknowledges, does not make them co-members of a global community of uprooted Indians; a collective with a distinct heritage or some sort of uniform core identity. Rather, it allows for an Indian diaspora to be discerned in a complexity of formations more or less structured (rather than structured in almost) the decentralised and hybrid fashion that – with reference to Deleuze and Guattari – some authors on diaspora have labelled 'rhizomatic' (e.g. Hall and Gilroy).

As the notion of rhizome already indicates, this eclectic Indian diaspora could be seen as the emergent outcome of a perpetual formative process. It involves formations that result from accumulative enterprises of (dis)connecting, relating, networking, mixing, imagining, and identifying at countless sites of 'settlement' across the globe. The particular contemporary conditions under which these formations today engage in such enterprise, and under which contemporary Indians overseas thus experience and express their dynamic diasporic-ness, have inspired the composition of this volume. More specifically, it can be argued that these conditions, mostly revolving around rapid and radical developments in the realms of mobility and connectivity, affect the making of diasporas (as well as the being of migrant) in such a profound way that empirically grounded reflections on the implications for their scholarly assessment are highly pertinent.

Conditions of Change

Analyses of transformative tendencies in literature on migration and diaspora often situate the dissection of change in a broad context of (intensified) globalisation. More specifically, change is linked to the restructuring of time and space that defines today's globalising processes. The profound impact of this restructuring in social and cultural realms was already mentioned in the work of both David Harvey and Anthony Giddens more than two decades ago. Harvey (1989), focusing on the effects of emerging flexible regimes of accumulation, has explained this restructuring as 'time-space compression'. As far as Harvey is concerned, the acceleration in the pace of economic processes is shrinking the world in a such a way that 'distance and time no longer appear to be major constraints on the organization of human activity' (Inda and Rosaldo 2008: 8). Giddens (1990) employs the notion of 'disembedding' to analyse the spatial-temporal effects of globalisation. According to him, developments in communication and the expansion of global systems of production and trade result in a stretching of social life across time and space. In other words, these developments lead to the disembedding or 'the "lifting-out" of social relations from local contexts of interaction and their restructuring across indefinite spans of time-space' (Giddens 1990: 21).

Giddens links the process of disembedding to the conceptualisation of place. He suggests that disembedding causes place – 'the physical settings of social activity as situated geographically' – to be increasingly phantasmagoric. Locales are thus evermore 'thoroughly penetrated by and shaped in terms of social influences quite distant from them' (Giddens 1990: 19). In fact, as some argue, human existence as such could be considered unprecedentedly deterritorialised; marked by the dislodging of forms and flows from anchored positions and fixed trajectories in space and time. Appadurai explains the apparently messy logistics of global interactions that result from this development by pointing at crucial 'disjunctures' between economy, culture and politics. He notes that 'people, machinery, money, images, and ideas now follow increasingly nonisomorphic paths' (Appadurai 1996: 11). According to Appadurai (1996: 11), a result of these growing disjunctures is the complication of continuity or, in his words, a prioritisation of 'the problem of reproduction'. This 'problem' is a crucial trait of globalisation that surfaces in numerous analyses. It relates to explorations of cultural processes that focus on mixing and exchange; on the manner in which fusion labelled as, for instance, creolisation or hybridisation generates new cultural forms (e.g. Hannerz 1992; Nederveen Pieterse 2009) and on the way in which revolutionary changes in the practice of imagination stir innovation (Appadurai 1996). The problem of reproduction also manifests in studies of economic systems and political configurations in contexts of globalisation. Particularly interesting here are shifts in anatomies of power that have inspired reflections on the role and future of the nation-state as well as on the emergence of new kinds citizenship that have been labelled, for instance, post-national and flexible (see Sassen 2002 and Ong 1999). Various authors argue that these shifts have ultimately produced some fundamental changes in the practice of politics and the organisation of social life. Contemplating systemic change in the realm of post 9/11 global politics, Appadurai (2006) describes the recent rise of 'cellular structures' as the cause of a destabilised political reality in which 'symmetrical principles' of conduct and transparent structures of coordination and organisation are challenged by fluid associations of flexibly managed and highly dynamic groups. Jeffrey Juris (2008), in his investigation of anti-corporate globalisation movements, vividly depicts the functioning of these cellular forms. He explains the fundamental changes in today's practice of politics in terms of emergent 'cultural politics of networking'. Counter-hegemonic initiatives, under conditions of mobility and connectivity, could thus involve the embrace of networking ideals such as grassroots participation, decentralised coordination, consensus decision making and the free flow of information.

Juris' focus on networks and networking connects to an extensive body of literature in which globalisation is studied by means of assessing transformations in social morphologies. In the 1990s Manuel Castells already claimed there was a shift in social organisation from relatively stable hierarchies to a more fluid network form composed of 'open structures, able to expand without limits' (1996: 469). More than anything, it was developments in information and communication technology that seemed to support this claim. In fact, the rise of the World Wide Web and especially its later incarnation as a user-centred system of interaction and collaboration (sometimes referred to as the 'social web') stirred ongoing debates on the nature of sociality and collectivity in hybrid (off/online) and deterritorialised settings. From utopian (and dystopian) reflections on the rise of virtual communities and explosion of exploitable ties in the 1990s,[1] these debates have matured into deliberations on, for instance, the impact of online presence

---

1 These were often inspired by the groundbreaking work of Howard Rheingold who coined the term virtual community in his 1993 book (of the same title), in which he explored the emergence of computer-mediated communications (starting with 'The Well').

on social capital (e.g. Boyd and Ellison 2007; Shah *et al.* 2001; Srinivasan 2006), the analytical limitations and potentialities of the concepts of network and community in online investigations (e.g. Postill 2008; Wellman 2001), and the influence of ICTs on processes of identification and identity formation[2] (e.g. Chan 2005; Wheeler 2000). On the whole, these studies narrate a departure from earlier revolutionary claims that presumed a fundamental transformation of society in the Age of the Internet. Most notably, it is generally acknowledged that 'the distinction of real and imagined or virtual is not a useful one' (Wilson and Peterson 2002). Simple online/offline dichotomies are thus gathered as unsustainable as empirical observations confront us with increasingly blurred boundaries and even the confluence of digital and physical existence, since especially mobile devices allow simultaneous presence in, and continuous interaction between, offline and online spheres. Rather than revolutionary change, these recent explorations of sociality and collectivity in hybrid fields of interaction focus on the matter of appropriation of social technologies and on the issue agency. In fact, in some way or another they usually include a contemplation of the way in which ICTs affects the desire and capacity for self-determination and self-construction/expression of groups and individuals. The urgency of such contemplation, especially in the study of particularly mobile populations, shows throughout this book.

Transnationalism

In line with the above, the texts presented in this volume thus do not suggest there is a specific type of transnationalism that exists online, or that web-based flows and forms result from a certain mode of transnational enterprise. Rather, they indicate that the study of human mobility requires an approach in which online interactive platforms ('social media') are recognised as crucial additions to the instrumentarium of connectivity of contemporary migrants and diasporas. The exploration of practices and constellations facilitated by or generated on these platforms should thus be an integral part of the study of so-called migrant transnationalism. Before briefly addressing some implications of this acknowledgement, it is obviously important to take a closer look at our core theme of transnationalism and assess existing theoretical contemplations of its manifestation online.

According to Peter Kvisto (2001), Nina Glick Schiller, Linda Basch and Christina Szanton Blanc (e.g. 1994, 1995) were the first to use the concept of transnationalism to capture the dynamics of contemporary migration. In their work, they identified a crucial shift in the character of migration that forces its reframing into a 'process by which immigrants forge and sustain simultaneous multi-stranded social relations that link together their societies of origin and

---

2 A prominent person-centred approach to the Internet-identity link was offered by clinical psychologist Sherry Turkle in 'Life on Screen: Identity in the Age of Internet' (1997).

settlement' (Glick Schiller *et al.* 1995: 48). This shift, which involves the emergence of a chronically interconnected 'transmigrant', requires a systematic and comprehensive exploration of 'the ongoing and continuing ways in which current-day immigrants [as transmigrants] construct and reconstitute their simultaneous embeddedness in more than one society' (Glick Schiller *et al.* 1995: 48). In the introduction to their reader on Indian diaspora and transnationalism, Baas *et al.* (2012: 3) observe that this recognition of a crucial development in the experience and practice of migration, along with the acknowledgement of the subsequent need to adjust our approach in terms of research and analysis, defines some of the most influential studies of transnationalism that followed the work of Glick Schiller, Basch and Blanc. Perhaps most prominent in these studies are efforts to delineate or classify and value the process of enquiry. These efforts were inspired by foundational questions such as: Is transnationalism indeed a new phenomenon or can examples of migrant transnationalism be found in the past? Do we actually need an alternative approach to the study of current-day migration? How do we specify the spatial component of transnationalism as an aggregate of trans-territorial connections and interactions? And, how inclusive should our definition of transnationalism be? What belongs to and what is excluded from the classification of contemporary transnationalism?

Portes, Guarnizo and Landolt (1999) as well as Faist (2000) argue that transnationalism is not a truly new phenomenon. Portes *et al.* (1999) mention, for instance, mediaeval trade diasporas composed of Venetian, Genoese and Hansa migrants as early examples of economic transnationalism. However, the authors agree that because of the relative ease of long-distance travel and because of revolutionary developments in communication technology, transnationalism today has gained elements of regularity, routine involvement and critical mass that make it far more extensive and consequential than its precursors. Thomas Faist stresses this structural nature of contemporary migrant interconnectedness in his definition of transnationalism. According to him, ties that are truly transnational are 'sustained ties of persons, networks and organizations across the borders of multiple nation-states, ranging from little to highly institutionalized forms' rather than the 'occasional and fleeting contacts' between migrants and relatively immobile others (Faist 2000: 189–190). A similar emphasis shows in Steven Vertovec's work. He also considers 'sustained linkages and ongoing exchanges' a crucial ingredient of those practices and formations that are labelled 'transnational' (Vertovec 2009: 3). In his exploration of the debate since the 'transnational turn' in the early 1990s, Vertovec (2009: 18) mentions a seemingly cacophonic process of conceptual tuning that has resulted in a range of typologies meant to capture the kinds of transnationalism produced by these 'sustained linkages' and 'ongoing exchanges'. He explains that these typologies concern 'modes, levels, extents and impacts of transnationalism' and differentiate between, for instance, transnationalism 'from above' and 'from below' (Smith and Guarnizo 1998), between 'great' and 'little' transnationalism (Gardner 2002), and between 'core' and 'expanded' transnational activity (Levitt 2001).

What such typologies or categorisations indicate – and what I would like to stress for the sake of the following assessment of the relevance of the Internet – is the heterogeneous manifestation of transnationalism. Practices and forms of transnationalism clearly vary from migrant to migrant (and from sphere of life to sphere of life) as well as across migrants groups (Faist 2000, Portes 2003, Vertovec 2009). Portes suggests this heterogeneity is heavily influenced by migratory experiences. According to him, 'the contexts of exit and reception' should be seen as a principal determinant of transnationalism because it conditions the propensity of migrants 'to engage in cross-border initiatives or even adopt them as their principal form of economic adaptation' (Portes 2003: 879). Essentially, Portes claims that high levels of incorporation in the host society and/or affective disconnection with the place of origin (as a result of instability or absence of strong ties) seem to discourage transnationalism while a limited incorporation in the host society and/or a strong emotional involvement in the context of exit boost the inclination to engage in transnational activities. Of course, besides such straightforward push and pull mechanisms, a range of other factors also help to determine transnationalism. An obvious yet crucial one concerns the practical ability to partake in border-crossing interactions and exchanges. In fact, as the earlier mentioned assessments of its newness show, radical changes in our instrumentarium of connectivity are the very reason we even consider transnationalism an unprecedented trait of contemporary migration.

Transnationalism Online

One of the most radical changes in the instrumentarium of connectivity involves improvements in communication technology. According to Vertovec (2009: 14–15), 'advances in the technology of contact' should be seen as a crucial novelty of migrant transnationalism as these affect the extent, intensity and speed of communication; allow an up-to-date awareness of situations elsewhere; and facilitate new forms of political engagement from a distance. The introduction of the Internet and the rapid evolution of the World Wide Web (only since 1991) are arguably the most important among the advances in technology of contact. Especially the Web's transformation into a user-oriented and user-generated platform and its continuously improving accessibility across the globe have turned the Internet in just two decades into a paramount tool for cross-border interactions and exchanges in diasporic settings.

Analyses of the online presence and practices of migrants seem to portray the Internet either as infrastructure or a site of transnationalism. As such, the Internet – increasingly often in the form of social media – is explained in terms of *(r) evolution* or *genesis*. On one hand, computer-mediated communication (CMC) is said to facilitate a revolutionary development of flows between distinct places (places of exit and settlement or places across the diaspora). CMC should thus be seen as a force that transforms the nature of linkage and affects the local impact of flows because it triggers a massive increase of speed and scale of exchanges. On the other hand, the Internet could be approached as an innovation that has implied the genesis of an entirely new social environment. In other words, concerning migrant transnationalism, the Internet thus means the materialisation of space that was previously non-existent and is constituted in a fundamentally novel fashion. This new ever-emergent space, which enables non-physical co-presence, is shaped by unusual temporal flexibility and by the residual nature of online conduct: it allows instantaneous as well as suspended interaction, and is determined by its users' awareness of the fact that online practice is inevitably an act of publication. Of course, Facebook profiles/posts and Twitter 'tweets' are the most obvious illustrations of the latter.

Irrespective of the approach taken to the Internet as a framework of transnationalism, cross-border sociality online should not be seen as behaviour that occurs in isolation. As Miller and Slater argued, we need to explore Internet use 'as continuous with and embedded in other social spaces' and acknowledge the fact that online interactions 'happen within mundane social structures and relations that they may transform but that they cannot escape into a self-enclosed cyberian apartness' (2000: 5). A crucial feature of transnationalism as online behaviour is its transformative potential. Perhaps most explorations of diasporic Internet use focus on this potential in some way or another. Essentially, these explorations indicate that the Internet generates important changes in: the experience of transnationalism; the practice of transnationalism; and the externalisation of transnationalism (as a practice).

The experience of transnationalism – The impact of the Internet on the experience of migrant transnationalism obviously relates to the spatial-temporal effects of online interactions. The Internet seems the epitome of time-space compression; a primary reason for the erosion of distance and time as crucial constraints on the organisation of human activity. As Hiller and Franz (2004: 732) state in their analysis of online relations among diasporic peoples: 'one of the compelling aspects of computer-mediated communication is that it transcends the limitations of time and space'. This faculty of CMC inspires the highly functional approach of migrants that surfaces in various studies of their Internet use (e.g. Hiller and Franz 2004; Parker and Song 2006; Everett 2009; Brinkerhoff 2009). What these studies suggest is, with regard to the challenges of dislocation and relocation, CMC should be seen as (part of) the coping strategy of migrants. Panagakos and Horst (2006: 118), for instance, say the Internet enables transnational migrants to 'expand their social space' and thus 'challenge the restrictive boundaries imposed by dominant host societies and the limitations of physical space and time'. This strategic use of the Internet seems to be inherently productive. It generates social formations and attachments, facilitates digital reconstructions of existing ties, and shapes processes of identity formation. Studies of the influence of social technologies on transnational family experiences are illustrative. For example, Bacigalupe and Cámara (2012) show how ICTs support the transformation of family networks into transnational (family) networks. They claim we have to acknowledge that, particularly in diasporic settings, some family processes are 'virtualised' (2012: 1431). This inevitably implies a reassessment of notions of presence and absence as well as a reconsideration of the relevance of physical proximity for the maintenance of close ties. Licoppe (2004) mentions the emergence of a new kind of social bond in this respect. According to him, social media or social technologies are 'exploited to provide a continuous pattern of mediated interactions [e.g. SNS posts, e-mails, WhatsApp messages] that combine into "connected relationships", in which the boundaries between absence and presence eventually get blurred' (2004: 136).

The experience of such blurred boundaries between absence and presence or between the here and there, along with the interrelated expanded possibilities of co-presence, also manifests in analyses of the impact of the Internet on migrant attachments. The Internet affects the 'dual frame of reference' that keeps migrants attached to their homelands (Guarnizo 1997). Panagakos and Horst speak of the influence of ICTs on migrant multi-positionality in this respect. They argue that 'the Internet, mobile phones and other ICTs add new dimensions to [migrants'] multi-positionality and allow for the cultivation of ethnic, cultural and national expressions with a global reach' (Panagakos and Horst 2006: 117). It seems to be the enhanced experience of this multi-dimensionality, rather than one of revolutionary virtual transnational existence, that the Internet produces. This echoes Manuel Castells (2000) reflections on 'the material organization of time-sharing social practices' in his contemplation of the network society. According to him, 'the space of flows does not permeate down to the whole realm of human experience in the networked society' as most people live in places and 'perceive their space as place-based' (Castells 2000: 453).

The practice of transnationalism – The space of flows defined by the Internet facilitates transnationalism as a communicative practice. Hepp (2009) employs the concept of 'diasporic communicative spaces' to assess the nature of such practice. He portrays the Internet as part of a 'transmedial' sphere in which different media – conventional mass media as well as personal communication media or 'small media' – help to create 'communicative networks' that result in a 'thickening of communication' which Hepp refers to as communicative spaces (Hepp 2009: 330). Empirical explorations show that these spaces should not be seen as colossal meeting grounds that unify fragmented diasporas (e.g. Georgiou 2006, 2007). As Hepp (2009: 330) states, 'communicative spaces are not homogeneous but [rather] marked by various contradictories and power relations'.

The contradictories and power relations that shape CMC are particularly prominent in assessments of transnational public spheres. In 1996, Appadurai already recognised the transformative impact of 'electronic mediation' on such spheres of opinion formation. He observed that the manner in which electronic communication affects diasporic subjectivities 'is deeply connected to politics' and has created sizeable and influential public spheres that shape the cultural dynamic of life across the globe (Appadurai 1996: 10). Parham (2004), in an analysis of the Haiti Global Village Forum, provides an illuminative empirical exploration of the deployment of new kinds of media to establish such infrastructures for cultivating transnational subjectivities and political discourse. According to her, the political potential of the Internet is quite significant:

> In contemporary times, diasporic websites and forums have become the newest social bases for cultivating national subjectivity and discourse across borders. Immigrants and exiles may be physically displaced from the geographic borders of the nation, but their ability to create independent reading publics provides them with space to analyse critically or express opposition to the policies of their home states. While community newspapers and radio stations within ethnic communities have always facilitated this kind of expression, their use and impact have generally been restricted to local or regional areas. The use of Internet forums introduces the potential for creating truly transnational public spheres within dispersed national communities. (Parham 2004, p. 202)

Parham argues that these 'truly transnational public spheres' result from the capacity of media to facilitate time- and space-distanciation among a community of authors and readers. More specifically, the Internet not only provides a space for expression but also inspires the formation of publics. According to Parham, these transnational publics can affect the anatomy of power at a national level as they may operate as 'interstitial networks of individuals and groups acting as citizens' (2004: 203). A similar perspective shows in Bernal's (2005, 2006) analyses of the Eritrean transnational public sphere. Like Parham, she argues that the skilful and frequent political use of the Internet by migrants means we need to 'reconsider the dynamics of sovereignty'. Bernal mentions the emergence of so-called counter-publics as an example. She explains how Eritrean websites have fostered the birth of these counter-publics and of creative 'spaces of dissent where unofficial views are voiced and alternative knowledges are produced' (Bernal 2006: 176).

It is hard to say how productive these counter-publics can be in their efforts to realise political change beyond virtual spheres. On one hand, the Internet supports the establishment and maintenance of empowering alliances that help marginal actors to express themselves, build networks, and gain support from civil society. On the other hand, these alliances tend to be comparatively fragile and ineffective because of their constitution and because of the distinct character of online involvement. For instance, the reformative potential of online opposition might suffer from challenges of regulation and access as well as mobilisation (due to fragmentation and limitations in commitment). Nevertheless, the political use of the Internet in diasporic settings is a crucial component of contemporary practices of transnationalism. It shows the importance of transnationalism online as a strategic effort and is linked to fundamental questions of networking, community and identity. Besides, it reveals the illusion of the Internet as an instrument of re-unification of dispersed populations and highlights its potential as a catalyst of change.

The externalisation of transnationalism – Modifications generated by the Internet as a catalyst of change concern social morphologies, cultural expressions, and migrant identifications and subjectivities. The specific manifestation of these modifications, as well as the underlying process of change, is the third and last take on transnationalism online that needs to be introduced. Crucial to the assessment of the way in which practices of transnationalism externalise as various structural modifications is the conceptualisation of 'the online' as a configuration of productive encounters and exchanges. Adams and Ghose (2003), in a study of Internet use by Indian migrants in the United States, explain this configuration as a virtual space between. According to them, such a virtual space between comprises a 'vast, international complex of interlinked websites used by [in their case] the "Indian diaspora" and by residents of India' that is part of an even larger space of transnational communication which can be called a 'bridgespace' (Adams and Ghose 2003: 415). Adams and Ghose define this bridgespace as an environment that is built in and through the Internet. This environment enables or supports flows and interactions between geographically separate locations and, pertaining to externalisations of transnationalism, thus helps to shape the limits of the possible.

Skop and Adams (2009: 130, 131) explain the creation of bridgespaces as a process of transduction; 'the binding of technologies, practices, representations and places by a particular group, defined by its involvement in two (or more) disparate places'. As Adams and Ghose (2003) show in their analysis of the Indo-American bridgespace, this process of transduction results in complex variegated configurations rather than in a homogeneous bridgespace. These interrelated configurations are used by different groups (e.g. national, ethnic, sub-ethnic) and serve purposes that range from cultural preservation and community organisation to intercultural mediation and religious participation. According to Skop and Adams (2003), the NRIs' use of or active involvement in bridgespaces could be seen as a cultural quest and a part of community- and identity-forming routines. Their research indicates that the Internet as part of bridgespaces is often used to satisfy conservative inclinations. They mention the work of Mathew and Prasad (2000) and Pathak (1998) as illustrations of this utilisation of the Internet for 'the purpose of confirming and perpetuating cultural values as traditional' (Skop and Adams 2009: 142). According to them, at least in the early days of online presence, highly skilled Indian immigrants in North America shaped virtual transnational spaces into podia for cultural preservation. Vinay Lal (1999) observes a similar tendency in his analysis of 'cyber-diasporic Hinduism'. He mentions the retrograde features of the Hinduism of Indian-Americans and argues that these 'devotees have developed an ossified conception of their faith' that ignores the dynamic nature of 'homeland Hinduism' (Lal 1999: 147). Quoting Lal (2003: 129), Skop and Adams state these online representations of tradition are in fact contemporary fabrications: attempts 'to give shape to a new Hindu history' that show the creative use of the Internet as an instrument of reality management. The particular manifestation of these attempts should be seen as a 'dynamic conceptualisation of Indian culture that is formed and transformed across and between national boundaries' (Skop and Adams 2009: 143). This process does not occur in isolation. It entails a performative constitution of identities – as well as the imagination of communities – structured by historical quests for self-definition and legacies of (imposed) ethno-cultural categorisation (see Rai 1995). As a project of identity and/or community it also shows continuities and interdependencies between transnational, national and local spaces. In fact, as Georgiou (2005: 483) states with regard to diasporic media in Europe; the local, national and transnational form the locations where 'diasporic particularism' is shaped in the production of media and in the consumption and appropriation of media and technologies. Expressions of, for instance, Indian-ness, Indo-Australian-ness, Punjabi-ness, and Sikhism online should thus be seen as the product of identifications that are (a) situational, coexistent and intertwined, and (b) shaped by the actors' accumulated experience of socialisation, involvement and positioning in various performative spaces.

The translation of complex experience-based urges and inclinations into (re)formative actions online is ultimately determined by users' assessment of the potential of the Internet. Studies of migrants' Internet use illustrate the prominence of functional contemplations of the Internet and its goal-oriented appropriation. An example concerns analyses of the online practice of Hinduism (e.g. Helland 2007; Scheifinger 2008; Herman 2010) The fact that devotees use 'the Web to take virtual tours of sacred temples, undergo virtual pilgrimages, and even have rituals conducted in real time in their most sacred temples and places' (Helland 2007: 974) indicates an awareness of the practical possibilities of the Internet and the willingness to customise cultural forms according to the attributes of a new environment. Recent studies show this utilitarian tendency inspires the creative exploration of the rapidly expanding possibilities of communication and representation online. Gajjala's reflections on Saris in Second Life (SL) provide an extreme example. The production of Saris and their consumption by SL 'avatars' of both Indian and non-Indian origin shows how Indian wear, as cultural artifact, becomes 'a floating signifier' used in processes of demarcation in a virtual world (Gajjala 2011).

Power and Identity

The dynamic nature of the Internet, its ever-increasing versatility as a catalyst of disembedding, complicates its dissection as an environment of migrant transnationalism. Transnationalism online today is, in many ways, different to the kind of transnationalism that early explorers of virtual spheres observed in the 1990s. An important development has been the emergence of the so-called 'social web'. According to Flew (2007: 36), this development meant 'the move from personal websites to blogs and blog site aggregation, from publishing to participation, from web content as the outcome of large up-front investment to an ongoing and interactive process, and from content management systems to links based on tagging (folksonomy)'. The major implications of such change in the fundamentals of the World Wide Web and the steady rise of Internet accessibility concern the issues of power and identity. Although these have long been identified as a crucial focus in explorations of the impact of the online (e.g. Mitra 1997, 2001), today's user-oriented and participatory Web prioritises reflections on the (re)organisation of power and on the constitution of what Anthony Giddens (1991) referred to as self-identity. The following nine chapters, in more or less explicit ways, reveal and analyse these reflections on identity and power. As a collection they delineate Indian transnationalism online as an echo of India as a constellation of interconnected and long-standing projects of community and identity; a dynamic environment of condensed social, cultural and political experimentation and contestation. This collection is inevitably incomplete, partially because it comprises pioneering work in a field that we have only just begun to explore, and partially because of the immense scale and diversity of the Indian diaspora. Nevertheless, the papers touch upon crucial themes that will undoubtedly serve as a foundation for future research. The themes include the nature of social organisation, the dynamics of sovereignty and agency, and the (re)formative practice of imagination.

The first section of the book focuses on the process of identity. It starts with two person-centred papers that explore the production of new selves as a result of the entrance of Indians into virtual spaces. Chapter 1 concerns an exploration of online manifestations of the individual experience of transnational existence. It analyses private blogs of migrant women as a means of constructing a virtual 'I'. Raman and Kasturi explain these constructions in the 'blogosphere' as instances of identity performance that show how the creative composition of online selves through text, imagery and visual aesthetic is inherently a reflective exercise. This exercise implies the imagination of an audience as well as the strategic contemplation of self-positioning. According to the authors, these reflective efforts result in transnational identities that are eclectic products of a juxta-positioning of local and global elements which reveal a liberation from rigid and constraining cultural labels and 'prove' the bloggers' ethno-cosmopolitanism. Mitra would undoubtedly label these bloggers 'Trans-Indian'. In Chapter 2, he introduces this notion of a hyphenated identity to assess the variety of ways in which contemporary Indians have become able to reformulate the self. A focus on Indians as Trans-Indians helps to reveal the increased agency of people who simultaneously navigate real and virtual spaces. The essence of such agency is discursive practice. According to Mitra, 'digital systems' help to empower individuals as they allow a selection of 'specific narrative hats' for the sake of creating a Trans-Indian self.

Mitra's notion of Trans-Indian suggests a reformulation of the self through a reinterpretation of the space in which the self dwells. As such, it points to a pertinence of reflections on space and place that shows throughout this volume. The following two chapters that explore the satisfaction of self-needs are indicative. Goel's analysis in Chapter 3, for instance, focuses on the emergence of a German virtual space called *Indernet*. She argues that this space, founded by people identifying themselves as (second generation) Indians, serves to satisfy its users' urge to belong and imagine linkages to a place that in practice is often beyond physical reach. According to Goel, this urge to belong is rooted in experiences of alienation and 'racist Othering' in Germany, Austria and Switzerland rather than the result of strong emotional attachments to a region of origin. Skop's paper on 'thirdspace', Chapter 4, also acknowledges the influence of migrants' lived-in space on their participation in virtual environment. According to her, senses of identity are constructed in an alternative space that is located between the here and there. This so-called thirdspace should be seen as a multifunctional resource that helps to build communities, that provides a material and symbolic homeplace, and that facilitates the maintenance of strong ties despite physical separation. By means of five vignettes, Skop reveals how participation in these thirdspaces varies and depends on, for instance, personal inclinations and life-stage. She explains this as a 'continuum of embeddedness' and recognises five degrees of involvement in the process of ethnic identity formation.

Although equally interested in understandings and experiences of place, the final two chapters on the process of identity focus on the motivating force of place of origin rather than context of settlement. Scheifinger's exploration of *Advaita Vedanta* online, in Chapter 5, analyses the potential of the Internet to neutralise discomforts of absence. His focus is on practical possibilities of transnational religious participation. By means of two case studies, he illustrates the way in which the Internet enables gurus to connect to devotees overseas and allows migrant followers to be 'virtually' part of religious events that take place in India. As such, his paper provides an illuminative empirical example of the blurred boundaries between offline and online spheres and occurrences.

Scheifinger's study also demonstrates the peculiar match of faith and format that Lal dissects in the last chapter of the section on projects of identity. According to Lal, 'among the world's principal religions, none appears to be so apposite for our digitally wired times as Hinduism'. He explains how Hinduism seems to anticipate the Internet's hallmark features such as its lack of central regulation and 'its intrinsic spirit of free inquiry and abhorrence of censorship'. Paradoxically, Lal argues, this congruence seems to have inspired a tendency to turn to the Internet to forge defensive and standardised forms of Hindu identity rather than an inclination to sell and celebrate Hindu diversity and anarchy. The 'internet Hinduism' that results from this tendency narrates a conceptualisation of religion that is reformatted to (systemically) resemble Abrahamic faiths so as to be taken seriously as a world religion and to serve and suit India as an emerging global power and its elites in their quests for economic and political gain. A different intersection of offline and online efforts is the subject of Mirian Santos Ribeiro de Oliveira's study of homegrown transnationalism in Chapter 7. In her analysis of convergences between the annual Pravasi Bharatiya Divas conference and an online initiative called NRI Power Podium, she explains the construction of a consistent and positive image of the Indian miracle migrant as largely a joint effort of state and India-based non-state actors. According to Santos, their common incentive is to 'reinforce the centrality of the sending country within transnational networks' and stress common histories, symbols and interests for the sake of diasporic loyalty and ultimately exploitation of the economic potential of Indians overseas.[3]

Such an effort of exploitation, as a project of power not so different from online *hindutva*, obviously serves elite interests and demonstrates the use of digital infrastructures to replicate national and offline systems of control in transnational and online spaces. Emilia Bachrach's chapter seeks to explore the ways in which individuals belonging to the Vallabh Sampraday, a Vaishnav sectarian community based in western India, negotiate between religious and social values inherited from their tradition's past and everyday life in the present via the Internet. A contrasting effort transpires in the final chapter in this volume. Saxena's exploration of transnational Dalit activism shows the relevance of the Internet as a space for opposition and emancipation. According to him, virtual space has facilitated the establishment of alliances for change that connect Indians to the Dalit diaspora and link Dalit activists to larger circuits of human rights activists and movements. The Internet, as such, is a means of empowerment that can bring about positive change as it facilitates information and reflection, helps to unite marginalised groups and provides alternative network opportunities, and allows representation and participation in processes of opinion-making and agenda-setting. This optimistic analysis represents a growing body of studies that explore the use of the Internet as an instrument of 'grassroots globalisation' and assess its impact as a catalyst of change.

References

Appadurai, A. 1996. *Modernity at Large: Cultural Dimensions of Globalization.* Minneapolis, MN: University of Minnesota Press.

Baas, M., Sahoo, A. K., and Faist, T. 2012. Indian Transnationalism: Theoretical Developments and Practical Implications. In: A. K. Sahoo, M. Baas and T. Faist (eds.), *Indian Diaspora and Transnationalism.* New Delhi: Rawat Publications, 1–15.

Faist, T. 2000. *The Volume and Dynamics of International Migration and Transnational Social Spaces.* Oxford: Oxford University Press.

Gajjala, R. 2011. Snapshots from Sari Trails: Cyborgs Old and New. *Social Identities*, 17, 393–408.

Ghorashi, H. and Boersma, K. 2009. The 'Iranian Diaspora' and the New Media: From Political Action to Humanitarian Help. *Development and Change*, 40 (4), 667–691.

---

3 See also Mallapragada (2006). She provides an interesting assessment of the (Indian-American) 'web' as a site for the construction (and dismantling) of official categories of NRI and PIO.

Giddens, A. 1990. *The Consequences of Modernity.* Stanford, CA: Stanford University Press.

Glick Schiller, N., Basch, L. and Blanc, C. S. 1995. From Immigrant to Transmigrant: Theorizing Transnational Migration. *Anthropological Quarterly,* 68 (1), 48–63.

Hannerz, U. 1992. *Cultural Complexity: Studies in the Social Organization of Meaning.* Columbia, NY: Columbia University Press.

Harvey, D. 1989. *The Condition of Postmodernity: An Enquiry into the Origins of Cultural Change.* Cambridge, MA: Blackwell.

Inda, J. X. and Rosaldo, R. 2008. Tracking Global Flows. In: J. X. Inda and R. Rosaldo (eds.), *The Anthropology of Globalisation (2nd Ed.).* London: Wiley, 3–46.

Mishra, V. 2005. The Diasporic Imaginary and the Indian Diaspora. *Asian Studies Institute Occasional Lecture 2*, Victoria University of Wellington, New Zealand.

Mitra, A. 1997. Diasporic Web sites: Ingroup and outgroup discourse. *Critical Studies in Mass Communication*, 14, 158–181.

Mitra, A. 2001. Diasporic voices in cyberspace. *New Media and Society*, 3 (1), 29–48.

Nederveen Pieterse, J. 2009. *Politics of globalization.* New Delhi: Sage.

Ong, A. 1999. *Flexible Citizenship: The Cultural Logics of Transnationality.* Durham: Duke University Press.

Portes, A., Guarnizo, L. E. and Landolt, P. 1999. The study of transnationalism: pitfalls and promise of an emergent research field. *Ethnic and Racial Studies*, 22 (2), 217–237.

Skop, E. and Adams, P. C. 2009. Creating and Inhabiting Virtual Places: Indian Immigrants in Cyberspace. *National Identities*, 11 (2): 127–147.

Smith, M. P. and Guarnizo, L. E. (eds.) 1998, *Transnationalism from Below*. New Brunswick, NJ: Transaction Publishers.

Vertovec, S. 1999. Conceiving and researching transnationalism. *Ethnic and Racial Studies*, 22 (2), 447–462.

SECTION I:
Identity

Chapter 1

Performing Transnational Identity Online: Women Blogging from Domestic Spaces

Usha Raman and Sumana Kasturi

Introduction

To say the Internet creates space beyond boundaries is perhaps simplistic. True, one can travel through images and text generated from different places on the globe, allow them to converge on your computer screen in tiled windows, skip from one to another, speak to a distant someone in a foreign language and have a text chat with someone else in your own tongue. You can be here and there, this and that, switch professional and personal selves, all without leaving your seat or switching keyboards. But within this unbounded space there are distinct states of being, each divided in ways as clear as fences in the physical world. There are 'sites' that you walk within and 'portals' you walk through. There are different codes of interaction, (re)presentation and retrieval in each of these demarcated spaces. As we travel through the Internet, we take on different shapes and forms, and we generate our being through the footprints we leave with clicks and moves and in text and image. This 'second self' (Turkle 1985) could be a projection of who we are in 'offline' or 'real life' but it could also be something else, an aspect of personality we create as we find our way through the Net, forge connections and create communities.

Much literature has been generated on the changing meanings and contexts generated by the Internet; the idea of mobility, the nature of self, and the formation and maintenance of community, as well as its meaning and efficacy (Holmes 1998). The Internet has complicated our ideas of location and space; where we are at any given moment is more a function of our cyber-imagination than our physical location. Once we enter the Net we could be anywhere and everywhere at the same time, but in some essential way we operate from an imagined set of coordinates that are very real to us at that moment. Our experience of relationships, with texts, and processes of education and entertainment is divided between the online and offline worlds, as opportunities to engage in multiple contexts (often through multiple aspects of our selves – or our multiple selves) dramatically increase. Negroponte (1995) notes that life in the digital age depends less and less on being at a particular place in time, but others (Whitty and Gavin 2001; Valentine 2006) contend that the experience of specific 'concrete' geographies constructed as they are by the particularities of language, and culture, is important to a sense of place. While incidental communication may not require contextualisation within the structure of space and time, sustained interaction necessitates 'fixing' the other and the self within boundaries of some nature, to enable interpretation and understanding. The online self therefore does require location, even if this location is digitally constructed, thus temporary and variable.

On the other hand, many groups of people are experiencing increasing physical mobility – migrant workers of various hues, a global upper class that shifts with the season, and others who are constrained or who choose to move from 'home' to 'elsewhere'. These moves do not necessarily result in disconnectedness or isolation for all those in this diasporic space. The Internet allows for a seamless re-rendering of communities online, through a variety of mechanisms ranging from email to voice and video chat to social media and mobile telephony. More and more of these postmodern migrants thus achieve continuity by generating a presence online and building links with other online presences, often others 'like themselves'.

As globalisation fuels the massive movement of capital and labour across continents, both the meanings and uses of technology and communication, culture and society, are transformed in the process. Traditional binaries of native and diasporic, or home country and host country, are overturned, to be replaced by a hybridity that goes beyond our conventional understandings of migration and assimilation, voluntary or forced. The fluid and dynamic nature of globalisation restructures not just time and space, but society and culture. In this continuously shifting environment, identity becomes an important anchoring mechanism, yet one must note that the traditional markers of identity (language, religion, nationality, ethnicity, etc.) are both heightened and reconfigured in new and transformative ways. Cultural critics such as Appadurai (1996) have noted the need for a redefinition and a renewed understanding of concepts such as diaspora, migration and transnationalism in the context of globalisation.

Within the growing body of research focusing on themes related to cultural and geographical dislocations, the idea of transnationalism has provided a conceptual category that at once goes beyond the national and subsumes the global. This allows the definition of an identity that combines elements of the national/native with 'international', an identity that moves with fluid ease across contexts, its parts intact, yet part of a larger seamless global flow of ideas, capital and culture. This has been theorised by scholars from different domains but we situate our analysis within the feminist studies approach following the definition by Kaplan and Grewal (2005). In their view, transnationalism requires an 'attentiveness to… linkages and travels of forms of representation as they intersect with movements of labour and capital in a multinational world' (Kaplan and Grewal 2005, p. 357). Transnationalism generates the transnational subject – one who is from and of more than one geographical, political and cultural space, one whose representations become an important element of creating and contributing to the culture of specific transnational groups.

Rajan and Sharma (2006) coin the term 'new cosmopolitans' for these transnational subjects, defining them thus:

> ...people who blur the edges of home and abroad by continuously moving physically, culturally, and socially, and by selectively using globalized forms of travel, communication, languages, and technology to position themselves in motion between at least two homes, sometimes even through dual forms of citizenship, but always in multiple locations (through travel, or through cultural, racial, or linguistic modalities). (p. 2)

The transnational self, then, is a combination of identities that exists in several realms at once; when this self presents itself online, in the space of flows (Castells 1999) that is the Internet, it draws from and projects a kaleidoscope of elements that are differentially integrated and translated by its audience, or those it transacts with. Apart from the complexities produced by reading identity, there is a process through which these elements are differentially selected by a consciously transnational being to construct a visible (or discernible) identity for an imagined (or consciously produced) transnational audience, or members of a co-created transnational community.

The production of self on the Net results from the ability to represent one's personality in a variety of modes and media – through abstract as well as realistic images, combinations of images and their manipulations, texts of different lengths and metaphorical structures, and through the display of linkages and associations (for instance, hyperlinked elements or 'friends' and 'shares' on social media platforms such as Facebook and Pinterest). In this chapter, we explore the creation of the transnational self by Indian women through the act of blogging – a popular means of generating and maintaining presence online, as well as a means of creating community.

'Being' on the Net

Many of us today are 'connected' in some way or other as we use the Internet in our daily lives in multiple ways. By the end of 2011, it was estimated that globally, as many as 2.68 billion people were using the Internet[1] – that is close to a quarter of the world's population. Just under a half of all users are from the Asian region, even though Internet penetration in this region is less than 26 per cent. North America accounts for around 12 per cent of Internet users worldwide, but this represents more than 78 per cent penetration in the region. The numbers grow almost daily, with more and more people accessing the Net on their mobile phones and other portable devices. Much of this use is instrumental and serves specific purposes: browsing for information or making commercial or professional

---

1   Source: www.internetworldstats.com. Numbers as of December 31, 2011.

transactions on the Internet, for instance. The interactive or 'social' portion of the Internet – popularly known as Web 2.0 – encourages users to generate and share content, form linkages and build communities. So on the social web, there are the self-constituting activities of engaging online through one or more of the following: creating email circles, joining discussion groups and social network sites, blogging and micro-blogging, sharing photographs and other information, indicating preferences in visible ways on web pages, and so on. Estimates are that worldwide, around 1.5 billion people will be using social networks like Facebook by 2012[2] – that is, around 60 per cent of all Internet users.

The social web plays an important role beyond information provision and exchange, which has been the key role of the Internet until the advent of social media. Forrester, a market research firm specialising in new media metrics, describes five eras of the social web, the first having begun in 1995 with the 'era of social relationships', progressing through eras where social functionality, social colonisation and social context are predominant, to an era of social commerce, realised by 2013, where these communities deliver commercial value.[3] In its current stage of evolution, the social web has become an important part of the Internet user's life, with an increasing percentage of those on the network spending some part of their lives within this social space. Data from social networking monitoring services suggest that this part of the Internet is registering much more growth than any other. Facebook use in India, for instance, grew by more than 20 per cent in 6 months between January and June 2012, with total users numbering over 8.4 million by the end of this period.[4]

Research and thinking about the social web has fallen into two broad camps (Curran 2012). One group contends that the Internet has created opportunities for people to connect in new and unprecedented ways, to go beyond the limitations imposed by physical presence on understanding the 'other'. The other holds that the Net has made our connections more superficial and transient. Sherry Turkle, for instance, began her work on online behaviour in the 1990s by hailing the Internet as holding promise for more 'emancipated sensibilities' (Turkle 1995). But in her more recent work, she notes that spending time on the Internet actually precludes us from developing richer, more fulfilling relationships offline (Turkle 2011). The debate as to whether the Internet – and more specifically, Web 2.0 – has affected the quality of offline relationships, and whether it is a benign or malign influence on society, is beyond the scope of this chapter. What we do accept is that the Internet does have a bearing on the way we live our lives, and the time we spend interacting with people and expressing ourselves online is important in and of itself. It is an important self-constituting space; it may play either a

---

2   Source: www.emarketer.com. Numbers as of February 2012.

3   Source: http://www.web-strategist.com/blog/2009/04/27/future-of-the-social-web.

4   Source: http://wearesocial.net/blog/2012/07/15-highest-growth-countries-facebook. Accessed 24 July 2012.

complementary or an additive (and in some instances even substitutive) role in how we deal with ourselves and with our social worlds.

Through the words, pictures and electronic thumbprints we leave as we leaf through others' sites, we build a 'literature of the self'. The status messages we post, the notes we write on social networks, the pictures and videos we post/upload to the 'Net', the blogs we maintain, and the Twitter feeds we write and follow all contribute to this. The 'narrative bits' or 'narbs' (Mitra 2010) that users generate on these platforms together serve to build a specific identity that then is put to service in creating a presence online and participating in communities online. The online self, in Mitra's words, is a 'discursive presence', constructed through the accumulation of these narbs over time.

Women are an important presence in the social web, more so than on the Internet in general, which is still dominated by men. A Pew Internet Survey in the United States estimated as early as 2005 that women used the Internet more for social purposes than did men, with women being more 'enthusiastic online communicators' than men (Pew Internet Research 2005). Women's participation in online forums, particularly in non-Western societies, has been linked with the growth of the women's movement in these regions (Curran 2012), particularly because online spaces provided a less 'visible' and therefore more 'safe' space from which to articulate ideas that may be labelled radical or progressive. By the same token, these spaces were also seen as more patriarchal, a sense probably compounded by the fact that fewer women read online content. Curran also notes (citing a study by Youna Kim 2011) that the Web offered women in conservative societies a space in which to imagine a different world, a 'utopian self-imagining' that allowed them to 'remake themselves in a Western context by placing themselves at the centre of their biography' (Kim 2011, quoted in Curran 2012). A study by Richard Joiner at Bath University found that women Internet users in the UK spent more time on social networking and 'communication' than did men (Joiner *et al.* 2012). Market surveys in India too have found that women tend to use the Web more for 'communication' than 'fact finding', and while there are more Indian men than women accessing the Internet overall, women are bigger users of social networking sites (43 per cent of web pages visited by women are social networking sites, compared to just 32 per cent for men).[5]

Given that women appear to spend more time online engaging in communicative functions – interacting with others, writing about their own lives, looking for support from other women or other groups – it would be logical to expect that they would also create more conscious representations of themselves online, or, to use Mitra's terminology, more consciously create 'discursive selves'. Add to this the transnational identity: women who live in adoptive homelands and straddle two and sometimes more worlds. Their relationships and their activities are a complex of two or more cultures; they may integrate into their sense of self their ethnic

---

5   Nielsen reports, http://blog.nielsen.com/nielsenwire/global/smartphones-in-india-web-browsing-is-for-men-texts-are-for-women.

roots and the cultural trappings and values of their adoptive social space. Their presence in a migrant geography often necessitates adaptation of domestic routines that incorporate elements of their homeland and the new country. For those who see themselves as 'international' or 'global' citizens, there is a conscious melding of various external and internal cultural characteristics – cuisine, fashion, leisure, parenting styles, etc. We contend that these find expression in communicative acts online, in their participation in social forums online, in the 'narbs' that they consciously and unconsciously leave behind in their online worlds.

Our interest is in those activities Indian women in the diaspora engage in online that directly relate to the construction and maintenance of identity. The next section discusses one of the many methods by which this discursive self may be constructed online – through blogging.

The Blog: Generating a Net-presence

A weblog, or blog for short, is at its most basic, an online journal that allows users to write and 'post' content in an easy manner. Early blogs required users to have knowledge of HTML and other web design and coding skills in order to build and maintain one. It was only in 1998–1999 that the technology for non-skilled users to build blogs was developed. Blog-hosting sites, Blogger and Live Journal, were launched around this time and allowed anyone who had basic email and word processing skills to start and run a blog. The blog host did the rest. Soon after, WordPress and other similar blog-hosting companies were begun, and there has been no looking back since then.

Technorati, a company that tracks Internet and blog use, has published an annual State of the Blogosphere report since 2004. As of December 2011 there were an estimated 178 million blogs on the Internet.[6] Technorati's 2011 report showed, among other things, that women comprise nearly half of all bloggers surveyed.[7]

The tremendous growth in the number of blogs indicates that it is a popular medium for both men and women. Accordingly, the 'blogosphere', as this is known, is rapidly gaining more importance in both public life and personal lives. Bloggers commenting on news and politics have come to wield increasing clout in the political process in the US (Drezner and Farrell 2004).

Since then, blogs representing ideas and opinions in very many areas besides politics (technology, consumer advocacy, business, news, health, etc.) continue to grow in importance. We may loosely describe these as 'public blogs' – those

---

6   http://www.socialmediaexaminer.com/tag/technorati-study.

7   The 2011 State of the Blogosphere report surveyed over 4000 respondents from all over the world, breaking them down by location, gender, age, employment, and other markers. Source: http://technorati.com/social-media/article/state-of-the-blogosphere-2011-part1.

that relate to matters circulating widely in the public sphere. In 2012, studies reported that there had been a dramatic increase from the previous year; 68 per cent of bloggers cited other blogs as having a greater influence than conversation with friends, which was the primary influence in 2011. The study also recorded a notable increase both in hours spent blogging as well as frequency of posting.[8]

However, there is more to the blogosphere than the 'public blogs' detailed above. New genres of blogs emerge every day. Categorised under the larger heading of 'personal/lifestyle blogs', popular genres of blogs include: food blogs, parenting blogs, fitness blogs, homeschool blogs, design blogs and 'mommy' blogs. Unlike public blogs, these blogs tend to focus on the 'private' or domestic aspects of people's lives. As yet, none of the influential blog survey companies have provided demographic details of bloggers broken down by blog genre/category. Nevertheless, preliminary exploration and general observation, as well as supporting statistics regarding social communication use by women (cited elsewhere in this chapter), lead one to believe that a very large number of bloggers in the personal/lifestyle category are women.

Blogging: Construction of the Virtual 'I'

As blogs become a more important part of our use of Web 2.0, there is a growing body of scholarship studying blogs and blogging. While some focus on the potential of blogs to shape community and the cultures surrounding these communities, other work looks at how the process of blogging helps to create identity. Survey-based research is also growing as scholars from different fields and interests attempt to understand the many uses that blogging can be put to: for instance, to enhance learning or social change, to build community or exchange ideas around specific hobbies, lifestyle choices, or ethnicities, or to develop/construct individual or group identity through the act of blogging itself (e.g. Farkus and Xu 2008; Kerawalla *et al.* 2008; Somolu 2007).

There are some structural aspects common to all blogs, whether public or private. The single most identifying characteristic of a blog is that entries or 'posts' are published in reverse chronological order. As the reader scrolls down the page, they are able to access older posts. A title banner, a main area for the posts to appear, and a side bar that provides additional information are also common to all blogs. The side bar usually contains an 'About Me' (profile of the blogger), a list of recent posts, a category cloud or list, and an archive. In addition, each post has provision for readers to comment and for the owner of the blog to respond to these comments. Frequently, the number of comments that a blog receives per post is used as a marker to gauge the popularity of that blog. Some of the elements may vary somewhat based on the kind of blog and personal choice of the blogger.

---

8 Source: http://happycodes.blogspot.in/2012/06/state-of-blogosphere-2012-introduction.html.

By positioning media as social practice, Hegde (2011) argues for the importance of 'the material specificities of everyday life' as an analytic space in which to study not only the production of individual and collective identities, but also to 'examine how the global is performed, reproduced, and contested' (Hegde 2011: 6).

The ease of use and the 'online diary' feel of a blog encourages personal/ lifestyle bloggers to use it as a record of events or happenings in their lives. These blogs thus become a fluid document of the thoughts, ideas, events and experiences in the lives of these women. As a dynamic and constantly evolving media 'text' of such material specificities, blogs thus become an important social and cultural artefact for researchers.

When one combines the politics inherent in blogging as an act, with the idea of a transnational self and an imagined audience that is also dislocated in time and space – and transnational – many questions arise. What is the self that one chooses to display? How are its different elements combined and what is the effect this creates? While we cannot with any degree of confidence attribute a definite intentionality to the blogger, it is certainly possible to unpack the discourse generated and contributed to by the blog and uncover some notions of self and how it plays out in this space of flows called cyberspace, in conjunction with notions of audience, community, and connection.

In this chapter, we look at the act of blogging; specifically, the private blogs of women and how 'self' or the virtual 'I' is constructed. Individual blogging may be seen as an essentially exhibitionistic act. It depends on a sense of audience, much more than a traditional paper diary, which is a space of confidences. The personal blog instead is a space of shared articulations that masquerade, in a certain sense, as intimate conversations.

One might use the metaphor of a private living room or salon. Geographically, the blogger is blogging in a physical space within the confines of her home. Virtually, she is constructing a space online and inviting the reader into this very personal domain in order to share thoughts, ideas and confidences, where one is invited to sit down and listen to a conversation about (one's) life.

Extending the metaphor, one can say that the writer constructs the blog in the way one might decorate a room, selecting the design, colour scheme, font, blog heading and banner, photographs, etc. Yet, as she constructs and maintains this space, she is very aware of her audience, of inviting her readers into her virtual living room. This is an act of voyeurism on the part of the reader/follower and an act of exhibitionism on the part of the blogger. In the case of the transnational blogger, the process and the result allows the definition of an identity that combines elements of the national/native with 'international', an identity that moves with fluid ease across contexts, its parts intact, yet part of a larger global seamless flow of ideas, capital and culture.

Following the feminist tradition of looking into the artefacts of everyday life to extract meaning and uncover politics, a personal blog can be considered a 'publicly personal' narrative. Within this space, the blogger is engaged in a strategic construction of 'self', creating an online persona that may or may not have elements of their offline selves. Personal bloggers are often consciously positioning themselves in a certain way. Bloggers tend to pick and choose the elements that contribute to their online personas by (usually) carefully choosing which aspects of their offline selves to present and which to eliminate or obscure (Hine 2000). McCaughey (2010) borrows from Goffman (1959) when she points out that bloggers consciously choose which mask to wear when they present themselves in the virtual world. There is (usually) some sense of the imagined audience, and the self is performed keeping this audience in mind. Put another way, there is a strategic identity building that is taking place. Our analysis does not intend in any way to compare the online self with the offline one, but to study the construction and positioning of self through the process of blogging.

Locating oneself in cyberspace is a specific act involving a careful choice of words and visual context. Imagining the audience is the next step: who is the 'you' the blogger will address, and who will be part of the 'we' in her narrative? Visual and textual elements are carefully chosen (albeit from a selection) to reflect personality. The content is limited only by the boundaries the blogger sets for herself.

Middle class, educated women of the diaspora form a significant group on the blogosphere and were among the early Indian adopters of this medium. Accessibility, education, and fluency of language all contribute to their activity online and their sense of ease with the technology, as well as their own strong sense of self.

In this chapter, we follow the identity performance of three bloggers, all women who are part of the Indian diaspora. One currently lives in the United States, the second has lived both in the US and India and has recently moved back to the US after spending the past six years in India; the third moved back to India from the US a few years ago. The blog offers a window into the woman's life, her comfortably polymorphic existence as a modern Indian woman living across cultures, cuisines, contexts. By studying the construction of self among women bloggers in the context of transnationalism, this chapter places itself within research in women's studies, globalisation, and new media.

Methodological and Theoretical Approach

Our methodological approach in this paper is multi-pronged and uses qualitative tools of inquiry. We use a combination of textual analysis of the blogs and interviews with the bloggers themselves. For the textual analysis, there was an initial reading of the entire blog(s) to get an overall idea of the look, content, and feel of the blog. Further, there was a close reading of randomly selected entries over time. This was accompanied by an analysis of the various elements (words, pictures, colours, graphics) and layout of the blog. An adapted version of Herring's (2010) model for Web Content Analysis (or Web CA) was used for this.

Next, two sets of questions were successively administered to the bloggers. The first set asked for some preliminary information and introduced some basic ideas we were trying to explore with regard to their blogging process, perceptions of audience, identity and community, privacy boundaries, etc. The second set of questions tried to probe deeper into issues of imagined location and identity positioning in relation to culture, ethnicity and other socio-political aspects, particularly those we found expressed in the blogs. Finally, we followed up with in-depth telephone interviews (with two bloggers) and a Skype interview (with the third) to clarify and explore these ideas further.

Our theoretical reference points were based on several different sources, some of which were more directly drawn upon for our analysis than others. For instance, a recognition of the importance of the everyday in women's lives was the starting point and initial inspiration of our study. The concepts of gender performativity (Butler 1990) and construction and performance of self (Goffman 1959) informed our analysis of the specific ways in which the bloggers constructed and performed identity online. Theories of globalisation and migration (e.g., Appadurai 1996) and their intersection with research into the role of new communication and information technologies in modern society (e.g. Castells 1999; Morley 2000 among others) were fundamental to our understanding of transnationalism and global identities. Research on media as practice (Hegde 2011; Couldry 2012) and new media as a tool for identity and community building (Morley and Robins 1995) were also useful in understanding how individuals interact with and within this space. Finally, new theories of diaspora (e.g. Rajan and Sharma 2007) and the building of digital diasporas (Brinkerhoff 2009) helped us greatly in our understanding of the changing meanings of diaspora and transnational identities.

In the context of this project, we reiterate that it is important to recognise that analysing the bloggers' portrayal of self is not an attempt to decode or interpret their offline identities, but to understand better how the blogger creates or performs herself in the online space – in fact it is the 'creation/performance' that is of most interest.

Understanding Transnational Identity Performance: Reading from the Blogs and Listening to the Bloggers

A careful reading of the three blogs and unpacking the conversations with the bloggers provides some clues to how these women, and possibly others in similar situations and with similar backgrounds, build their presence online and hence construct an identity in this transnational (or global) online space. The three blogs each have a distinct identity, dealing with different topics with highly individual styles. Our task here was to look for clues to identity, given that all of them are part of what we might understand as the diaspora – one has been living abroad for many years, the second has lived abroad for most of her life but returned to India

Blog Host: Blogger   Blogging since 2005
Blogger: Nupur   Location: New York City and St. Louis, USA
Category – Food Blog

The blog has a short, punchy name, with a clean, simple look: a white background, a small photograph and black title form the banner. The simple yet effective design is very representative of both the blogger and the blog content. The posts document cooking experiments, recipes, menus and ingredients from Indian, Asian and Western cuisine.

Apart from pictures of the food she cooks, this blogger only shows pictures of her dog on the blog. Her husband is only referred to by an initial and there are no pictures of herself, her family or friends, or her house or any other location. There is a conscious separation between her online and offline lives.

About Me: 'My name is Nupur. I am an Indian woman currently living in the United States. I started writing this blog in February 2005 when I was living in New York City. Since 2007, *One Hot Stove* comes to you from St. Louis, Missouri. This blog is a diary of my adventures in home cooking. I have a love for all things home-made and hand-made and a special interest in Indian regional cuisine. Join me as I write about whatever is cooking in my home, from simple everyday meals to attempts to replicate restaurant dishes, baking experiments and tastes of cuisines around the world'.

Figure 1.1   One Hot Stove

Blog Host: Blogger   Blogging since 2007
Blogger: Sangeetha   Location: Chennai, India
Category – Natural Living Blog

The name conveys a sense of freshness and lightness, appropriate for a blog on natural living and mindfulness. The colour scheme is maroon, pale yellow and white – simple, yet with a sense of depth. This blogger writes about parenting, homeschooling, natural living, organic gardening and other related topics. The posts are planned in advance, and carefully thought through as well as researched extensively before being posted. This blogger primarily posts articles she has written about a topic she is interested in – often in a series – or posts about her daily activities related to conscious choices she makes regarding how she wants to live her life.

She occasionally includes photographs of herself or her daughter engaged in an activity, but there are no photos of anyone else in her family or friend circle. The blog tends to be text intensive. The only names mentioned are those of herself and her daughter. For this blogger, there is a small overlap between her offline and online selves, though it is clear that her boundaries are carefully set and followed.

About Me: 'I wait for dawn so I can wake up and do stuff that heal and create. Write about what I care about. Mulch the soil. Sit in silence. Grow herbs. Hand wash clothes. Organise my kitchen. Compost. Experiment with food and healthy living. Research on keeping ants away the natural way. Harvest my backyard spinach. Hang out with people I connect with. Explore collaborations and co-creations. Read. Sew. Host purposeful gatherings. Smile. Cry. Laugh. Grieve. Celebrate. Sing. Dance. Pray. I'm immensely grateful to be able to share my journey through this blog!'

Figure 1.2   **Love, Fresh Air, and Sunshine**

Blog Host: Blogger   Blogging since 2010
Blogger: Kamini   Location: Hyderabad, India and Seattle, USA
Category – Art, Design and Travel Blog

The name evokes a sense of luxury, along with rich colour and texture. Saffron is both colour and spice, indicating intensity of both hue and flavour. In keeping with this, the 'Look' is dark, moody, and rich with a range of maroons, saffron and golds in the background and banner picture. The focus of this blog is on art, design and travel seen through the eyes of a global citizen with eclectic as well as an ethnic aesthetic. The blog showcases the blogger's own home, Indian arts and crafts, other beautiful homes, as well as offering virtual tours of expensive homes and high-end hotels around the world. The online and offline lives of this blogger frequently merge: the blog has lots of personal names, photos and anecdotes.

About Me: '...my name is Kamini. I am an Interior designer by profession and live in Seattle. My husband and I relocated back to India in the summer of 2006 after living in the US for 23 years....It was supposed to be a permanent move...(but) suddenly we were faced with the chance to go back to the US. Though design is my first passion, I am also an avid yogaphile and an artist in a constant state of learning! I am blunt, outspoken, hot headed, impulsive, sometimes a bit irreverent, could care less what others think, but also generous, loving, and hopefully kind and compassionate. I am a vegan, I absolutely LOVE dogs and live here with my husband and 2 dachshund dogs, Lucy a fiery red dog and Junglee, a lazy black dog!'

Figure 1.3   Saffron and Silk

for an extended stay before returning again to the United States, and the third is part of what we might call the reverse migration, returning home after many years in the United States. Their experience of making and remaking home in different places gives them an easy confidence in dealing with a variety of contexts, ideas and people.

The blog is, as mentioned earlier, a space of ideas consciously put together by the blogger, thus serving as an interface with readers – thereby becoming a mark of her identity. Textual and visual elements on the blogs, along with a variety of cultural, social, ethnic, and philosophical/political references, contribute to this construction of identity. The transnational self and its visible identification operates on several dimensions, some of which appear to be consciously adopted/ added, while others may be more unconscious/incidental. Our reading revealed five main threads or aspects of personality/identity building that seemed to run through the three blogs we studied, despite their individual differences. These aspects of transnational identity construction are discussed in detail below.

Theme 1: Positioning the Transnational Self

In the context of transnationalism, we see that all three bloggers have a well-defined sense of their positioning within this global interactive space, where they can be seen by people across geographies and cultures. The positioning is achieved in various ways: the visual aesthetic of the blog; the colours and motifs used; the photographs and font. The textual elements also contribute to this positioning – the name of the blog and the short description, the wording of the 'About Me', the metaphors used and the idiom, as well as references to events, places and personalities and other elements of culture/politics. In short, all elements of the blog are selected to convey a certain impression of 'who' the blogger is. These elements position her socially, politically and culturally, and to some extent, also geographically. The locale plays a role to a varying extent in her writing, and is brought in when it is the reason for a particular post.

For instance, the 'look' of One Hot Stove (OHS) is simple and streamlined. The background is white, the font is basic and black, and the buttons at the top are just black outlined rectangles with the categories in the same font size as the text. The title of each post is in a pale blue, with an occasional highlighted sentence in dark purple. The banner is likewise uncluttered. The banner title (One Hot Stove) and a tag line ('…a celebration of home cooking') are also in a simple black font. Next to it is a small photograph of a hand-crocheted 'Indian Meal' laid out on a traditional banana leaf. All the individual foods as well as the leaf itself have been handmade using different coloured wools. In the About Me section, Nupur, the blogger, explains that it was made by an unknown artist in India and 'represents my interest in home-style food, made and shared with love'. The look of the blog is in keeping with both its content and style. The recipes she shares tend to be simple and quick to put together, and her prose is well written, straightforward and comes across as genuine.

Similarly, the 'look' of Saffron and Silk (SAS) is also indicative of the 'what' and the 'who' of the blog/blogger. The name evokes a sense of luxury, along with rich colour and texture. Saffron is both colour and spice – indicating intensity of hue and flavour. The colours of the blog – dark grey, reds and maroons, orange and golden yellow – are dark, moody and saturated, and convey a sense of richness and high-end style. The photographs in the banner are snapshots of 'vignettes' around the blogger's house that suggest an ethnic-chic aesthetic that is very indicative of the blogger's style. In the same manner, in Love, Fresh Air and Sunshine (LFAS), the choice of colours and design give us a sense of what to expect. A simple blog heading and font choice – both heading and post are in white, and the category buttons in pale yellow. While the title and the colour of the text evoke a feeling of lightness and joy, the background colour of deep red provides depth and some seriousness that is in keeping with the deeply personal and heartfelt ideas and issues that the blogger writes about.

The transnational 'self' at first looks difficult to attach a cultural or national label to – it is unremarkably international in spirit and appearance; the tone and content match that found in the lifestyle or living columns of mainstream Western magazines. On closer look, some of the posts demonstrate a sense of being comfortably Indian yet consciously global in perspective and experience. The bloggers display a rootedness in the domestic (or 'home nation') space, yet are able to integrate global cultures of food, living, leisure and aesthetics, with frequent references to an easy movement across these varied geographic and cultural locations.

As Sangeetha of LFAS says,

> I think I talk about very global issues – for example when I talk about urban farming it is equally relevant to Chennai or India or someone in the US. Of course, if I'm talking about plant species and planting seasons, then it's very local…so it's very specific to the post. (Sangeetha, Interview)

In her blog, Sangeetha displays deep concern about very many matters of global concern – agriculture, education, and women's health are some topics she frequently writes about. She draws from a wide range of sources around the world to research the topic, yet her search for solutions is almost always rooted in her own native culture – be it regional (Tamil Nadu) or national (Indian). For instance, a series titled 'Who are first generation learners?' is inspired by a conversation she has with a store worker. In it she talks about what education means and how indigenous knowledge needs to be more valued. She quotes from Einstein and Justus Von Liebig (known as the Father of the Fertilizer Industry) and then gives real-life examples from Madagascar and India. In this context she relates an anecdote where an infection of the eyelids that her mother had was cured by a Siddha (an Indian system of medicine) remedy when antibiotics had failed to work.

> She stepped out of the doctor's clinic and said 'When my illiterate maid saw my infected eyelid ten days ago, this is what she asked me to do. But I didn't follow her advise (sic) and went to the doctor instead!' (Sangeetha, Blog Post)

On OHS, in a post titled 'Idli, Dosa, Chutney: Brunch Perfection', blogger Nupur describes a brunch with friends where she made Idli, Sambar and Chutney (she gives recipes for these) and her friends brought 'challah (bread) French toast with sliced strawberries'. This multi-ethnic meal is a signature aspect of this blog, where the blogger displays an easy familiarity with cooking, presenting and talking about foods from multiple cultures.

The writing in all three blogs clearly indicates a complete ease and fluency with English, suggesting an urban 'English medium/Convent school' education. The prose is easy to read, articulate and engaging. Nupur and Kamini move easily between 'convent English' (Indian) and American expressions, demonstrating not only their familiarity with it, but also a hybridity and a (conscious) act of assimilation that is a key element of a certain category of diasporic experience. Their prose also sometimes reveals a quirky sense of humour as when Kamini of SAS says in her About Me:

> ALL…(Starbucks)…employees…do a one day barista training…so if you ever need a 5 shot venti, 2/5th decaf, ristretto shot, 1pump Vanilla, 1pump Hazelnut, breve, 1 sugar in the raw, with whip, caramel drizzle on top, free poured, 4 pump mocha – I can make you one! (Kamini, Blog)

In contrast, while Sangeetha's writing is also fluent and articulate, she is somewhat self-conscious about having to write in English.

> Yes, I write in English because it's the language I write and think fastest in. And it's convenient because of the keyboard too. I wish I could write in Tamil like that. (Sangeetha, Interview)

It should be noted that her discomfort is not with the fact that she is fluent in English, but with the fact that she is not equally at ease in her mother tongue. In fact it is this unease that signals Sangeetha's awareness of her transnational identity. Talking to her revealed the deep sense of responsibility she feels towards society and people both in the larger context of the world and in the specific context of her own life. She explains,

> We need to share stories – new stories. We're all part of this big machine – we've been told what questions to ask and we're given the 'right' answers. But we need to ask new questions. It's very important. (Sangeetha, Interview)

While comfortable with their transnational identity, there is a clear sense of the 'I', a performative transnationalism that involves a juxtapositioning (that may be either conscious or incidental) of local and global elements. In Saffron and Silk, for instance, this is achieved by the rich textures and colours of the blog, and the choice of photographs, or by the header in One Hot Stove described earlier. In Love, Fresh Air and Sunshine, words take precedence over design, and the local (or native) flavour comes through in specific references to lifestyle or in the use of ideas from Indian thinkers.

The posts in LFAS draw ideas, quotes and inspiration from thinkers both local and global. There's an interview with educator·John Holt, mention of Vinoba Bhave's philosophy, and Einstein's opinions on religion and science.

> I've grown a lot by reading about others who share their journeys in a fearless way. I find it very inspirational. For instance, Gandhi. He wrote about so many personal things in such a fearless way. I find that very inspiring. (Sangeetha, Interview)

When asked to describe her identity, Nupur of OHS says she is '50-50', one half Indian woman and the other, world citizen. 'This fits me', she says, of her location, where she can choose which elements of 'Indianness' to keep. To be truly transnational in practice, one must be in a place where there is the liberty to selectively retain or practice only those elements of identity that, in Nupur's term, 'fit'. In a space where one is undeniably rooted in body, if not in mind, it could become more difficult to become transnational in practice and feeling. Nupur, for instance, admits that she would have to do many things that are not in conformity with her own beliefs, if she were to live in India.

The juxtapositioning of local and global stands out clearly (and often visually) in SAS as well. A post titled 'My Seattle Home Tour' shows glimpses of a modern American home with wooden floors, a fireplace, and contemporary fittings. Yet the wooden floors are covered with Persian and Indian carpets, a favourite old Indian-style armchair sits next to the fireplace, and the American 'daybed' is covered with colourful Indian cushions and flanked by an antique copper vessel into which are stuffed more ethnic fabric cushions. The house displays a casual yet elegant and strikingly 'global' aesthetic that suggests its occupants are comfortable with both their local (i.e. native) and global identities.

Theme 2: Self-Conscious Reflection

The blog posts are often questioning and inward looking, with the bloggers asking questions of themselves and meeting the responsibility of answering them. The local-global identity that they display makes them aware of the possibility of differential readings. This is addressed by invoking/explaining cultural references at appropriate points.

Responding to a question about her perceived audience, Kamini said that she thinks that the majority of her readers are somewhat equally divided between India and the US. A widget on her sidebar tracks readers and their geographical location in real time and displays as a continuously updating list of readers from around the globe. Her posts are similarly geared towards a differentiated audience: a post on the gulmohar tree introduces this Indian species to non-Indian readers, and one about the festival of Navratri explains how it is celebrated. Similarly, there are posts about life in the US, visits to places all over the world, and an easy familiarity with foods, activities, cities and cultures from both India and the US. Interestingly, both Kamini and Sangeetha do not explicitly address the reader in their posts. There are very few instances where they specifically explain a cultural reference to the 'other'. All descriptions and explanations are part of the larger context of the topic and words, foods, artefacts, and ideas are introduced in a happy mix of both native and diasporic references.

In contrast, Nupur affirms that she occasionally feels the need to explain cultural references to the two sides of her readership – 'Westernized Indians or Indians living in the United States who are looking for different kinds of recipes, and Americans who are interested in Indian food'. The level and kind of explanation varies according to the needs of specific recipes.

> Sometimes I do not go into much detail with an explanation, for instance if the recipe is of the kind that only someone who is keenly interested in a certain kind of cuisine would pay attention to. (Nupur, Interview)

The self-consciousness therefore extends to a consciousness of the reader and her expectations and requirements. Nupur notes that the process of blogging forces one to pay attention to the content and the presentation:

> People are spending time to read what I write, and I have to respect that. I take care about what I say and how I say it; the writing has to be high quality…it shouldn't just be a rant about something. (Nupur, Interview)

Kamini echoes that feeling when she says:

> …the more people you know are reading your blog, well you change the words a little. I don't change what I want to say, but when I'm aware that someone is going to read it, then I 'adapt' it a little so it's more interesting to read, so people want to come back to read it. (Kamini, Interview)

The bloggers display a conscious 'rootedness' in culture and the ethnic aesthetic, and an appreciation of all things ancient and natural, and as in the case of Sangeetha of LFAS, also spiritual. While the narratives may in the case of OHS and LFAS be restricted to themes that are 'domestic', the exposition is articulate, often funny, wry and very aware of larger ideologies and movements. SAS, on the other hand, offers a different window into the blogger's mind. Kamini invites us to see the world as she does, informed as she is by a strong sense of an Indian aesthetic that has been successfully melded with a Western sensibility. SAS goes outside the home more often than not, but the home too has its doors and windows open to the arts of the world.

The muted liberalism and absence of political statements on the blogs demonstrate a (self) conscious reflectiveness, in their choices and their articulation of those choices, as well as a certain awareness of audience that may inform the non-articulation of their underlying ideologies. The bloggers often address a certain 'you' and include an expansive 'we' in this personal reflective space that is at once 'here' and 'not here', but one in which they are comfortable in being who they want to be.

Theme 3: Building Blocks of the 'I'

So what are the aspects of self that make up the transnational person, the 'global citizen' that the blogger represents? The natural/ancient/spiritual aspect is juxtaposed with an equal zest for the modern, technological, exploratory life. The blogs provide a sense of the everyday, lived experience of the diasporic – or migrant – woman. Talking about food, an essential part of this everyday, allows Nupur to bring to the table – quite literally – her experience of assimilation. It also allows her to connect with others whose lives are similarly enmeshed in a multiplicity of cultural networks. While taking about food, she is also able to bring in her role as a mother, a friend, a wife and a professional. In other words, her recipes are couched within these other material contexts.

Talking about how she makes baby food, she explains that she only uses commercial baby food for travel or emergencies, and makes most of the food for her daughter at home and gives an example of what she makes. In other posts she explains how she needs quick recipes to make on weeknights when she comes home tired and hungry from work.

For Kamini, giving the reader entry to her home also provides access to the many aspects of her aesthetic sensibility: the specific objects that she showcases from around the world. There is a careful bringing together of the old (evidence of family history) and the new (adoption of new ideas about food and consumption), the respect for tradition-from-home (religious artefacts) while also being very clued into the contemporary and the here-and-now (shopping at local crafts bazaars). Much of Kamini's blog is highly visual, carefully composed photographs that provide interesting frames of her ideas – and identity.

A photograph of a display table in her Seattle home is accompanied by the following text:

> ...or as meaningful as these wooden ceremonial spoons which our family priest has been using in all our religious family events for the last 50 years, worn out and burnt at the edges from so many years of pouring spoonfuls of hot ghee into the sacred fires...So it has a lot of significance to us. (Kamini, Blog Post)

The global self is about an appreciation of diverse expressions of beauty – in art, in thinking, in living. It is also about consciously and in a carefully considered manner assimilating the best the world has to offer. This casual balancing act that brings together a variety of elements is further evidence of a conscious yet comfortable transnational identity.

Theme 4: Invisible Words, Visible Alignments

Each of the blogs we studied is tightly focused around certain themes. Nupur's One Hot Stove is, in her own words, about 'her everyday, middle class life in an American city', but within this it mainly features recipes for everyday cooking. Sangeetha's Love, Fresh Air and Sunshine is about the life of the mind and the everyday struggle to live a meaningful life. Kamini's Saffron and Silk is about things of beauty, that 'touch her senses', and displays a strong visual aesthetic in appearance and content. But food, spirituality and art and craft cannot be divorced from cultural context. And there are invisible threads that tie the bloggers' writing about food, life and art to a deeply felt cultural core.

Although conversations with the bloggers revealed definite liberal politics (also proclaimed in the About Me section of the blog) and a decidedly eclectic lifestyle, there is little or no specifically political discussion on the blogs themselves.

Interestingly, the ethnic rootedness and respect for 'culture' almost never strays into the realm of religion (this is in direct contrast to domestic blogs of many white American women, which often have a dominant and strongly articulated Christian affiliation). Kamini does not hesitate to say, 'I am extremely liberal, as far to the left as possible. I'm sure people would have concluded from my posts that I'm not religious'.

Similarly, while their numerous references to specific choices with regard to consumption and lifestyle (natural foods, organic gardening, yoga, homeschooling, etc.) indicate largely liberal ideas, there is rarely a direct discussion of the larger politics underlying these choices. We learn where they shop, the kind of foods they buy, the art they display and the school choices they make (or unmake), but there is no connection made between these and the sources of their choices or how they link to the larger socio-political milieu.

Sangeetha broadly refers to the words of major educational thinkers but stops short of contrasting them with the politics of the day – thus avoiding a political positioning which might compromise the equivocality inherent in someone who is in search of a deeper meaning in all aspects of life. Kamini links to other similar bloggers whose penchant is beauty in different spheres of life and the arts and there is an eclecticism that disavows visible alignment to any single body of thought or school of practice. But the reader needs only to unravel a few strands of her writing to understand and grasp where she stands; socially and culturally, and by extension, also politically.

The previously mentioned post about baby food speaks to a larger discourse of promoting natural foods and healthy lifestyles with regard to diet choices. Nupur demonstrates this in her occasional references to local foods, farmer's markets, healthy recipes, and natural ingredients. A regular reader quickly gets a sense of what her opinions are regarding these food and lifestyle-related issues even though she never overtly refers to her politics in this regard.

Taking this a little further, Kamini explains:

> I mostly write about design, but when I mention other things – like my son's wedding (to his partner) – then I want to make people think about something they may have never thought of before. In India, we tend to... (ignore)...these things, but if I, an Indian mother can be happy and supportive of this, then it's possible for others too. I wanted to show that it's the obvious thing to do – I'm his mother and I want my son to be happy. That's all it is. (Kamini, Interview)

Yet, despite photographs and descriptions of events, she never explicitly explains where she stands on the issue. To her, it is enough to just show who she is. The politics are understood.

Sangeetha posts frequently about her interactions with her daughter who she and her husband homeschool. She mentions visits to the organic food store and the things they do there and other similar activities. While she does address head-on the reasons for her choices in some posts, she does not openly declare an ideology or refer to ongoing contemporary political debates on the blog. However, she explained herself a little more clearly during the interview:

> I am part of an extended family (of friends) which seeks to bridge the gap between 'radical politics' and 'radical spirituality'. For instance, homeschooling or eating organic is a political act for me as much as it is one about 'what is good for my family'. (Sangeetha, interview)

The global citizen reflected in these blogs is liberal, free-thinking, deeply introspective and appreciative of the linkages between the hand, heart and mind. This impression is achieved without recourse to direct political discourse, simply by choosing to exhibit certain kinds of behaviours, by letting drop casual references to the way celebrations are conducted (or not), and by responses to events in the domestic domain.

This alignment is also discernible in the linkages made with other bloggers, through comments on posts and responses to these comments, and to the blogger's own sense of community. Nupur, for instance, when asked how she would define her community (of readers), distinguished between those who 'identify with my lifestyle and this group would include people *like me who are liberal* and who like to read' and those who 'come to my blog for recipes alone and do not care about the rest of the content' (emphasis added).

Theme 5: Rendered Virtually Whole

For the blogger, blogging thus brings together on a common platform the various aspects of the self – a way of reconciling the local and global consciousness. There is a strong awareness among bloggers regarding their multiple selves. Some even have multiple blogs, in a sense demonstrating that one online space alone is not enough to articulate all aspects of one's identity (or identities). This could be a way of saying 'there's more to me...'. Kamini, for instance, has in addition to SAS a travel blog and links to her blogs from other social media as well (Facebook, Twitter, Tumblr and Pinterest).

If a conscious or unconscious identity is essentially about transacting with the other, then these online performances allow one to stay in touch with the many aspects of one's hyphenated identity.

> I feel a sense of urgency – when I think of something, I sometimes can't wait to write my next post. I feel it's very important to share. I tell my husband, I might die today and so there's no time to lose – I have to be of some use. (Sangeetha, Interview)

Here, Sangeetha is deeply aware of a certain responsibility she feels as a citizen of the world. She extends her identity of woman-wife-mother-friend, etc. to citizen-activist-thinker/philosopher-educator-learner. For instance, she later explains how she feels about parenting as more than care-giving or nurturing, 'I see my role as a parent as a form of service'. Her blog then becomes another way for her to fulfil the many roles she envisions for herself.

It is important to recognise that hyphenated identity does not refer only to one's ethnic-national associations but also other roles that one fulfils both by choice and constraint. These could include roles within the family and without, profession, neighbourhood and other social obligations, as is the case for the blogger quoted above.

Add to this the further complication of varied interests and politics that may be incompatible with their formal roles and require other spaces to be indulged.

For Kamini,

> The blog is a place for me to write down what I see, pen my thoughts. It's just a place to record my life and thoughts. Sometimes I'll go back and read a post that I wrote 2 years ago and I'll think, oh that's what was going on at that time, that's what I was thinking about. (Kamini, Interview)

And for Nupur,

> At this point, my blog has become an important resource to me because it contains my favourite recipes from the last 7 years, and also a diary of some of my best moments from these years. (Nupur, Interview)

Sangeetha extends this idea by explaining how she uses the blog:

> When I want to say something that may be threatening or embarrassing – it's easier to write a post about it – readers can choose to read or not, respond or not. I can just put it out there and it's done. It's very non-threatening– writing. To the other person. (Sangeetha, Interview)

The blogosphere then becomes the unifier, a space where she can be really herself, a global citizen who can express multiple and sometimes seemingly contradictory facets of her personality. She has no need of labels that constrain her within ethnic, cultural, social, geographic boundaries. On the blog, she is 'at home' in a boundless space that does not need to be defined in these restrictive ways.

Sangeetha explains:

> Sometimes when I have a thought or idea,…you want to say something to someone immediately, but there's no one there. Then the blog allows you to capture that…fleeting insight, works as an outlet so you can talk about it as much as you need to. It helps me…reflect. (Sangeetha, Interview)

Further, blogging becomes a way of finding community – blogging circles and followers – in this neither-here-nor-there space.

> You sort of build a community. You have the same commenters who respond each time…we're all good friends and do everything we can to promote one another's blogs. (Kamini, Interview)

There is the possibility of recovering/reclaiming on one platform the various fractured aspects of self through an engagement with this community. In effect, the blogger is rendered virtually whole.

Conclusion

This limited study of identity performance in the blogosphere gives us a sense of the complex yet comfortable transnational or 'global' personalities of women who, while writing from their domestic spaces, feel a liberating connectivity as online actors. Not only are they able to reconcile the often contradictory values that come with being an immigrant, but they are able to celebrate who they are, and draw together elements from two and sometimes more cultures to make a global whole. The transnational identity is something that goes beyond how the diasporic Indian has been understood; it operates not only among the diaspora, but also among those who have returned home, only to find that they have left it yet again. It is a sense of being both detached from and attached to the local context yet part of a larger world culture.

Women have always been recognised as bringing an important socialising influence to the family, particularly in terms of 'passing on' culture to children. For the diasporic woman, the absence of milieu and the extended family network makes her the key link in the chain of traditional and cultural practices that need to be passed on to the next generation. So the women bloggers in our study may feel the need to engage in traditional practices in their offline lives, but their online identities emerge as areligious, liberal, politically engaged. This domestic narrative of liberality is not only a space of resistance for her individual self, it also represents an oppositional narrative to the 'public' digital accounts that are playing out in the diasporic space, recalling more conservative, often fundamentalist, versions of a nationalist pride. The blogs offer us a view into what may be a kernel of the kind of liberalism that can perhaps go beyond the sometimes divisive and isolating nature of offline immigrant cultures.

Much research into the lives of diasporic women focuses on the ways in which culture is preserved, transmitted, or negotiated with in their everyday encounter with the foreign and new (e.g. Rayaprol 1997; Abraham 2000; Iyer and Haslam 2006). In today's mediated and interconnected context, the lines of cultural difference are easier to cross and smudge. There is a growing transnational population whose everyday is about mixture, about assimilation while maintaining distinctiveness, and about a harmonious coming together of a variety of elements which in the process of adoption become newly local. Rajan and Sharma (2007) contend that 'new cosmopolitans do not depend upon geographical location or the eventual return home to maintain or practice a distinct South Asian identity'. While this has been seen to be true, our insight and research brings us to the conclusion that the reverse is true as well. The 'new cosmopolitans' do not depend on geographical location – i.e. living in a foreign land – in order to practise a liberal, multicultural, transnational identity.

References

Abraham, M. 2000. *Speaking the unspeakable: Marital violence among South Asian immigrants in the US.* Newark, NJ: Rutgers University Press.

Appadurai, A. 1996. *Modernity at large: Cultural dimensions of globalization.* Minneapolis, MN: University of Minnesota Press.

Brinkerhoff, J. M. 2009. *Digital diasporas: Identity and transnational engagement.* New York: Cambridge University Press.

Butler, J. 1990. *Gender trouble: Feminism and the subversion of identity.* London: Routledge.

Castells, M. 1996. *The rise of the network society.* Malden, MA: Blackwell.

Curran J., Fenton, N. and Freedman, D. 2012. *Misunderstanding the Internet.* London: Routledge.

Drezner, D. and Farrell, H. 2004. The power and politics of blogs. *Downloaded from:* http://www.utsc.utoronto.ca/~farrell/blogpaperfinal.pdf. Last accessed: 4 August 2012.

Farkas, D. and Xu, K. 2008. Blogging as a Rhetorical Act. *Downloaded from*: http://www.kejunxu.com/work sample/the_blogs.pdf. Last accessed: 15 May 2011.

Goffman, E. 1959. *The presentation of self in everyday life.* Garden City, NY: Doubleday.

Hegde, R. 2011. *Circuits of visibility: Gender and transnational media cultures.* New York: New York University Press.

Herring, S. C. 2010. Web content analysis: Expanding the paradigm. In: J. Hunsinger, L. Klastrup and M. Allen (eds.), *International Handbook of Internet Research* (Chapter 11). New York: Springer.

Hine, C. 2000. *Virtual ethnography.* London: Sage.

Holmes, D. 1998. *Virtual politics: Identity and community in cyberspace.* London: Sage.

Iyer, D. S. and Haslam, N. 2007. The psychological cost of new cosmopolitanism: Eating disorders in the context of globalization. In: G. Rajan and S. Sharma (eds.), *New cosmopolitans, South Asians in the US.* Hyderabad: Orient Longman.

Joiner, R., Gavin, J., Brosnan, M., Cromby, J., Gegory, H., Guiller, J., Maras, P. and Moon, A. 2012. Gender, internet experience, internet identification and internet anxiety: a ten year follow-up. *Cyber Psychology, Behaviour, and Social Networking*, 15 (7), 370–372.

Kaplan, C. and Grewal, I. 2005. *An introduction to women's studies: gender in a transnational world.* Columbus, OH: McGraw-Hill Higher Education.

Kerawalla, L., Minocha, S., Kirkup, G., and Conole, G. 2008. Characterising the different blogging behaviours of students on an online distance learning course. *Learning, Media and Technology*, 33 (1), 21–33

Kim, Y. 2011. Female cosmopolitanism? Media talk and identity of transnational Asian women. *Communication Theory*, 21 (3), 279–298.

McCaughey, K. 2010. Food in Binary: Identity and Interaction in Two German Food Blogs. *Cultural Analysis*, 9, 69–98.

Mitra, A. 2010. Creating a presence on social networks via Narbs. *Global Media Journal*, 9 (16), 1–18.

Morley, D. 2000. *Home territories: Media, mobility and identity.* London: Routledge.

Morley, D. and Robins, K. 1995. *Spaces of identity: Global media, electronic landscapes and cultural boundaries.* London: Routledge.

Negroponte, N. 1995. *Being digital.* New York: Knopf Doubleday.

Pew Internet and American Life Project. 2005. How women and men use the Internet. http://www.pewinternet.org/Reports/2005/How-Women-and-Men-Use-the-Internet/01-Summary-of-Findings.aspx. Last accessed: 24 July 2012.

Rajan, G. and Sharma, S. (eds.) 2007. *New cosmopolitans, South Asians in the US.* Hyderabad: Orient Longman.

Rayaprol, A. 1997. *Negotiating identities: Women in the Indian diaspora.* New Delhi: Oxford University Press.

Somolu, O. 2007. Telling our own stories: African women blogging for social change. *Gender and Development*, 15 (3), 477–489.

Turkle, S. 1995. *The second self: computers and the human spirit.* New York: Simon & Schuster.

Turkle, S. 1999. Cyberspace and identity. *Contemporary Sociology*, 28 (6), 643–648.

Turkle, S. 2011. *Alone Together*. New York: Basic Books.

Valentine, G. 2006. Globalizing intimacy: the role of information and communication technologies in maintaining relationships. *Women's Studies Quarterly*, 34 (1/2), 365–393.

Whitty, M. and Gavin, J. 2001. Age/sex/location: uncovering the social cues in the development of online relationships. *Cyber Psychology and Behaviour*, 4 (5), 623–630.

Chapter 2

The Trans-Indian: Perspectives on Real vs. Virtual Identity in the Age of the Internet

Ananda Mitra

This chapter considers some of the key constructs and ideas that I have developed over the past two decades[1] and makes the argument that in the emergent digital age, a real-life person is being transformed from a 'real-life' individual to a 'digitally produced' presence that dwells in a cybernetic space that is produced at the congruence of the real and the digital.[2] For the Indian, this transformation is connected with a reconsideration of the term 'transnational' to suggest that another way of considering the term is to hyphenate it and argue for a 'trans-national' who has expanded opportunities to reformulate both the self and the place that the self dwells in.

To support this argument, I begin with the re-thinking of the 'person' by offering the proposition that a person will soon exist in two realms – one of the organic carbon-based 'real' and the other of the binary-based 'virtual'. Consequently, identity is becoming a contested site which can be created, ripped apart and re-created in the digital realm. While the flesh and blood continues to carry the burdens of evolution, the digital has the opportunity of constantly trans-forming its own infinitely hyphenated identity. To begin with, it is useful to consider identity in the real.

Identity in the Real

As anyone looking at me will see, I am a middle-aged, brown-skinned, short-statured being with grey hair and brown eyes. Indeed my driver's license, issued by the State of North Carolina in America, states my eye colour explicitly. My real body, in its living state, is a dead giveaway that I am neither white with its historic privileges nor black with its history of oppression. I am physiologically

---

1 See for a list of selected publications (Mitra 1999, 2000, 2001, 2002, 2003, 2004, 2005, 2006, 2008, 2010, 2011, 2012; Mitra and Watts 2002; Mitra and Schwartz 2001; Mitra and Cohen 1998).

2 The notion of cybernetic space refers to the emergent condition where an individual simultaneously dwells in the real space produced by the surroundings and a cyber space that is entered discursively through a digital tool like a computer or a smartphone.

somewhere in between as are nearly a billion other people from India and neighbouring regions. In the real, I belong to the group called 'Indians' whose real characteristics, as embodied in the organic being, are easily measured and well documented as demonstrated, for instance, by medical research which makes much of my body. Medical researchers will assert that Indians have different sets of diseases, they have unique sets of immunities and are known to eat specific kinds of food that help or hinder their physiological processes. An Indian growing up in India also knows what it means to be a biological Indian in India – we have to deal with environmental threats such as unsafe water and polluted air, we have to be cautious of unreliable medicine at our medical stores, and we have immunities that no one in the developed world can even dream of. When that body is offered clean air and water, it thrives, and diseases that might have assailed the body in India simply do not matter anymore. On the other hand, the body has to accept other threats ranging from unfamiliar weather to unwelcoming stares in public places. The experience of the body is intimately connected to its appearance and where the body is.

The same body is well catalogued in the Indian system of creating a structural social system where people are placed where they belong. A fair-skinned girl is still assured a wealthy husband in the marketplace of arranged marriage, and a female foetus may never be born, just as the colour of the skin of a man would place him in an exact place in the north-south axis of India. These factors of identity are grounded in real life where the fortunate can avoid the body odours of the third-class compartment in the train, just as any Indian-looking person is fair game for a conversation in Gujarati at O'Hare airport in Chicago. It is impossible to deny that we are Indians by look and physiology. To me, this becomes crystal clear when I take a group of students from Wake Forest University to India every summer. We have a parlour game we play – which one of the students can I pass for Indian in India. The question comes down to who looks Indian – or how brown is your skin, how black is your hair, how short are you? This, incidentally, has some real consequences – an Indian-looking American can enter the Taj Mahal at a fraction of the price that the blonde, blue-eyed, white girl will pay to enter that site. It does not take complicated analysis to recognise that a person in the real is grounded by very tangible characteristics of the body – skin colour, body odour, height, colour of eye and hair, and susceptibility to diseases – and those can neither be ignored nor successfully hidden in real life and in the real spaces that we must inhabit.

Spaces in the Real

The real body is placed in a real space because we have to live somewhere. Even the destitute and homeless would claim to live in Calcutta, Chicago or Mexico City. These spaces are defined in many different ways, the most important being the boundaries that place us in a place. Places are defined by mountains, oceans, rivers and other natural borders. These act as real definers of a specific space even before the space has been colonised, fought over, charted and divided by new borders made up of fences and walls. These are the real spaces we inhabit.

While we might not always be aware of the larger borders, we surely make it a point to define our personal borders. Homeowners build boundary walls, shopkeepers put up tables and counters to separate the storage area from the customer, and we often make it a point of knowing the geography of the space we inhabit. When we travel away from the zone of comfort in real spaces we make it a point to learn of the new spaces we might have to go to or travel to. The transgression into real other spaces is often fraught with anxiety as the real body will have to occupy a real space where the body would encounter an unfamiliar geography, environment and climate. Indeed there are carefully arranged mechanisms that allow for such movements where the stress on the real body is minimised. Consider, for instance, the way in which the real body needs to be protected when in real spaces. The Centre for Disease Control (CDC) in Atlanta, USA reminds Americans that 'before visiting India, you may need to get the following vaccinations and medications for vaccine-preventable diseases and other diseases you might be at risk for at your destination'. The discourse is about disease, risk and the real space called India.[3] The real American body is reminded that the real Indian space is different, unfamiliar and risk prone and the body can reduce the anxiety of going to a new place by taking the vaccinations. In this day and age we are constantly called upon to go to new places and at all such moments the real body must prepare for the real place.

The preparation can be at many different levels – from vaccination to acculturation. We read travel guides and consult maps, we ask people who have been there before, and we seek out information about the new space hoping to find a comfort and safe zone in the new place. Indeed Anderson makes much of the ways in which we can describe a place (Anderson 1983). He suggests that real spaces are not only made up of geographic boundaries and characteristics but they are also defined by shared practices of the real people in the real space. People in some countries speak only one language and that fundamental practice defines the space just as its boundaries do. For instance, in Japan most of the people speak Japanese and not any other language. That language defines the real space just as the nation is defined by the five islands. For a real person to carve out a living place in Japan, it could be essential to be able to speak the language that defines the place. Real spaces place these demands on the real person.

These demands are important even if a person never moves out of a place of origin ever in a lifetime. We learn to belong to a place. Even if one is born into a place, one has to become a part of the place and that is a cultural process that happens somewhat naturally. In other cases, we naturally learn to belong to a place where one might not have been born, and when that learning is complete we are allowed to become 'naturalised' citizens of that place – ratified by a passport that

---

3   This information is available at the Destinations Web site of the CDC at: http://wwwnc.cdc.gov/travel/destinations/india.htm.

proves naturalisation. This passport eventually becomes the representation of the real person as the individual crosses real spatial boundaries. It is not enough to present the real person at the border for free passage; one must have a passport – a legal facsimile of the real person – to be permitted the border transgression. In the passport, and similar travel papers and identification documents, we legitimise the real body in real spaces. Yet these papers are mere representations – discourse and text – that define the real person who has to remain constantly cognisant of the borders and boundaries that make up the real spaces as the body moves from one place to another.

Movement

History would show that there have always been reasons for real people to cross real spatial boundaries, leaving a place of birth to occupy a space of adoption. This movement or diaspora has been a historical fact beginning with the movement of Jews when the Egyptian Pharaohs abolished them from Egypt. The concept of diaspora becomes useful in understanding the consequences of such movement. In the contemporary use of the term diaspora, the focus is both on the process of movement and the conditions that the diasporic encounter. The condition is independent of what motivated the movement – need for wealth, avoiding political unrest, escaping natural disaster, family imperatives. Indians who have left India can claim all of the different reasons for the movement away from the place India to other places that include all parts of the world.[4]

In all cases the Indian body, with all its characteristics, moves to a different space which is foreign to the body. Imagine the awe felt by my Indian body, which lived for 24 years in Calcutta, when it encountered snow in North Carolina for the first time. This is not only a moment of cultural discovery or that of culture shock; it is a diasporic moment when the body must acclimatise to weather it has never seen before. On a very visceral level, diaspora brings with it the physical and physiological conditions that become a significant portion of the diasporic condition. Those physiological shocks accompany the cultural shock that is a part of the diasporic experience as well. Everything is new to the diasporic Indian body. The accumulation of snow to the mysteries of the cultural mores of the new place are all equally shocking.

History has shown that the outcome of the shocking process is the search for a safe and comfortable place in the new space. Just like others who have experienced movement, the diasporic Indian must eventually find such a place in Sydney, Chicago, London or Cape Town. This process too has been one of creating new real spaces and places that offer comfort. The Indians learnt from what people had

---

4   There is a vast literature on diaspora and identity formation and much of the argument has been that the diasporic condition leads to some unique lived conditions that have a permanent influence on identity.

done before and quickly colonised places in the new space. Southall happened on the outskirts of London, a portion of Devon Avenue is renamed Gandhi Marg in Chicago, Hindi language store signs have become commonplace in markets of Dubai and children in schools in UK complain that all their group mates in a class project speak Urdu. Indians, and people from neighbouring countries, produced the new areas in the new places and in the combination of the geographic ghettoing and the preservation of language and culture Indians, like others, have produced their new identity by co-opting the real new space.

Such has been things for a long time. However, the status quo gets called into question with the invention of the Internet and the opportunities presented by the age of creation and distribution of digital discourse. I argue that the normalised term – transnational – morphs into a hyphenated identity narrative where people become Trans-National, i.e., Trans-Indian.

The Discursive Internet

It is often confusing to refer to the technological innovations that create the digital world possible by a single term – the Internet. Indeed, this much maligned word, along with its compatriots such as cyber-space and virtual-space, is often simplified too much and synonymised with the term Web. I urge some caution in the use of the language, and for the purpose of this chapter, I would separate out the terms. First, when I use the term 'Internet' I mean the technological system of connectivity that allows numerous computers to be able to communicate with each other. Second, when I use the term 'Web' I mean a specific computer application that operates on the Internet platform. And finally, I use the term 'cyber or virtual space' as the imaginary place where digital discourse resides. In this parsing, the key is the discourse. The computers on the Internet running some variation of the Web program would be inconsequential unless there was meaningful discourse that populated the hard drives of the millions of computers. Eventually, it is this discourse that becomes the point of analysis and inquiry.

It is this discourse that resides on real hard drives as binary data that produce the cyber space because the Internet connects the hard drives and the Web allows universal access to the discourse. For the most part, the discourse is produced by real people living in real spaces using real digital tools to produce the discourse that populates cyber space. Absent the people in their places, and the digital world becomes barren. Thus real people produce the virtual places. And the real people live both in the real world as well as the virtual world they create – veritably living in a cybernetic space that happens at the congruence of the real and the virtual.

To understand cybernetic space it is important to consider the ways in which the digital discourse is produced and circulated. It is real people who produce this discourse. These are people who sit at a keyboard and use tools such as the Web to create home pages, blogs, vlogs, and profiles on social media. These are the people who find a personal voice because they are now empowered to be able to speak in a forum where they have gained an affordable way of voicing themselves.[5] Their personal discourse makes up the content of Web sites and podcasts. Not only is each individual speaking, they are also getting access to the voices of others who are also creating digital discourse on cybernetic space. Eventually, we have the equivalent of digital heteroglossia unlike anything Bakhtin could have imagined (Bakhtin 1981).

Examination of the discourse would show that there are two primary tendencies that are evident in the process of creating the discourse. First, the process produces a discursive digital self, and the second is the creation of discursive cybernetic space where the digital discourse and the real space come together to produce a place where the real person can hope to fit in, independent of where the real place is located on the globe.

The first tendency creates the digital presence of the person in virtual space. The real individual becomes transmuted by the digital discourse into a digital person that resides in cybernetic space. It is this digital representation that seeks relationships and friendships based on the digital presence the real person has created.

The second tendency deals with the way in which digital discourse can produce specific real spaces that alter the nature of the real space. Consider, for instance, the way in which digital tools such as television programs delivered by the Internet, easy access to Voice over IP software and similar other tools shape our real lived experience by providing the discourses that surround us. It is both these tendencies that help to shape the Indian who lives in cybernetic space. In the next part of the chapter, I examine these tendencies with respect to the Indian body placed in real spaces in and outside India. In order to do this I will create hypothetical people with claims of Indianhood placed in many places.

Indians Everywhere

For Indians who choose to leave India and go away to a different place for an elongated length of time, the diasporic experience is not unlike what other migrants have faced. Historically, Indians have tended to move to places where English is the primary language, making the transition to the new place somewhat smoother for Indians who can speak and understand English. In the post-World War II and post-Indian Independence period, particularly starting in 1969, there was a significant movement of people from India to America. I will use America as the destination for my hypothetical Indian abroad. The movement to America has continued since the early 1970s, waning and expanding with changes in American

---

5   The key argument is that new technologies empower people to be able to voice themselves. Examples of that happening can be traced from the early days of the development of digital communication tools and it continues as new technologies allow common people to access the tools to propagate their voices.

immigration policies, Indian economic opportunities, and global political changes. However, if one were to consider a young Indian professional who moves to the USA in the early 2000s, we would encounter some specific cultural components that have been made possible by the emergence of digital tools.

To begin with, the actual process of moving the body from India to America is a relatively smooth process requiring the negotiating specific border control protocols and eventually travelling in relative comfort and in a short time to reach New York from Calcutta. However, prior to the geographic move, the real person could easily have created a digital presence, perhaps a Web site or a blog, which resides in cyber space. This does not move with the movement of the real body. The blog does not need to negotiate any national boundaries and that discourse remains fixed exactly where the real person had produced it before leaving India. The Web site exists as a Web address that remains accessible to anyone in the world, independent of where the real body that created the Web site might be. Indeed, my previous work with blogs has demonstrated that it is notoriously difficult to tease out real body location from the discourse of the blog. It is quite possible that the real body would never disclose the movement and all those who relate to the real body via the digital presence in blogosphere might not even be aware of that portion of the narrative about the person. To those observers, diaspora has not even happened for the protagonist of this hypothetical tale.

This process is also true for another aspect of the digital presence of an individual – the address to which e-mails could be sent. By the early part of the twenty-first century e-mail addresses were insensitive to geographic location. The popularity of systems such as 'gmail.com' and 'hotmail.com' was making it possible to maintain relationships without disclosing location. The connections established via e-mail contact are insensitive to where the body is as long as e-mails can be sent and received. An e-mail sent from New York or Delhi appears the same to the receiver who might be in London. For instance, even when I am travelling outside of the USA I retain access to my e-mail and unless I wanted to let others know, there would be no way for many to know that I am not in the USA. In this condition I can retain all my relationships as long as I have access to my e-mail. Similarly, as long as people receive my responses there is no reason to 'miss' me or even notice my absence. The era of relationships forged on meeting face to face, at a coffee shop, in the neighbouring market, in the 'real' is supplemented by meeting in the virtual where the meeting is between the discourses we produce and the tales we tell about who we are as we produce our digital selves.

Perhaps nothing at this time does this better than the explosive popularity of social media.[6] It is quite likely that our hypothetical Indian would have had a presence on one or more social media platforms and that presence too is unhindered by physical movement. Regular updates of status using the narrative

---

6 There are numerous resources that describe the growth of social media. For instance, current statistics demonstrate that the number of people who are on Facebook add up to be the third largest country in the world (http://www.socialbakers.com/facebook-statistics/).

bits, or narbs, which the person produces keeps him in view of his friends.[7] As long as one is narbing there is no reason to miss the person or question the person's real whereabouts. It might indeed be true to say that if the person is narbing then the person is relating. To all the friends in the social media sphere the person is very much 'there' as long as there are narbs emanating from the individual. The old days of acutely missing a loved one who has gone away are replaced by a persistent digital presence where every minute detail of the person's life might be visible in the narbs. Where the person is in 'real' could become irrelevant in this new condition except for a small number of people who were physically close to the person – perhaps living under the same real roof in India. For the others whose relationship with our protagonist was based purely on digital discourses, the issue of physical displacement is a non-event.

The possibility of digital stability actually mitigates one of the key challenges of the diasporic condition which is the loss of familiar relationships. Early European immigrants to the USA would longingly wait for letters from loved ones in the old country to retain a sense of connection with the old place. Even recent immigrants like me, who reached the USA in 1984, would have to wait days to get an aerogramme from my father. It was those hand-written discourses that maintained the relationships and allowed for retaining a balance between adaptation and retention. It is the dwindling of those connections that leads to the need to make new connections in the new land, making the diasporic experience acutely palpable. The digital tools call those historical diasporic processes into question. Our protagonist would need access to a computer, even a smartphone would suffice, to retain any digital connections that were produced before leaving India. Nothing has changed in the digital realm because there has been no movement in that part of the cybernetic existence of the protagonist. Just like those who are observing the person in digital space do not need to know of the physical movement, our imaginary individual can deny any movement too. The body might suffer through jet lag and might need to acclimatise to different weathers, but the digital Indian is exactly where he was before she left India and arrived in America. There is no diaspora at that moment because a significant component of the self has not moved anywhere. It is up to the real person to even acknowledge the movement when creating the digital presence. One need not narb about movement, one need not reveal it in an e-mail, one can turn off location services on the smartphone and there is no evidence of movement. It is as if the real body refuses to accept the movement and the body only needs to adapt to the geography but in all other aspects the self is in India, digitally glued to the everyday relationships that were born digitally and flourish in the virtual.

While the relationships are central to the negotiation of the diasporic experience, there is also the concern with the real space in which the real body

---

7   The notion of the narb refers to a tiny digital narrative, or a 'narrative bit'. The narb offers a theoretically stable way to consider how the discourse of social media can become meaningful and analysable (www.narbs.info).

is now inserted. The space is different from India. Our protagonist in America is faced with numerous new cultural elements that need to be negotiated in order to have a reasonable quality of life in America. For this too, the digital realm becomes peculiarly important. First, the real body which was in India in the early 2000s was always and already digitally connected with the West. One of the most important aspects of this connection is created on the computer screen which becomes the conduit to produce virtual discursive spaces where many media formations meet.[8] With the availability of mediated messages from all over the world, the Indian in India is no longer restricted to media produced in India. Without a doubt the media ecology of India has changed, especially with respect to broadcast and cable television from the 1980s, but those changes need to be superimposed with the changes in the way in which the Western cultural practices have entered the personalised media space created around the computer screen. It is no surprise that one of the most popular shows in 2011, watched on television screens and the computer screen in India, was the American situation comedy 'How I Met Your Mother'. This show discursively brings America into the homes of the Indians who eventually go to America. The availability of such shows on the Web has also been coupled with video social media applications such as YouTube where the Indian in India has already discursively experienced the place where the body is now really located.

America is not the mystery it might have been to the immigrants of the early years looking up at proverbial awe at the Statue of Liberty as the ship pulled into Hudson Bay, nor does it have the mystique that it held to graduate students from India like me who looked with astonishment at the Manhattan skyline, with its Twin Towers, as the plane landed at Kennedy airport in 1984. With the flow of digital discourse and the expansion of global multi-national capitalism, America and its practices are accessible at the local mall in any metro in India. The diasporic moment of discomfort is now replaced by a sense of seeing and experiencing the same hamburger with a local twist or watching an American sports show surrounded by people who look like the people playing the sport. The discursive America was already a part of our traveller's life.

There is, however, another way in which the diasporic nostalgia of the real place left behind is mitigated by digital means by the Indian who has now arrived in America. Just as American sitcoms are available through the computer screen, 'Chikni Chameli' and 'Why so Kolaveri di' are also seamlessly available on the computer screen on the dinner table in the apartment in Manhattan. Much like ESPN streaming in on the home TV in Delhi, the combination of services such as Yupp TV, Dish Network, live streaming of the latest Bollywood music on Pandora, and the multiple versions of the same song on YouTube creates a digital Indian bubble where the real body is immersed in a virtual discursive place where the

---

8   The idea of the media formation goes beyond the examination of a single medium. Here the focus is on the ways in which different elements come together to create a set of cultural connections and around that create a media formation.

real place recedes into the background and only becomes visible when one steps out into the cold December evening to go to the Indian grocery store to pick up frozen samosas to be had with tea while watching the latest Bollywood release on BWCinema. The real Indian in America in the twenty-first century can completely create an India in America that is produced precisely in the way that Anderson described nations – around practices.

Consequently, my hypothetical character only goes to America when he has to go out to earn a living and she is back in India as soon as she comes 'home'. This individual in Los Angeles lives a life much like the call centre worker in Hyderabad who manages incoming service calls for HP and goes to work in 'America' every night at the swank call centre office in Hyderabad and then goes home to India at the end of the night. Diaspora is equally true for both these individuals as they cross through imaginary and discursive lines as they move through real space. What the Indian in America has produced are multiple spaces in cybernetic space where the spaces have different levels of alienation yet none of the spaces are uncomfortable. The fundamental anxiety related to traditional diaspora begins to disappear for the new Trans-Indian.

However, the transformation of the Indian into the Trans-Indian is not only true for the body that has physically moved but discursively remained where it chooses to be. Mobilising the idea of the Trans-Indian offers an opportunity to expand the identity of any individual who might have claims to India. The next part of the chapter demonstrates the way in which the idea of Trans-Indian can help re-think the entirety of a person's identity narrative.

The Trans-Indian

The new person in the end Trans-forms into many people in many places. This is evident in a recent blog by Martin Bryant in the blogosphere called 'The Next Web' who seeks to find a passport for Internet citizenship.[9] The blogger claims that in many ways, for many of us who are living in cybernetic space, some of the aspects of nationhood and nationality are becoming irrelevant. These are the identities that are depicted in Figure 2.1.

Starting at the bottom left side of the box, the lower left quadrant is the only part of the identity where the real body is in real India and can claim to be a national Indian rooted in the real space of India. This is a vast India but is certainly not always the privileged India. Movies such as 'Khaap' and 'Rewaz' are made of this place. Or this place is romanticised as the 'real' India, whereas the development of tools such as Akash and the penetration of smartphones is quickly drawing this place into the digital realm. Once the body leaves this place and enters the India made up of McDonalds and The Colours of Benetton, the identity narrative of the

---

9   This is available at: http://thenextweb.com/insider/2012/03/11/im-a-citizen-of-the-internet-where-do-i-get-my-passport/.

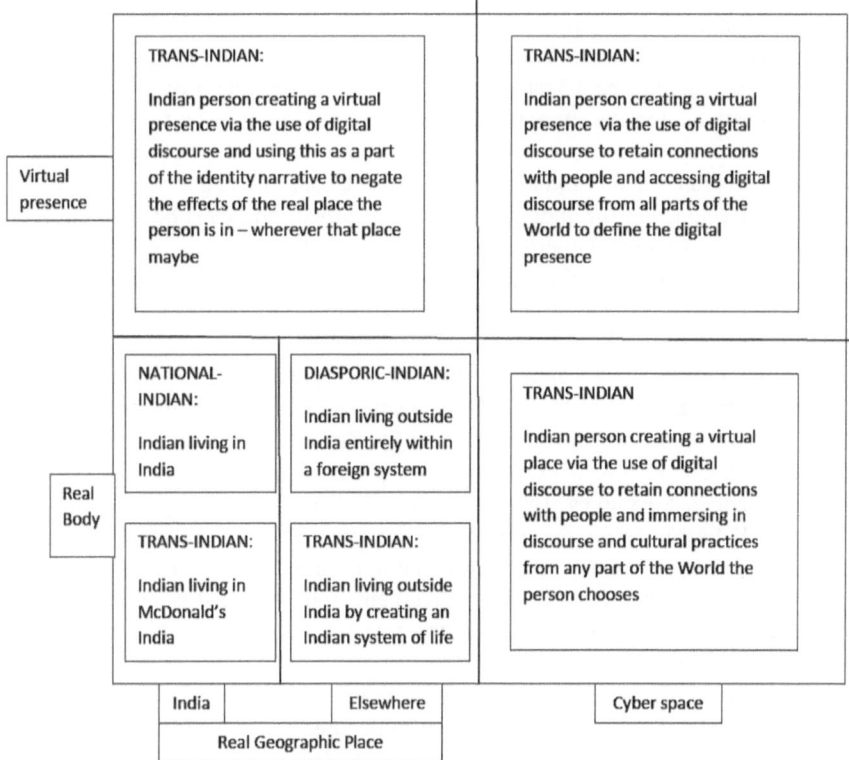

Figure 2.1 The Identity Components of the New Indian in the Early 21st Century

body begins to take on a specific version of the Trans-Indian. This Trans-Indian is the person to whom everyday life is influenced by global products and services, and to be the person the individual must be, the person must re-construct the self without ever leaving the national boundaries. Some industries in India glorify this Trans-Indian. Consider, for instance, the way in which employees of call centres across India are reminded that they must become Western in order to best handle the Western customers.[10] To the Trans-Indians working in this industry, the change in the identity narrative is palpable – Ananda must become Andy, and Saraswati must remember to introduce herself as Sara when on the phone.

Once we leave this segment of the lower left part of the quadrant, we have left the Indian national identity narrative and all the other narratives are indeed Trans-National. Each of these identities are also different from each other. For instance, continuing to focus on the bottom left part of the quadrant, the greater the access

---

10   There is sufficient evidence to claim that there is a concerted effort to 'Westernise' the call centre worker, often with negative impact (see readings on call centre).

to Indian culture outside India, the greater is the opportunity to reject diaspora. Some Trans-Indians who run businesses on Devon Avenue in Chicago might never feel that their identity as a Trans-Indian has to shed too much of the traditional Indian narratives. On the other hand, those who are stuck in parts of the World where there is little access to Indians and Indian practices in the space around them might create a Trans-Indian identity that is closer to being a person from the place of adoption. Yet the Indian part of the identity can never be shed entirely because of physiological imperatives. I would argue that diaspora for Indians does not take the Indian out of the narrative but offers the opportunity to construct a Trans-identity that becomes most appropriate for the individual at a specific place and time.

The other parts of the quadrant all create different kinds of Trans-Indians. In the bottom right part of the quadrant, where the real body is in virtual space, the person has many ways of constructing themselves. The Trans component of the identity becomes pliable as the real body produces itself in the different kinds of digital spaces it occupies. This is the Trans-Indian who is always rooted in the discursive but cannot deny the real body it occupies. This is the Trans-Indian who surprises friends and family, who know the real body, by disclosing feelings on social media sites that appear new or divergent from the identity created by the real body. Within this quadrant, the identity narrative is influenced both by the real body and the digital discourse it produces.

In the top right part of the quadrant, where the discursive self dwells in cyber space, the opportunities for creating Trans-Indian narratives are limitless, and this is the place where the Indian part of the narrative could completely disappear. The discursive self, untethered from the real body and the real space, has countless ways of constructing identity. This is not a process that only Indians participate in. Indeed, one of the most popular multi-player virtual games in the world is Second Life where any real person can create a persona, called an avatar, which becomes a new identity for the person in the second life gained in cyber space.[11] In places like Second Life, the person does not have to be from any place at all because the person is already in a virtual place. The Trans-Indian here comes closest to being the global Internet citizen whose identity is completely created by discourse controlled by the real body which never has to disclose the real characteristics of the body or the real place where the body is located.

Finally, in the top left quadrant, where the discursive self is located in a real space, the Trans-Indian can retain any component of the discursive self that the person wants. Here the real place becomes acutely evident as the body creates its discursive presence. The Trans-Indian can create the identity narrative around the place they are in. This is not unlike the process of creating social media updates

---

11   Second Life has been a focus of attention as it has garnered an increasing number of people who live the other life on this 'game' site. It has led to significant controversies as described in: http://www.wired.com/culture/lifestyle/commentary/sexdrive/2007/05/sex drive_0504.

that talk of the place the person is in. A person from India travelling to a different place can create the Trans-Indian self by chronicling the influences of the place on one's identity. In being the Trans-Indian, the person does not deny the real space the person is situated in, but allows the real place to help construct the discursive self and allows discourse to re-construct the real place. A person doing a nostalgic blog about Bollywood while watching a Bollywood music video sitting in Sydney is the Trans-Indian who resides in this quadrant.

It is important to note that while these quadrants offer ways of thinking of the emergent identities, one individual can possess any of these identities components and move between them. A person is not tied to any one of these identities and indeed a person can move smoothly between these identities. Other than the national Indian identity, each one of the other identities offers the opportunity to answer the question: 'Who will I be today?' as opposed to the far more stable answer to 'Who am I already and always?' The traditional position of a subject in ideology, somewhat powerless and subjectified into a specific position in a structure, is being problematised as the digital systems and greater opportunities

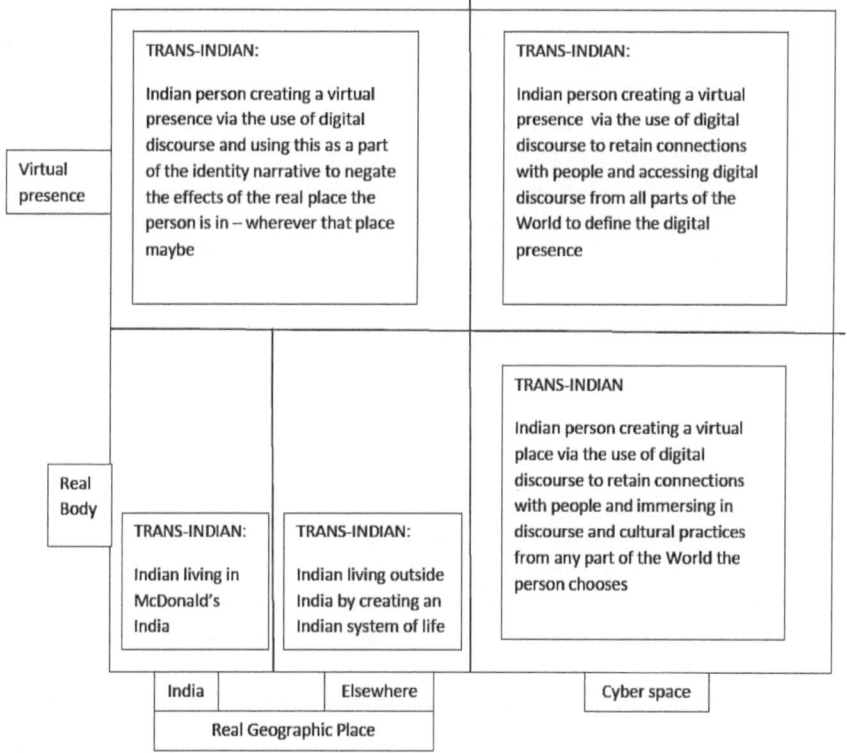

Figure 2.2   The Identity Components of the New Indian in the Middle of the 21st Century

for movement are empowering the individual to wear specific identity narrative hats to create the Trans-Indian.

There are many consequences of the production of the Trans-Indian, of which I touch upon only one – how the rest of the world looks at this Trans-Indian. I focus primarily on the economic glance. The evidence would suggest that the pliable Trans-Indian is an increasing object of desire for global capital. It is this Trans-Indian who is now bombarded with advertising at 'home' and 'abroad' as the Trans-Indian adopts and shapes everyday lived practices that are fluid and open for re-formation. Western products are pushed out on television in India just as satellite networks in America would advertise basmati rice available at the neighbourhood 'Patel Brothers Grocery Store'. The Trans-Indian travels seamlessly between London, Paris, New York and Sydney and Bollywood is able to play that out at its best, just as Tom Cruise comes to Trans-India to accomplish the impossible mission in a parking lot of Mumbai. There is no turning the process around. The Trans-Indian and Trans-India are here to stay and will remain propped up by all those who see the potential of this new national and identity formation.

The future would be worthy of examination. As Figure 2.2 shows, it could be a matter of time and technology before the bottom left quadrant, where the national Indian identity found a place, disappears. The evidence for that movement is found in a recent *New York Times* article about the entry of Starbucks and Amazon into the Indian market where the author notes, 'It signals the latest episode in India's remarkable process of Americanization'.[12] What started as a trickle in the 1990s has now become a flood of global capital entering the Indian real space. It is up to the economists and politicians to debate the influence of this on the Indian infrastructure, but at the level of everyday life practices that produce the narratives and discourses we live by, the Trans-Indian is probably going to be the majority identity narrative for people who would otherwise have said 'I am from India' in an introduction at a cocktail party in Chicago. A couple of decades in the future, that utterance might be as appropriate at a cocktail party in Hyderabad. So, in closing, I simply ask, 'Will the real Indian please stand up?'

References

Anderson, B. 1991. *Imagined Communities: Reflections on the Origin and Spread of Nationalism*. London: Verso.
Bakhtin, M. M. 1981. *The Dialogic Imagination: Four Essays*. Ed. Michael Holquist. Trans. Caryl Emerson and Michael Holquist. Austin: University of Texas Press.
Mitra, A. 1999. Characteristics of the WWW Text: Tracing Discursive Strategies. *Journal of Computer Mediated Communication*, 5 (1).

---

12   Thisisavailableat:http://www.nytimes.com/2012/03/11/opinion/sunday/how-india-became-america.html.

Mitra, A. 2000. Virtual commonality: Looking for India on the Internet. In: D. Bell and B. M. Kennedy (eds.), *The Cyberculture Reader*. New York: Routledge, 676–694.

Mitra, A. 2001. Diasporic voices in cyberspace. *New Media and Society*, 3 (1), 29–48.

Mitra, A. 2002. Trust, authenticity and discursive power in cyberspace. Communications of the Association for Computing Machinery (ACM).

Mitra, A. 2003. Diasporic online communities. In: K. Christensen and D. Levinson (eds.), *Encyclopaedia of Community*. Thousand Oaks, CA: Sage, 1019–1020.

Mitra, A. 2004. Voice of the marginalised on the Web. *Journal of Communication*, 54 (3).

Mitra, A. 2005. Creating Immigrant Identities in Cybernetic space: Examples from a Non Resident Indian Website. *Media, Culture and Society*, 27 (3), 371–390.

Mitra, A. 2006. Towards finding a cybernetic safe place: Illustrations from People of Indian Origin. *New Media and Society*, 8 (2), 251–268.

Mitra, A. 2008. Using blogs to create cybernetic space. *Convergence*, 14 (4), 457–452.

Mitra, A. 2010. Creating a Presence on Social Networks via Narbs. *Global Media Journal*, 9 (16).

Mitra, A. 2011. Collective Narrative Expertise and Using the Narbs of Social Media. In: Takseva (ed.), *Social Software and the Evolution of User Expertise: Future Trends in Knowledge Creation and Dissemination*. Hershey, PA: IGI Global.

Mitra, A. 2012. Using narratives from social network to manage teacher-student interaction. In: Méndez-Vilas (ed.), *Education in a technological world: communicating current and emerging research and technological efforts*. Formatex Research Center.

Mitra, A. and Cohen, E. 1998. Analysing the Web: Directions and Challenges. In: S. Jones (ed.), *Doing Internet Research*. Newbury Park, CA: Sage.

Mitra, A. and Schwartz, R. L. 2001. From Cyber Space to Cybernetic Space: Rethinking the Relationship between Real and Virtual Spaces. *Journal of Computer Mediated Communication*, 7 (1).

Mitra, A. and Watts, E. 2002. Theorizing cyberspace: The idea of voice applied to the Internet discourse. *New Media and Society*, 4 (4), 479–498.

Chapter 3

From the German Periphery – On Ethnographic Explorations of Indian Transnationalism Online

Urmila Goel

The aim of this chapter is to reflect on the formulation of research questions as well as the processes and consequences of research. This focus has been inspired by discussions at the international seminar 'Indian transnationalism online: ethnographic explorations' in Hyderabad in 2012. Accordingly I am taking the title of this international seminar and explore it in three stages. Firstly, I question the concept of 'Indian transnationalism', in particular the meaning of 'Indian' outside of India. Secondly, I look at barriers to 'transnationalism online'. Thirdly, I discuss 'ethnographic explorations' of virtual spaces. At each of these stages I add to my theoretical deliberations material from my research about the *Indernet*. This is a virtual space founded by people identifying themselves as (second generation) Indians in Germany, which started in summer 2000 as a meeting place for others who were similar to them in terms of this linkage of India and Germany. Following the discussion of 'Indian transnationalism' I show, firstly, how the users and editors of the *Indernet* relate to the concepts of Indian and German. Secondly, in exemplifying 'transnationalism online' I discuss how far the *Indernet* can be considered as transnational. Thirdly, I describe my ethnographic explorations of the *Indernet*. After thus having discussed the three parts of the seminar title, I conclude by looking at the figure of the ethnic entrepreneur (Brubaker 2004), in particular in the form of the webmaster and the researcher, whose projects are coded in ethnic terms.

Indian Transnationalism

The phrase 'Indian transnationalism' can be understood to refer to the migration from India to other parts of the world and the consequences thereof. This interpretation as well as the phrase itself, however, raises questions.

The first one is: What is India and who is an Indian? Does India refer to the Republic of India? Or to what used to be British India? What defines an Indian? Citizenship, birth place, ancestors, culture, physiognomy and/or something else? And if so, what exactly defines these? Which ancestors, what culture, which physiognomy and what else? Is Indianness something embodied, passed on by the genes of the parents and thus a biological category? When does one qualify as an Indian and when not (Goel 2008a)? Is Indianness something homogenous and if so, what about the differences between people? Do we use the term Indian as a category of practice or a category of analysis (Brubaker 2004: 31–33)? Who has legitimation to define Indianness for what purpose? Which categorisations are we using when and why?[1]

Brubaker (2004: 31–32) argues that (ethnic) identity is used as a category of practice

> by political entrepreneurs to persuade people to understand themselves, their interests, and their predicaments in a certain way, to persuade certain people that they are (for certain purposes) 'identical' with one another and at the same time different from others, and to organise and justify collective action along certain lines.

These ethnic (political) entrepreneurs pursue economic, political and/or social aims, which are coded in ethnic terms and thus mobilise in these terms. Researchers might also act as ethnic entrepreneurs, creating the category they are investigating. Thus, it needs to be asked why researchers use concepts like Indian as categories and what aims they pursue by this. How far is their category of Indian linked to nationalist projects? And to which? Which role does, for example, Hindu nationalism play in it? Who is included in the category and who excluded, and why? What political, economic, social aims are pursued thus in the research?

When I think about 'migration from India' or 'Indian transnationalism', I am guided by constructivist theories of social identities, among others Jenkins' (1997) concept of transactional ethnicity as well as Barth's (1996) and Cohen's (1985) theorisations of ethnic groups or Brubaker's (2004) of ethnicity without groups. Ethnic identity according to them is not something essential but the outcome of social interactions. Furthermore, this transaction takes place in societies structured unequally through power relations such as racism, heteronormativity or classism.[2] The ascriptions are thus not innocent but rather place the individual in a more or a less powerful position within the society. I am interested in these power inequalities, their consequences for societies and individuals and how individuals deal with them. Thus in my research I focus on the transactional nature of Indianness, i.e. I do research about people who are marked as Indians. This means they are considered on the basis of some physiognomic and/or social markers to be

---

1   For a more detailed discussion see Goel (2007, 2008). Compare also Brubaker (2004) for a discussion of ethnicity without groups and Anthias (1998: 564) for a questioning of the concept of Greek diaspora.

2   Authors such as Anthias (1998) criticise the focus on ethnic identity for ignoring other factors determining individual lives (such as gender or class) and argue for an intersectional approach.

Indians and/or consider themselves being Indians. As these ascriptions are specific to particular spatial and temporal contexts, it is necessary to further specify the latter: in my research this is contemporary German-speaking Europe (with a focus on Germany).

Thus entering the context of the transnational, the second question is raised: What does Indian transnationalism mean? If the term Indian refers to the Republic of India or an Indian nation, then the phrase combines the nation and the transnational. It does not transcend a national logic, but actually continues it. It seems to be linked to the notion of diaspora in the sense of dispersal from one place of origin (Cohen 1997; Safran 1991) with India at the centre and the transnational linked to and through it. This notion, however, has been criticised for overemphasising the role of the centre (Clifford 1997) and essentialising identities in terms of nation or ethnicity (Anthias 1998; Goel 2007). Furthermore, the concept of diaspora can be (mis)used in nationalist projects. An example of this is *The Encyclopaedia of the Indian Diaspora* (Lal 2006): My article on Germany (Goel 2006) was changed by the editors without my authorisation to include a passage titled *Netaji* about Subhas Chandra Bose's activities in Germany and the Indian legion there. While my original text[3] highlighted Bose's problematic coalition with the Nazi regime, the inserted passage wrote heroic Indian history. An aspect of German (and Indian) history has thus been decontextualised and its violence negated.

Furthermore, while Lal (2006) tries to map the whole world, covering each continent and even places like Eastern Europe, most literature about the Indian or South Asian diaspora(s) focuses on the regions with large populations traced back to South Asia, in particular Great Britain and the USA as well as the countries in which Indians were brought as contract labourers and to some extent also Canada, Australia and West Asia (e.g. van der Veer 1995; Bates 2001 or Oonk 2007). It is left to the researchers from the (European) periphery[4] to include analyses from there (e.g. Jacobsen and Kumar 2004; Jacobsen and Raj 2008). Coming from the peripheries it is thus difficult to find analyses from other peripheries to which one can compare one's work. Another issue is that of language: if academic literature is written in languages other than English, the accessibility of it is transnationally much restricted. For (academic) transnationality, the English language is necessary, which, however, means that local audiences (both academic and non-academic) are potentially excluded.

Indian Transnationalism and the *Indernet*

The name *Indernet* is a play on words, taking the German word for Indian 'Inder' and combining it with the English internet abbreviation net for network. It thus

---

3   http://www.urmila.de/UDG/Forschung/texte/encyclopedia.html (accessed on 25 July 2012).

4   Other peripheries are probably even less internationally noticed.

signifies a network of Indians. This meaning, however, can be understood only by those understanding German (and English).

Although the *Indernet* started trilingually in German, English and Hindi, only German was actively used (and by now Hindi has totally disappeared). The language German is not only linked to Germany but also to Switzerland and Austria. Thus despite the editorial focus on Germany, there have always been active users from the other two countries as well as users in other places of the world who grew up with German. The usage of German was not only a consequence of language competence, as many users also did know English quite well and did use English language spaces as well, but reflected the localised context of their interaction, which was best expressed in German and probably also only made sense in German (Goel 2008c).[5]

Like the notion of German, that of Indian was interpreted quite flexibly by different people on the *Indernet*. There were those with one or two parents, who migrated from India to Germany, but also users, whose parents were from Pakistan or who were adopted from Sri Lanka (Goel 2005, 2008a). In spite of their heterogeneity, these users and editors were marked by physiognomic and/or social markers as (imagined) Indians in German-speaking Europe. Accordingly, this is the category of analysis I am using for them although their categories of practice might have been quite different. Those marked as Indians in German-speaking Europe are transnational in the sense that they belong to several natio-ethno-cultural[6] contexts of belongingness at the same time and move between these at least in imagination (Mecheril 2004: 73). I thus adopt and adapt the phrase 'Indian transnationalism' to refer to a biographical link to India imagined from a location in some other natio-ethno-cultural context.

Transnationalism Online

Internet technologies from early on have been seen as tools to cross (not only national) borders, make them less important and connect people over long distances. Ethnographic studies like Miller and Slater (2000), Greschke (2012), and Miller (2011) show that the internet is used by migrants to keep or develop transnational ties. They show that the internet is used in particular for everyday interactions and that in these several different technologies are combined. But internet technologies cannot cross all borders; many borders do remain or become even stronger and new ones develop.

Fundamental to internet usage is access to technology and technological competence, which determines who can go online and who cannot (Morley 2000: 186–188; Tawil-Souri 2009). Once technological access is given, the question of

---

5   For the importance of the location see also Anthias (2009: 12–13).

6   I use Mecheril's (2003) term natio-ethno-cultural for the ascriptions made with respect to the diffuse concepts of nation, ethnicity and culture.

language competence becomes crucial. Even though the internet increasingly offers video and audio technologies, still internet communication is focused very much on language (written and increasingly spoken). To participate in the communication one needs to read and understand the language used as well as be able to write and speak it oneself (Tawil-Souri 2009: 32). Goggin and McLelland (2009) show that the internet is much more multilingual than anglophone internet studies suggest. They collect analyses both about widely used internet languages such as Chinese or Korean as well as about languages spoken by very few persons such as Welsh or Catalan. They show that the anglophone focus of internet research cannot be legitimated by the false claim that English is the most important language of the internet. It is much more an issue of the language competences and interests of the researchers as well as the unequal power relations in the world. Jeganathan (1998: 517–518), for example, shows how an American company can imagine itself online as placeless and universal, even though the location in the USA is implicitly made clear not only by using English but also by offering destinations all over the world with the exception of the USA (from which the other destinations are to be reached).

Besides the language, the issues dealt with in the virtual spaces set barriers. The topics dealt with depend on the location of the people involved, not only their geographical but also their class, gender, natio-ethnic-cultural, etc. location (Anthias 2009: 12). Not all people are interested in the same things, not all people can relate to the same things. Thus Greschke (2012: 23) argues that although in principle anybody could access the internet space *Cibervalle*, in practice it does not only need a particular language competence, but one also must be able to find the space in the depth of the internet. She goes on to argue that the people who are most likely to find *Cibervalle* are those who are searching particularly for information about Paraguay. They must share a specific interest with the others in the space not only to interact, but first of all to find it.

Research about online communication of people considered Indian outside of India (or to use the language of the seminar: Indian transnationalism online) similarly has certain biases. When I started my research, I found mainly USA-centred research (e.g. Rai 1995; Mitra 1997 or Mallapragada 2000), although often this focus was not explicitly stated but rather became obvious implicitly. I also found much on Hindu nationalism online (e.g. Lal 1999 or Brosius 2004), which again was very much USA-centric. At the international seminar, at which this work was first presented, this dominance of locations and topics was to some degree reproduced. All this research is valuable for me, because it deals with the question of migration and the internet, but the Indianness of it hardly relates to the Indianness of my research field in Germany. Thus this work on Indian transnationalism online is hardly more relevant to mine than Miller and Slater (2000) or Greschke (2012), which share my ethnographic interest. Similarly, Gajjala's (2004) *Feminist ethnographies of South Asian women* are important for me not so much because of the natio-ethno-cultural ascription of the research field, but much more because of the critical feminist and postcolonial perspective (like

Kuntsman 2004, 2009). There might be research on similarly peripheral Indian transnationalism online as mine, which would be more relevant to me. But so far I am not aware of it (most probably both because of my lacking language competence and the limited accessibility of research from the peripheries of anglophone academia).

The *Indernet's* Transnationalism

As said above, the *Indernet* started trilingually, but only flourished in one language: German. The language and the topics linked to it made the *Indernet* special for its users. It made it different from English language online spaces used by people in Germany, such as the transnational *shaadi.com* or the mailing list *GINDS* (Indians in Germany). For those socialised in German-speaking Europe and marked as Indian, the *Indernet* provided a virtual space in which they could use their everyday language to discuss issues linked to their everyday lives and to chill out with others like them. It provided a space of the second generation, in which they could imagine being natio-ethno-culturally like everybody else within the space and where they were safe from racist Othering (Goel 2005, 2009).[7]

The *Indernet* was a transnational space in the sense of catering for the multiple natio-ethno-cultural belongingness of its users and giving them the possibility to jointly imagine their belongingness to India in German-speaking Europe. On the *Indernet* they could talk about India and develop their own image of India in reaction to dominant images of India in German-speaking Europe and the images of their parents. Here they could also acquire and develop information they needed to succeed in everyday interactions. People marked as Indians are often ascribed an expert knowledge about India and they are asked questions that, being socialised in German-speaking Europe, many cannot easily answer. To avoid admitting ignorance, acquiring the necessary answers for the most frequent questions is a helpful strategy. The *Indernet* was thus a space of negotiating, debating and developing one's own position on issues somehow linked to India. Here the editors and users could reject, adopt and adapt images according to their needs. All of this happened in German and based on the experiences in Germany, Austria and Switzerland negotiated with others from this region about an India, which in its realities was far away for most of them.[8]

The *Indernet* was very localised not only by the language and the contents discussed there, but also in terms of its users and editors. There was no significant interaction online with people from India or Indians outside of German-speaking Europe. Nonetheless the *Indernet* opened the possibility of being in German-speaking Europe and imagining oneself part of a global Indian diaspora. It did so

---

7   For similar analyses see Mandaville (2003: 146), Greschke (2012: 100–106) and Kuntsman (2009: 13–15).

8   For a more detailed discussion of the imagining of India see Goel (2008b).

by symbolically offering the three languages through the project description and by offering information about Indian popular culture in the UK.[9]

Besides this imaginative transnationalism, there was also interaction, which crossed natio-ethno-cultural as well as national borders, on the *Indernet*. In this virtual space not only young people with parents from different parts of India came together, but to some extent there was also pan-South Asian interaction, in particular with users, whose parents came from Pakistan. Furthermore, the *Indernet* linked young people in Germany with those in Austria and Switzerland and it allowed people who were brought up in these countries and who were temporarily abroad (studying in the USA or UK or doing an internship in India) to stay in contact with those back home. The *Indernet* transnationally connected those who felt themselves somehow connected to India and German – a very localised transnationalism.[10]

The description so far has been in the past tense, because the zenith of the internet portal *Indernet* lasted from its foundation in the summer of 2000 until about 2006/07. After this there was a phase of near standstill, during which the interactive parts of the portal were inactive and the editorial section was hardly updated. In autumn 2011 suddenly the *Indernet* was reactivated. A blog has taken the place of the internet portal and is interlinked with a Facebook page. Thus a new *Indernet* is developing, which is much less centred on enabling communication between Indians of the second generation and more on providing information about India (in Germany). It might well be that with the new opportunities social networks like Facebook offer, those marked as Indians in German-speaking Europe now have much less need of a virtual space like the internet portal *Indernet* to communicate with others like themselves. Within Facebook they can develop and maintain their own networks of communication. This is something they also already did, while the *Indernet* functioned as a space of the second generation. Not only did they communicate publicly in forums or chat rooms, they also used other features of the *Indernet* to get in touch with people. They consulted in particular the events calendar to meet people offline and used a media mix of forum, chat, private messages, email, instant messenger and phone to communicate with others. The *Indernet* was the place where information about Indians in Germany and their meeting places could be found and where one could initially meet. This function might now be taken over by Facebook, where there are several spaces and paths to find others like oneself. Looking at Facebook walls and friends list (as far as they are public to me), many of my former interview partners are interacting both with others marked as Indian in German-speaking Europe and those marked as Indians elsewhere. In some sense this is more visible in Facebook than it was on the *Indernet*. Facebook also seems to provide better opportunities to address different friends differently, both in terms of language and topics.

---

9 For a more detailed discussion of the Indernet's transnationalism see Goel (2008c).

10 For more discussion see again Goel (2008c).

The coexistence of different users and different usages is not a new phenomenon. Besides those marked as Indians and socialised in German-speaking Europe, there have always also been users from the dominant societies in Germany, Switzerland and Austria (increasingly so from the middle of the 2000s) and to some extent also Indian IT professionals, who recently migrated to German-speaking Europe, have been using the *Indernet*. While according to my material for many of the first category, the *Indernet* served as a space of the second generation (Goel 2005, 2009), this was by no means the only function it fulfilled for them. Like for members of the other two categories, the *Indernet* was able to cater for many differing interests. Among these are getting information about India, showing interest in India, discussing India (Reggi 2010) and looking for information about India and Indians in Germany. In fact, I was told by a number of my informants (both white and marked as Indian) that they primarily observed the *Indernet* to learn and stay informed about the second generation in Germany.

The virtual space of belongingness was thus only one (or maybe also several) subspace(s) that could be found under the roof of the *Indernet*. It/they coexisted with other spaces catering for other interests. Since there were different entry points into the *Indernet* (the homepage, the forum, the chat, etc.) and paths through it, users could use the portal in quite different ways without noticing these differences and imagining doing the same as everybody else. The users marked as Indians and socialised in German-speaking Europe could thus navigate the *Indernet* without interacting much with users of the other two categories (for the latter this was probably less possible). When people of the different categories, however, met and interacted, this might also be understood as a transnational interaction in some sense. It seems that in particular the white users imagined themselves to enter on the *Indernet* a transnational space, giving them the possibility to interact with Indians who they imagined to be fundamentally different from themselves (Goel 2008b; Reggi 2010).

Ethnographic Explorations

Many internet scholars now claim to do ethnographic studies. In most cases this seems to mean that they conduct interviews and/or observe internet usage for some limited time. They use methods from social and cultural anthropology, but stay rooted both methodologically and theoretically in their own disciplines (such as media and communication studies, sociology, etc.).

My interest in ethnographic explorations, however, is much more rooted in the discipline of social and cultural anthropology and in developing its methods for the virtual space further. In particular, my interest is in the embeddedness of the use of internet technologies in the offline world. Accordingly, I drew heavily on and was influenced by Miller and Slater (2000), who starting from an offline place (Trinidad) followed different paths of internet usage. They argue that 'the Internet is not a monolithic or placeless "cyberspace"; rather, it is numerous new technologies, used by diverse people, in diverse real-world locations' (Miller and Slater 2000: 1) and that accordingly internet usage should be analysed in its particular contexts (in their case in Trinidad and its diaspora). Furthermore, Miller and Slater (2000: 1–23) demand a full-fledged ethnographic approach, criticising the arbitrary use of some ethnographic methods:

> We assume ethnography means a long-term involvement amongst people, through a variety of methods, such that any one aspect of their lives can be properly contextualized in others. (Miller and Slater 2000: 21)

In their case,[11] their study of the internet in Trinidad built on former ethnographic research by Miller in Trinidad and internet research by Slater. They combined fieldwork in Trinidad itself with a longer period of fieldwork online. Offline they conducted interviews, hung around cybercafés and places of friends, chatted with people, used informal encounters and a questionnaire. Online they did much of the same, hanging around, chatting and emailing as well as analysing internet data. Ethnography for them, however, not only requires a variety of methods, but a lasting 'immersion in a particular case' (Miller and Slater 2000: 21), which is needed for as much contextualisation of the material as possible. This in-depth analysis of a special case they argue can then be used as part of a comparative analysis to formulate generalisations. It can also be used to analyse long-term developments as Miller's (2011) study on Facebook usage in Trinidad illustrates.

Rather than starting from an offline space like Miller and Slater (2000), the ethnographic explorations of Greschke (2012), Kuntsman (2009) and Shahani (2008) start (like mine) from a virtual space (the transnational Paraguayan forum *Cibervalle*, *The Pan-Israeli Portal of Russian-speaking Gays, Lesbians, Bisexuals and Transsexuals* and the mailing list *Gay Bombay*) and then follow paths and topics from there. Like Miller and Slater (2000) they look at the embeddedness of the online in the offline world, do multi-sited long-term in-depth analyses and take into account several perspectives. In their openness to the field, their ethnographic analyses follow clear theoretical questions. Greschke (2012) is, based on theories about world society, interested in the role of the internet in migrants' everyday life and the emergence of global communities. Shahani (2008) looks at globalisation, gay love and (be)longing in contemporary India and bases his analysis on internet, queer and globalisation studies. Kuntsman (2009) starts off with an interest in queerness, migranthood and nationalism in Israeli on- and offline spaces and ends by analysing figurations of violence and belonging in contemporary Israel. She does so based in feminist, queer and postcolonial theory. Their interests thus all go beyond just analysing the internet. They are interested in questions relevant to the respective societies and thus contextualise their material in the respective time, space, political, etc. context. Their ethnographic explorations thus provide

---

11   Miller and Slater (2000, pp. 21–22) describes their ethnographic approach, which I summarise in the following.

localised analyses of communication crossing (not only natio-ethno-cultural) borders.

The difference between using ethnographic methods and doing an ethnography might be summarised by the focus on the long-term multi-perspective involvement in a particular offline or online space, which allows the researcher to notice subtleties and developments. In order to do this, the research, even if it is multi-sited, must carefully contextualise the material according to the particular localities analysed. Coming from critical racism, postcolonial and queer feminist theory I add that, furthermore, it should be guided by a clear epistemological interest beyond the pure observation of the internet.

The Ethnographic Exploration of the *Indernet*

In my ethnographic work I started from the virtual space *Indernet*. From there I pursued different paths linking different on- and offline spaces, attempting to understand more about how the *Indernet* was used by different people and what relevance this usage had for them.

But first I had to get to know the internet portal in order to make it the centre of my research. The path to the *Indernet* began long before its foundation in the summer of 2000. It began by getting involved in seminars for second generation Indians organised by the Indo-German society (DIG) since 1994. Through these I got in contact with others of the second generation from all over Germany, learned about their biographies, experiences and activities and thus became interested in researching the situation of Indian migrants and their children in Germany. I started to publish articles in an Indo-German magazine and during my master's course in London conducted small research projects on issues related to this group of people. Due to the particular migration history from India to Germany in the mid-1990s, for the first time a sizable number of children from migrants from India were old enough not only to search for their own spaces, but also to found them themselves. Thus not only the seminars of the DIG took place, but also local youth groups developed, several club nights of Indians of the second generation for the second generation were organised and young people experimented with the internet. In November 2000 the youth group of the DIG (of which I was a part) organised a networking seminar for the second generation, in order to get to know each other and improve cooperation.

It was at this seminar that I got to know the founders of the *Indernet* and became interested in the internet portal, of which I had heard a short time before. Shortly afterwards I started to observe the portal, and sometime later I applied for research funds and began the full-time research project *The virtual second generation* in spring 2004.[12] I was interested in why and how people socialised

---

12   For more information about the research project see http://www.urmila.de/english/research/virtual/virtualindex.html (accessed 6 June 2012).

in Germany related to India and what determined their ethnic self-description.[13] Already being influenced by constructivist theories, I questioned an essential Indianness and accordingly used the term 'virtual' in a double meaning, referring both to the online space where the 'second generation' met and to the imagination of a 'second generation'.

In my research process I was guided by the principles of grounded theory (Creswell 1998), adapting my approach, methods and analysis in accordance with the empirical material and my theoretical deliberations. Thus came, influenced in particular by Mecheril (2003), a shift in interest from ethnic identity construction to racism. Critical racism theory provided me with an analytical tool to understand why the *Indernet* attracted users, who were in many ways very heterogeneous and could not be described well by referring to (constructed) ethnicity (Goel 2008a). However, what most of my interview partners and those whom I observed had in common was that in German-speaking Europe they were ascribed as Indians by others. It linked the *Indernet* user, who had spent part of his/her schooling in India with her/his parents and family, with the user, who was adopted as an infant from Sri Lanka by white parents and never since had contact with South Asia. Racist ascription and not a joint ethnic identity formed their (implicit) commonality.

Since 2000 I have been observing the Indernet and have archived different parts of it. In particular in the time between 2004 and 2006 I occasionally participated in forum discussions, contributed articles to the editorial section, was on a few occasions in the chat, have exchanged personal messages and emails with other users and editors as well as attended offline events (organised by both *Indernet* editors and users). I also visited Indian offline events organised by other ethnic entrepreneurs and irregularly visited other websites administered by young people socialised in Germany and marked as Indians there (such as *digaachen*, *indianfootball*, *happyindia* and *pak24*).

My participation on the *Indernet* was mainly one of a distanced lurker, staying most of the time an observer and hardly considering myself part of the *Indernet*.[14] That said, in the time of my most intensive observation from 2004 to 2006, I became so used to the virtual space and its practices that I felt quite at home there and was emotionally involved in what was happening. It also happened often and still happens that people assume that I am part of running the *Indernet*. In order for the other users to know or remember that a researcher is observing them (Rutter and Smith 2005), I tried to make myself visible from time to time. Once in a while I posted an article in the editorial section or posted in the forum. My signature in the forum informed users about my research and provided a link to

---

13 I had already pursued this question in my master's dissertation on citizenship and identity (see http://www.urmila.de/UDG/Biblio/Citizenship.pdf (accessed 27 July 2012).

14 Greschke (2012, p. 43) argues that lurking is one form of participating in online spaces and thus is a legitimate form of participant observation. She, however, also argues that the researcher will thus only get a restricted insight into the space – the perspective of the lurker.

my homepage,[15] where detailed information about the research project could be found. When I joined the chat, I told those chatting with me that I was a researcher.

In 2006 during a technical crisis of the *Indernet* a standby forum was opened by a user, which then developed into an independent forum used by several former users of the *Indernet*. I started observing this forum as well, registered with the same nickname, but stayed a pure lurker, i.e. read the posting but did not post myself. For a short time I was also registered in *StudiVZ*, a German social network similar to Facebook, which was in 2006/07 much more popular than Facebook. In October 2011 I finally joined Facebook to follow more closely the *Indernet* Facebook page, which was started by the editors in 2010, as well as the *Indernet* group started by users in the same year. I also used my Facebook account to get back in touch with people I had interviewed and was quite successful in this.

Between 2004 and 2006 I conducted more than 80 open interviews about the *Indernet* with the three founders, current and former editors, users (from occasional lurkers to very active posters) and observers. Among the latter category were researchers, journalists who had written about the *Indernet* or were interested in India, as well as webmasters of other South Asian spaces, DJs, musicians and club night organisers, i.e. young ethnic entrepreneurs. Most of the interviews were conducted face to face. When this was not possible, either because the interview partner wanted to stay anonymous or I did not have the resources to meet her/him, I conducted email or personal message interviews.[16] For contacting interview partners I used my own networks among people socialised in Germany and marked as Indians there, contacted *Indernet* editors and users, posted a call in the editorial section of the *Indernet* and followed interesting traces found on the internet portal. Most of my interview partners were brought up in Germany (a few also in Switzerland or Austria) and were ascribed there on the basis of different physiognomic and social attributes as Indians. I interviewed only a few white Germans, most of them observers, but also two users, who had answered my call: an anonymous poster and a former editor. This dominance of those marked as Indian among my interview partners was mainly determined by my research question and my networks. It should not be taken as a clear indication of the composition of the users of the *Indernet*.

The long-term observation provided me with the possibility of becoming familiar with the space and its users, to notice subtle and considerable changes and developments. I observed that the subspaces of, entry points to and paths through the *Indernet* were continually changing, sometimes slowly and sometimes abruptly. I noticed users coming and going, becoming more or less active. I saw changes in the project description of the *Indernet* as well as in the editorial team and the type of articles posted. I had to adjust to changes in technology, features coming and going, the forum organisation changing and occasional technical crises. My

---

15   http://www.urmila.de/UDG/Forschung/forschungindex.html (accessed 27 July 2012).

16   For the difficulty of asynchronous online interviewing see Kivits (2005).

long-term involvement also made possible chance encounters in other contexts with people somehow linked to the *Indernet*. So, for example, when I met a person in 2008 for an interview in a different research project, s/he told me that s/he knew me from the *Indernet*. Furthermore, the long-term interaction with me gave my interview partners and other informants the chance to get to know me and my research better. Some of them followed my blog or contacted me for information and support. Several followed the news on my website about the research project and sometimes they interacted with me critically about my research. This also happened occasionally when I sent interview partners a published article, in which I had quoted them. Befriending many of my former interview partners on Facebook, I had the impression that several carefully chose their privacy settings for me in order to avoid me analysing their contents. It seemed to me that they had learned to adopt a controlled interaction with research over the years and were less naive.[17] Also the editorial team was always careful about which information it disclosed to me and which it did not. At the same time it used my research for their marketing, advertising it as a proof of the *Indernet*'s excellence.

The *Indernet* changed from an internet portal to a blog and Facebook page and thus from providing one roof for many independent subspaces to offering two nodes in a network. From offering a space for the second generation, it changed to being one of several suppliers of information about India (in Germany). These changes have several reasons: technological change, (dis)continuities in the management of the *Indernet*, biographical developments of the editors, demographic change with respect to the second generation, changes in the interest of the white German audience, etc. These developments could be analysed from many different perspectives: internal organisation, types of usage, types of users, forms and content of communication, forms and content of representation, etc. The choice of the research question is not straightforward but an epistemological choice to be made, and one that needs to consider research ethics (e.g. Gajjala 2004; Kuntsman 2009: 12, 27; Rutter and Smith 2005; Miller 2011: xv). At the periphery of Indian migration in Germany the number of those marked as Indians is rather small and people can be easily identified. Accordingly, it has to be carefully decided which information is published and how to effectively anonymise the informants as much as possible.

The Role of Ethnic Entrepreneurs

Having started with the construction of India, Indian and Indian transnationalism and its protagonists, i.e. the ethnic entrepreneurs, I want to come back to them now. There are many ways in which people outside India are involved in constructing something Indian. They can initiate Indian spaces, produce Indian products, foster

---

17 Compare Gajjala (2004: 19–27) on how the insider by becoming a researcher becomes an outsider and is treated with more caution.

Indian ideas, etc. All this can be done for a number of reasons and with quite diverse aims from altruism to economic benefit. But all of them are involved in (re)producing Indianness outside of India discursively.

In the case of the *Indernet* it was in particular the founders but also the editors who jointly and in interaction with the users created an Indian space, in which users (and editors) could negotiate and develop their ideas of Indianness in German-speaking Europe. The different persons involved will have done so for their own reasons and with differing intentions; both will also have changed over time. In particular at the beginning it seems that the founders created the space they wanted themselves, providing the possibility to meet others like themselves and also to experiment with the new medium internet. There seemed to be a genuine interest of many involved to do something for the community. However, it might be argued that this community did not exist as such before the *Indernet*, but rather was developed through the internet portal. But there most probably were also other aims pursued by the engagement for the *Indernet*: recognition from peers, parents and the German public, the wish to change the image of India and Indian in German-speaking Europe, access to events and important people, etc. From the beginning onwards and in the last years increasingly, it seems that there was also an interest in being taken seriously as a business partner, getting advertisements and media partnerships, being hired for marketing issues and potentially for earning money.[18]

Similarly the webmasters of other Indian virtual spaces, Indian DJs, musicians and event organisers, journalists as well as others involved in ethnic entrepreneurship in German-speaking Europe will pursue their projects for a number of reasons such as the love of music, the racist exclusion in mainstream clubs, a genuine interest in Indian politics, the impression of a business opportunity, etc., and with differing aims such as anti-racist politics, Hindu nationalism, economic interest, etc.

Also the researchers, who work on those marked as Indians in German-speaking Europe, have to be included here. They are also ethnic entrepreneurs involved in constructing Indians and Indianness, even if their aim is the deconstruction of ethnic identity (as it is mine). With my research I am placing the categories of my research within the academic realm (which in German-speaking Europe did not consider them before), making them relevant and fixing them in my terms. My research, furthermore, can be used by other ethnic entrepreneurs like the *Indernet* editors or Lal (2006) for their own ends, which are outside my influence. Like other ethnic entrepreneurs, my reasons for doing research are numerous: to earn recognition, to help my career, to earn money, out of an interest in others natio-ethno-culturally like myself, to deconstruct Indianness, to understand the mechanisms and consequences of racism, etc.

---

18   The Indernet founders and editors never shared information about their financial situation with me. They only always stressed that they were not making money from the Indernet. The Indernet, however, always displays several advertisements, is part of media partnerships, conducts raffles and addresses advertisers very professionally.

All of us ethnic entrepreneurs offer products that are coded in ethnic terms, market them and hope that there will be enough demand to make our efforts worthwhile. When we are successful with this, when people take our goods, then the transaction, which is necessary for transactional ethnicity to materialise, takes place. India, Indian, Indianness become a reality when people relate to our products, take them as something real and thus make them real. But in the German-speaking periphery of Indian migration, this is a precarious business. The numbers of people marked as Indians are rather small and the persons live scattered over Germany, Switzerland and Austria. Thus most everyday interactions take place with little contact with others marked as Indians. There is thus only restricted potential for social control and community building. On the one hand this is the reason why Indian spaces are of interest to many; on the other, this means that people can also live well without them. Thus the ethnic entrepreneurs have to make sure the interest in their goods is continuing and people do not choose another offer for identity and community building (around their profession, hobbies, gender, etc.).

One of the reasons for the standstill of the *Indernet* in the second half of the 2000s was probably that many Indians of the second generation no longer had such a high demand for Indian identity and community (negotiation). After some time on the *Indernet*, progress in education and maturing as adults, other issues will have become more important for many.[19]

Because of the role of ethnic entrepreneurs in constructing India, Indian and Indianness, it makes sense to research this figure and in particular the projects of the entrepreneurs, because the latter are the ones that (re)produce the realities. In this sense researching Indian transnationalism online (including the periphery) is highly relevant. Ethnography with its in-depth and long-term analysis can be very productive, in particular when it is done self-reflexively and in awareness of the researcher's own role in (re)constructing the object of research.

References

Anthias, F. 1998. Evaluating 'diaspora': beyond ethnicity? *Sociology*, 32 (3): 557–580.
Anthias, F. 2009. Translocational belonging, identity and generation: Questions and problems in migration and ethnic studies. *Finnish Journal of Ethnicity and Migration*, 4 (1), 6–15.
Barth, F. 1996. Ethnic groups and boundaries. In: J. Hutchinson and A. D. Smith (eds.), *Ethnicity.* Oxford: Oxford University Press, 75–82.
Bates, C. (ed.) 2001. *Community, empire and migration: South Asians in diaspora.* New Delhi: Orient Longman.

19 Due to demographic reasons they can be replaced only to a limited extent with younger people socialised in German-speaking Europe and marked as Indians there. The younger ones will want their own spaces with other styles.

Brosius, C. 2004. Of Nasty Pictures and 'Nice Guys': The Surreality of Online Hindutva. In: S. Sengupta and M. Narula (eds.), *Media Crisis*. New Delhi: Sarai Reader 4, 138–151.

Brubaker, R. 2004. *Ethnicity without groups*. Cambridge, MA: Harvard University Press.

Clifford, J. 1997. *Routes: Travel and translation in the late twentieth century.* Cambridge, MA: Harvard University Press.

Cohen, A. 1985. *The symbolic construction of community.* London: Routledge.

Cohen, R. 1997. *Global diasporas: An introduction.* London: UCL Press.

Creswell, J. 1998. *Qualitative inquiry and research design: Choosing among five traditions.* Thousand Oaks, CA: Sage Publications.

Gajjala, R. 2004. *Cyber selves – Feminist ethnographies of South Asian women.* Walnut Creek, CA: Altamira Press.

Goel, U. 2005. Fatima and theinder.net – A refuge in virtual space. In: A. Fitz, M. Kröger, A. Schneider and D. Wenner (eds.), *Import Export – Cultural Transfer – India, Germany, Austria*. Berlin: Parthas Verlag, 201–207. Available from: http://www.urmila.de/UDG/Biblio/Fatima%20and%20theindernet.pdf (accessed 25 July 2012).

Goel, U. 2006. Germany. In: B. V. Lal (ed.), *Encyclopaedia of the Indian Diaspora.* Singapore: Edition Didier Millet, 358–360 (The original text available from: http://www.urmila.de/UDG/Forschung/texte/encyclopedia.html (accessed 25 July 2012).

Goel, U. 2007. Indians in Germany – The imagination of a community. *UNEAC Asia Papers*, No. 20. Available from: http://www.une.edu.au/asiacentre/PDF/No20.pdf (accessed 25 July 2012).

Goel, U. 2008a. 'Half Indians', Adopted 'Germans' and 'Afghan Indians' – On claims of 'Indianness' and their contestations in Germany. *Transforming Cultures eJournal*, 3 (1). Available from: http://epress.lib.uts.edu.au/ojs/index.php/TfC/article/view/676/605 (accessed 24 July 2012).

Goel, U. 2008b. Imagining India Online: Second-Generation Indians in Germany. In: J. Esleben, C. Kraenzle and S. Kulkarni (eds.), *Mapping Channels between Ganges and Rhein: German-Indian Cross-Cultural Relations.* Newcastle: Cambridge Scholars Publishing, 210–232. Available from: http://www.urmila.de/UDG/Forschung/texte/GoelImagining.pdf (accessed 25 July 2012).

Goel, U. 2008c. The Indernet – A German network in a transnational space. In: R. G. Anghel, E. Gerharz, G. Rescher and M. Sazlbrunn (eds.), *The Making of World Society – Perspectives from Transnational Research.* Bielefeld: transcript, 291–309. Available from: http://www.urmila.de/UDG/Forschung/texte/transnational.html (accessed 25 July 2012).

Goel, U. 2009. The German internet portal Indernet – A space for multiple belongingness. In: G. Goggin and M. McLelland (eds.), *Internationalizing Internet Studies.* New York: Routledge, 128–144.

Greschke, H. M. 2012. *Is there a home in cyberspace? The internet in migrants' everyday life and the emergence of global communities.* New York: Routledge.

Goggin, G. and McLelland, M. (eds.) 2009. *Internationalizing Internet Studies.* New York: Routledge.

Jacobsen, K. A. and Kumar, P. P. (eds.) 2004. *South Asians in the diaspora: histories and religious traditions.* Leiden: Brill.

Jacobsen, K. A. and Raj, S. J. (eds.) 2008. *South Asian Christian diaspora: Invisible diaspora in Europe and North America.* Farnham: Ashgate.

Jeganathan, P. 1998. eelam.com: Place, nation, and imagination in cyberspace. *Public Culture*, 10 (3), 515–528.

Jenkins, R. 1997. *Rethinking ethnicity – arguments and explorations.* London: Sage Publications.

Kivits, J. 2005. Online interviewing and the research relationship. In: C. Hine (ed.), *Virtual methods. Issues in social research on the internet.* Oxford: Berg, 35–49.

Kuntsman, A. 2004. Cyberethnography as home-work. *Anthropology Matters Journal*,6(2).Availablefrom:http://www.anthropologymatters.com/index.php?journal=anth_matters&page=article&op=view&path%5B%5D=97 (accessed 27 July 2012).

Kuntsman, A. 2009. *Figurations of violence and belonging – Queerness, migranthood and nationalism in cyberspace and beyond.* Bern: Peter Lang.

Lal, V. 1999. The politics of history on the internet: Cyber-diasporic Hinduism and the North American Hindu Diaspora. *Diaspora*, 8 (2), 137–173.

Lal, B. V. (ed.) 2006. *Encyclopaedia of the Indian Diaspora.* Singapore: Edition Didier Millet.

Mallapragada, M. 2000. The Indian diaspora in the USA and around the web. In: D. Gauntlett (ed.), *Web.Studies: Rewiring media studies for the digital age.* London: Arnold, 179–185.

Mandaville, P. 2003. Communication and diasporic Islam: a virtual ummah? In: K. Karim (ed.), *The media of diaspora.* London: Routledge, 135–147.

Mecheril, P. 2003. *Prekäre Verhältnisse – Über natio-ethno-kulturelle (Mehrfach-) Zugehörigkeiten.* Münster: Waxmann.

Mecheril, P. 2004. *Einführung in die Migrationspädagogik.* Weinheim: Beltz.

Miller, D. 2011. *Tales from Facebook.* Cambridge: Polity.

Miller, D. and Slater, D. 2000. *The Internet: An Ethnographic Approach.* Oxford: Berg.

Mitra, A. 1997. Virtual commonality: Looking for India on the internet. In: S. Jones (ed.), *Virtual Culture: Identity and communication in cybersociety.* London: Sage, 55–79.

Morley, D. 2000. *Home territories: Media, mobility and identity.* London: Routledge.

Oonk, G. (ed.) 2007. *Global Indian diasporas: Exploring trajectories of migration and theory.* Amsterdam: Amsterdam University Press.

Rai, A. 1995. India online: Electronic bulletin boards and the construction of a diasporic Hindu identity. *Diaspora*, 4 (1), 31–57.

Reggi, N. 2010. theinder.net: Wenn globalisierte Alltage online gehen. In: S. Hess and M. Schwertl (eds.), *München migrantisch – migrantisches München.* München: Herbert Utz Verlag, 117–134.

Rutter, J. and Smith, G. 2005. Ethnographic presence in a nebulous setting. In: C. Hine (ed.), *Virtual methods: Issues in social research on the internet.* Oxford: Berg, 81–92.

Safran, W. 1991. Diasporas in modern societies: Myths of homeland and return. *Diaspora*, 1 (1), 83–99.

Tawil-Souri, H. 2009. Americanizing Palestine through internet development. In: G. Goggin and M. McClelland (eds.), *Internationalizing Internet Studies.* New York: Routledge, 48–61.

van der Veer, P. (ed.) 1995. *Nation and Migration: The Politics of Space in the South Asian Diaspora.* Philadelphia, PA: University of Pennsylvania Press.

Chapter 4
'ThirdSpace' as Transnational Space

Emily Skop

For many migrants who relocate across national boundaries, the transition can create a sense of cultural limbo as individuals attempt to reconcile their lifestyles and customs in a new social context. A recurring trend in migration studies has been to examine the ways in which migrants fashion alternative social spaces located between the two poles of 'here' and 'there'. Within these 'thirdspaces' migrants often engage in transnational activities that create new spheres of interaction. 'This "thirdspace"' write geographers Marie Price and Sarah Whitworth, 'comes from the duality of migrant existence, a tension between a lived-in space and a distant, remembered space' (Price and Whitworth 2004: 185).

The Internet as a 'thirdspace' has become imbued with symbolic meaning as it becomes the digital terrain upon which many migrants build and reproduce important community ties and relationships on a regular basis. While some argue that cyberspace provides only a surrogate for community, because 'communities are shaped by a sense of belonging to a place, a geographical location, by shared values, by common struggles, by tradition and history of a location' (Sardar 1996: 29), many scholars (including those in this volume) have illustrated that in practice the Internet as 'thirdspace' is often appropriated by individuals and groups seeking to preserve, develop, expand or celebrate their distinctiveness even as the same technology becomes in other circumstances a means for dissolving cultural differences. Internet chat rooms, discussion forums, and websites serve a dazzling array of purposes from advertising to grassroots mobilisation, from the sharing of political views to the dissemination of research findings. The medium has no particular essence; instead, diverse Internet users invest multiple 'thirdspaces' with varied meanings.

This research recognises that the Internet is undeniable as a 'thirdspace' which unites many Asian Indian migrants in the United States, providing them both a leisure activity and a shared outlet in which to socialise, network, and collectively reminisce on life back home as well as to imagine life in the future.[1] Through the results of in-depth interviews, I present the range of uses of the Internet by

---

1 This research represents a segment of the author's broader project on the Indian diaspora in the US. For other discussions, see Skop 2012; Skop and Adams 2009; and Adams and Skop 2008.

migrants to the US from India.[2] I suggest that convening together in 'thirdspaces' beyond the jurisdiction of their new physical environments creates an empowering sense of community. Additionally, in the realm of 'thirdspaces', many migrants take advantage of their cyberlinks to socialise with co-ethnics. Indeed, gatherings in 'thirdspace' give transnational networks both a material and a symbolic homeplace. Simultaneously, the gatherings in 'thirdspace' become activities that further cement the emotional bonds among migrants and their embeddedness in ever-increasing transnational networks. Nonetheless, I also argue that for some migrants, utilisation of Internet technologies are ambivalent; their incorporation within social processes of economic exchange, and political contestation, along with community formation and identity construction does not take a predictable course but varies from person to person and from place to place (Montgomery 2008; Dodge and Kitchin 2005; Staeheli *et al.* 2002; Crang *et al.* 1999; Castells 1999; Graham and Marvin 1996). Additionally, I contend that these 'thirdspaces' provide new arenas to promulgate old divisions based on social structures and hierarchies that once only existed 'here' and 'there', but now exist 'everywhere'.

Thus, the paper begins by describing several distinct characteristics that make Indian migrants particularly interesting for studies of the use of the Internet. Following this I briefly explain my research questions and methodology. Then, I provide vignettes that illustrate typical engagements with technology as a part of identity construction in cyberspace. Lastly, I introduce a continuum of embeddedness to discuss the varying ways in which migrants come to utilise the Internet as 'thirdspace'. Throughout the chapter, I contend that the Internet as 'thirdspace' is one of many resources at the disposal of Indian migrants for overcoming separation at intra- and international scales, for creating a variety of connections across space, and for constructing particular identities.

Technology and the Indian Community[3]

From a small contingent of 2000 in 1960, the number of individuals of Indian origin living in the US grew to nearly two million by the year 2010, doubling every five

---

2   It is important to note that even though a small subset of individuals is included in this chapter, my results are also informed by in-depth interviews and participant observation done in over ten years of research (see Skop 2012; Skop and Adams 2009; Adams and Skop 2008; Adams and Ghose 2003; Skop 2002).

3   Even though one may be tempted to refer in such a discussion to the 'community' of Indian immigrants living in the US, the term is poorly suited to this population in a way that raises an important issue with regard to this migration stream. Indeed, over a billion people comprise the nation of India – a sixth of the human population, divided into 25 states and speaking some 15 official languages and 200 languages overall. It is not surprising that for many Indians, the nation holds less of a purchase on personal identity than the local state, place, or region, and these smaller foundations of community remain important in diaspora (see recent discussions of Indian migrant diversity in Skop 2012; Sharma 2010; Bhatia

years on average during this period. This rapid and recent growth is indicated by the fact that more than 80 per cent of the Indian migrants living in the US arrived between 1990 and 2009 (U.S. Office of Immigration Statistics 2011; and U.S. Citizenship and Immigration Services 2010). Increasing numerical importance in American society is complemented by several other distinct characteristics that make this migrant group particularly interesting for studies of the use of Internet, including the groups' geographic dispersion, their overall socioeconomic success, and their technological orientation.

A distinctive feature of the Indian population in the US is its spatially dispersed settlement pattern. The migrants' high degree of population dispersion is particularly evident on the urban scale, where rather than a plethora of 'Little Indias' what we tend to see are 'saffron suburbs' (Skop 2002). Drawn to high-tech employment and therefore possessing the economic means to achieve the American dream of suburban home-ownership, many Indian migrant families have become scattered throughout ethnically mixed neighbourhoods where they rub shoulders mainly with representatives of other Asian migration streams, as well as members of the native-born white population (Sheth 2010; Skop and Li 2005).

Such suburban settings seldom offer a strong sense of Indian ethnic identity. So, in an effort to maintain a sense of community, some Indians have begun to use information and communication technologies for the purpose of *virtual gathering* (see Adams and Ghose 2003; Varghese 2003; Lal 2003, 1999; Mathew and Prasad 1996; Montgomery 2008). Various media, but particularly the Internet, can provide a sense of togetherness, engagement in cultural traditions, and exchange of in-group information – in short, a sense of place. The Internet serves as an alternative to physical gathering because overcoming the friction of distance permits dispersed groups to communicate regularly. Various individual migrants, as well as local and regional sub-ethnic group organisations, are linked via their websites to major Internet portals in India, as well as to various services in the US and India that cater to their corresponding migrant populations. At the same time, transboundary networking oftentimes facilitates physical gathering (for example, at festivals, films, musical performances, and business meetings that are advertised online) even as the Internet constitutes a form of gathering in itself, with certain key attributes of place-based interaction (Adams 1997, 1998).

2007; Dhingra 2007). Rather than coalescing to form a single ethnic community in the US, immigrants from India remain segmented into sub-ethnic communities derived from various source regions within India, which give rise to particular linguistic and religious characteristics in particular segments of the population.

Table 4.1   Socioeconomic Characteristics in the United States by Gender, 2009

	Male Indian Migrants	Female Indian Migrants	US Indian Migrant Total*	US Total**
Per cent with Bachelor's Degree or Higher	75.6%	72.0%	73.6%	27.9%
Per cent Labour Force Participation	85.1%	55.5%	70.3%	65.3%
Per cent Highly Skilled Occupation	69.7%	60.5%	65.1%	35.7%
Per cent Speak English Well or Very Well	–	–	71.6%	–

Source: U.S. Bureau of the Census, *2009 American Community Survey 1-Year Estimate, PUMS 1% Sample* (Washington, D.C.: U.S. Government Printing Office, 2009a).

**Source*: U.S. Bureau of the Census, *2009 American Community Survey 1-Year Estimate* (Washington, D.C.: U.S. Government Printing Office, 2009b).

Importantly, it is the economic success and high levels of education of Indian migrants that lower many of the barriers considered essential for Internet use. Indeed, Indians in the US are striking in terms of their social and economic resources, as Table 4.1 illustrates. According to the 2009 US Bureau of the Census American Community Survey, the majority have a bachelor's degree or higher. By virtue of their high educational level, most Indians also hold good jobs and earn high incomes. In fact, as a group, Indians earned substantially higher household incomes than the US population in general. Both males and females generally have high levels of participation in the labour force and they are more highly represented in professional occupations than any other ethnic group. Among the members of this group who are working, almost 60 per cent are engaged in managerial, professional, or related occupations. As a result, it is likely that most of the migrants have the means to adopt the Internet in their professional and private lives (Skop 2012; Bhattacharya 2011; Sahoo *et al.*, 2010).

This is not to say that there is not any disparity within the Indian migrant population. It is true that a significant number come to the United States with high levels of education and occupational skills, but there are also a growing number of migrants with less education and lower occupational status (Sharma 2010; Mathew 2008; Rudrappa 2008; Skop and Altman 2006). Though this research tends to focus on these more technically savvy, highly skilled migrants in the US, I in no way want to add to the myth of the 'model minority' that already circles around this national group by suggesting that all migrants from India are well off and technologically savvy. Indeed, circumstances surrounding migration and settlement force some migrants from India to become segregated from others in their ethnic community, whether physically or symbolically in 'thirdspace'. Oftentimes, lower-middle and lower-class migrants living in the US find themselves isolated and marginalised from both upper-middle- and middle-class Indians and from other lower-middle and lower-class non-Indian neighbours as well as co-workers. The migrants' lack of English proficiency, lack of technical know-how, and employment in service jobs as restaurant cooks, waiters, taxi-cab drivers, and convenience store clerks create divisions in the community. Their partiality for donning more traditional garb in their everyday public lives (like saris, salwar kameez, and turbans) in turn becomes the object through which these individuals become marked as Other. Few commonalities connect them to surrounding neighbours and co-workers (whether Indian origin or not). Even in those spaces where migrants of all social classes come together, especially during key holidays, lower-status newcomers often feel snubbed by their wealthier compatriots. Indeed, Indian community leaders sometimes marginalise this group even more by suggesting that the less fortunate in working class jobs are somehow atypical or have brought their troubles on themselves.[4]

Still, there is much evidence to suggest that many Indian immigrants are actively recruited by both the US government and US multinational corporations for their technical know-how, entrepreneurial skills, and business connections to fast-growing overseas markets, which in turn means that many of the migrants are favourably disposed toward technology (Lakha 1992; Lowell 2000; Cornelius and Espenshade 2001; Xiang 2004; Saxenian 2006). In 2009, for instance, nearly 263,000 migrants from India were admitted via the various visa programmes, making India the leading contributor of both employment-based immigrants and H-1B temporary workers (U.S. Office of Immigration Statistics 2011). Remarkably, India is now the second largest source country of migrants to the United States, just after Mexico. Thus, many Indian immigrants arrive in the US with high levels of education, professional training, and/or computer skills that may prove vital in how this particular group appropriates the Internet for cultural uses.

Research Questions, Data and Methodology

Below, I explore the interesting variability in the degree to which Indian migrants become integrated in and attached to the Internet as a 'thirdspace'. I suggest that individual migrants do not necessarily make use of the various sites of interaction,

---

4 For more on socioeconomic stratification amongst Indian migrants in the US, see Skop 2012; Sharma 2010; Mathew 2008; Rudrappa 2008.

nor do they inevitably work tenaciously toward preserving a sense of 'Indian-ness'. Even though a handful of migrants are actively involved in this project, there is also a level of indifference and angst within the Indian community.

'Indian-ness' implies a certain historical connection to a geographical area now called India, though as Khilnani would argue, 'India' is hardly a unifying concept even within the country's own borders (Khilnani 1999). In its new US context, this primordial attachment to a nation-state is expected to provide the means by which migrants and their children define themselves and their identity. This 'ethnogenetic presumption', as I call it, idealises the notion of ethnicity and the ethnic community and perpetuates the premise that ethnic identity exists outside and above individuals. In this framing, migrants embark on their experiences in the United States with an inherent sense of ethnic identity and a certain emotional connection to an ethnic or national group.

This 'ethnogenetic presumption' results in a narrow understanding of identity and is inconsistent with the everyday lives of migrants who can be found negotiating within innumerable social fields. The reality is that those migrants arriving from India continuously struggle between various definitions of what it means to be Indian. The bond that should act as an influential force (according to the 'ethnogenetic presumption') does not always function in this way. Sometimes, labels imposed because of ancestry and/or by what other people think can be resisted and reinvented. Thus, individuals may use the same ethnic label, but they construct their ethnicity based on their own shifting notions and interpretations of their cultural heritage. Ethnicity becomes a creative and complex response to both individual and societal forces, which changes through time and within varying contexts.

In my conversations with migrants, I discovered that individuals sustain and assert their identities as 'Indians' unevenly and with varying intensity. My observations result from the in-depth interviews that I conducted with 30 individual migrants, which took place during my intensive research involving Indian migrant spaces. While that investigation focused on the role of mid-level organisations and broader national dynamics, as well as international forces in the process of community formation and the ways in which ethnic boundaries, and thus identities, are constructed, these interviews also provided me with invaluable information regarding the lives of individual migrants, as well as information on how they employ 'thirdspaces' to reinforce their identities. Indeed, my conversations with recently arrived Indian migrants revealed vastly different experiences with regard to the use of IT in daily life. When I present – using their words as much as possible – the vignettes of some of the migrants themselves below, I highlight the differential manner in which individuals express their identities as 'Indians' in 'thirdspace'.

Constructing Identity in Virtual Place: Vignettes

Vignette 1: Kiran

Kiran is a retired computer programmer, born in Karnataka and now living with his wife in a major American city. He received his Master's degree from the Indian Institute of Technology and was admitted to the United States on an H-1B visa. He very quickly decided that he wanted to petition for a permanent immigrant visa and his employer was happy to sponsor him. The couple has raised two children in the US, both of whom now attend college.

Kiran visits India every other year in order to see members of his extended family. He also uses various forms of communication to stay in touch with his 'Indian side' and with life and society in India. He sends remittances of several hundred dollars to his parents a few times a year. His main information sources about the world are television and the Internet. While television provides a window on American society, the Internet allows Kiran to maintain ties to Indian culture. He accesses the Internet from both home and work, and is a frequent user of websites intended mainly for people living in India, born in India, or of Indian ancestry. On a daily basis he visits three websites that are intended for Asian Indians: two of which are online newspapers (*Prajavani*, the Kannada version of the *Deccan Herald*, and the *Economic Times*, one of India's leading financial newspapers). The other is a site devoted to Indian sports. These sites are also favourites among his friends who are from Bangalore. Over the course of the last year, he also visited each of the following types of sites several times a month: sites related to immigration and to living in the US as an immigrant, sites about traditional Indian culture (festivals, carnatic music, literature, etc.), sites dedicated to an Indian political party, sites with information about Indian history, and sites for buying specialty items (saris, spices, books, food, videos, songs).

Kiran also recently became the webmaster for his local Kannada Sangha, an association that brings together nearly 300 speakers of Kannada, a South Indian language. He expressed his hope that the Internet site would serve as 'an online, one-stop resource for finding businesses, keeping an up-to-date, interactive calendar of community events, and linking up to local and national organisation websites'. He also uses the site to inform other members about upcoming social events in the Kannada community in and around his adopted American city, especially the local movie viewings sponsored by the association.

Kiran does not use Indian matrimonial sites because he is already married. His values are generally rather traditional. For example, he believes it is a pressing issue for people of Indian ancestry living in the US to do everything possible to preserve Indian culture and customs (aside from maintaining the caste system). Still, in the realm of marriage, he does not see a need to preserve the custom of arranged marriage and considers 'non-traditional' qualities such as values and personality to be more important in a prospective spouse than 'traditional' qualities such as income and caste. His commitment to Indian culture stems, in part, from the belief that world civilisation owes more to the inventions and discoveries of India than of Europe. This belief translates into a cosmopolitan lifestyle: regular travel to India, frequent use of ethnically targeted Internet sites, consumption of Indian movies on a monthly basis, use of the Kannada language at home with his children and wife, and the observance of Hindu festivals and holy days at the local Hindu temple. For Kiran, the Internet serves as one of the most important tools for the maintenance of a strong attachment to India and a strong sense of ethnic identity, not only for himself but for his entire family. 'Thirdspace' enhances mobility and a geographically and culturally bifurcated lifestyle.

Vignette 2: Prasanna

Prasanna is a 26-year-old with a Master's degree in electrical engineering at a major state university. She was born and raised in Tamil Nadu. Prasanna's original goal was to get her Master's degree as well as some practical experience in the United States before returning to India. She finished school and has been working for a local building firm as an engineering consultant ever since. When I first asked about her employment future in the United States, Prasanna expressed her intention to return to India within five years:

> P: Since I'm only going to stay here temporary, I say I will work in this specialised field...After this big project – I want to finish that – and then I want to get into pure architecture and get that experience and then go back to India.

Prasanna's words and actions have been mixed ever since that initial conversation. She has finished that 'big' project, yet she continues to work for the same company despite her previous intentions to garner more experience elsewhere in the United States.

Prasanna acknowledges that so far her experience in the United States has been sheltered. She has spent the past five years mostly with other Indian migrants. She admits to an initial feeling of discomfort with members outside her ethnic group. As a result, she spends nearly all of her free time with compatriots – many of whom are involved with the local Tamil Sangam, an association organised by migrants from Tamil Nadu, which has both national and local chapters. She especially likes going to the local movie viewings sponsored by the association. Prasanna also has a 'whole bunch of friends' that belong to a charity group that is dedicated to providing education to underprivileged children in India. She participates in those club activities once or twice a month, especially when there are festivals celebrating Indian holidays.

She feels that Indian migrants like her should try to preserve their involvement in Indian culture, and occasionally argues with her friends about how to do this. Some of her female friends are annoyed that they were expected to learn Indian dances and cooking techniques, and they feel liberated by leaving home and aspiring to full economic and cultural assimilation. Others take an active role in organising Hindu festivals and other Indian student activities on campus. One thing that all of her friends agree on, however, is that American attitudes on determining a marriage partner are more reasonable than traditional Indian attitudes.

With the help of the Internet, Prasanna keeps up with current events in her hometown as well as in other parts of India. She has saved several 'favourite' websites, including direct links to Indian film magazines, the matrimony columns, and Indian newspapers:

> P: Normally, I go to the India newspapers, back in India, to pick out the temperatures, current news, and things like that. I mean, my home newspapers in my place, just to be in touch. Like, when I talk on the phone, they are, like, 'You know the temperature here is?' and I say, 'Yeah I read the newspaper'.

She appreciates the Internet's offerings in such areas as Indian music (via downloads), information about Indian history and politics, news from India, and products aimed at consumers of Indian ethnicity, as well as various resources supporting the Hindu faith. In each of these cases, she feels more connected to her family and friends back home.

Through the Internet, she remains interested in India and Indian culture. She sees the Internet as a tool to learn more about her parents' and grandparents' world and to keep up with news of important events in India. She also enjoys participating in online chat with other Indians of her age about once a week. But her use of email is limited to a few times a week and she rarely participates in blogs, discussion forums, or online games.

All in all, Prasanna's 'Indian-ness' is a matter of personal identity, as well as a symbolic construct and response to external categorisation. Her use of the Internet – to access Indian news and music, to learn about the history of India, and to maintain her Hindu faith – provides an important element of her identity. 'Thirdspace', then, stands in for direct experience of India and therefore fulfils a role in her life that is out of proportion to the small amount of time she spends there.

Vignette 3: Venu

Venu married her husband, Syed, in India and then after just one month, moved to a major city in the western United States, as a result of her husband being recruited by a major high-tech firm. Their parents arranged their marriage, as is the custom in Tamil Nadu, where the two are from. She visits India every four or five years and has a strong sense of dual cultural attachment, though she is increasingly experiencing conflicting feelings about 'Indian' vs. 'American' culture as her son enters his high school years.

Venu belongs to two local Indian associations. She tries to participate in both organisations' events, though in the past three years, she has only infrequently found time to attend. Flyers of various local events cover the door to her refrigerator.

Venu explains that the many festivals and holidays that mark the social calendar in India also serve to bring together migrants in Phoenix:

> V: There are a whole bunch of festivals in India, and the India Association ends up celebrating all of these Indian functions, even though maybe not at the exact same day we celebrate at the closest weekend as possible.

Venu also gets invited to events put on by the local Tamil Sangam. The association not only gives migrants a chance to speak Tamil (Venu's native language), it also serves as a way to meet with other migrants from home. Unfortunately, Venu has been so busy with raising her son and work-related projects that the couple has not gone to any functions recently.

The couple is even less involved with events back in India. They do not have subscriptions to any Indian newspapers or magazines, and Syed uses the Internet to go to some Indian newspapers and magazines 'only every once in a while'. Despite her use of the Internet on a daily basis from both work and home, and her reliance on it for news about world affairs, she does not make use of any of the diverse array of online offerings specifically for diasporic Indians. She has never visited websites related to living in the US as an immigrant, and rarely uses sites with news from India, sites relating to Indian traditional or popular culture, sites supporting Indian political parties, sites for buying specialty items (saris, spices, books, food, videos, songs), or sites geared towards Indian students. For her, the Internet simply is not a tool for accessing Indian culture or community or for maintaining an Indian self-identity. Instead, to keep in contact with family and friends in India, Venu usually uses the telephone. They call her family every week, while Syed calls his relatives less frequently. The couple hardly writes any letters; they usually end up calling instead.

While they often have heated discussions about the future, both Syed and Venu agree that they intend to stay in the United States, especially now that their son is growing up. Both miss India sometimes, but they have developed a strong attachment to the United States as well, as Venu indicates:

> V: We've got lots of American friends, and we like the American style of living – the independence – and also the opportunities, the technology advancements, things like that. So, I would say we are like, in-between; we like to be a part of the American culture by enjoying what is available to us, but at the same time, we also want to keep in touch with all the Indian traditions.

Venu's attitudes toward cultural preservation generally are neutral to pro-assimilation. She is proud of Indian culture and society, but would not go so far as to assert that India's role in world history is more important than that of Europe. She is not disappointed to see that children of immigrants grow up acting and thinking like other American kids, and while she is inclined to believe that immigrants to the US should preserve their Indian cultural roots, she is not strongly committed to a lifestyle oriented around these roots. Her stance on arranged marriage and on the necessary qualities in a spouse are similar to those of mainstream American society, and in other ways she also demonstrates an inclination towards assimilation rather than cultural preservation. It would appear that, through time, she has begun to disrupt her ties to Indian culture and favours her non-ethnic uses of the Internet, and that this 'thirdspace' does not function as a tool for identity construction in her case.

Vignette 4: Prasad and Amrita

Prasad is 33 years old and is from the state of Andhra Pradesh in Southern India. He never intended to come to the United States, but got his Master's degree in computer science and now works for a major multinational firm. Since we first met, Prasad has been promoted several times at the company. He is now a project manager, with more than 10 employees working under his supervision. He finds great satisfaction in his occupation and even refers to himself as a 'company man'.

He married his wife, Amrita, just three years ago when their parents got together and arranged their marriage. According to his retelling of their courtship, it was a straightforward, uncomplicated process:

> P: We are old family friends, and we never thought we would get married. We, once my parents thought that this would be good, I went to India, met her a couple of times, and she came over and visited me a couple of times – it was not like this long dating thing…Things looked good, so we finally decided that we would move ahead and we were married.

Amrita was young when they got married – just 21 – and felt that she 'had no choice' when she came to the United States. When she first got to Phoenix, she complains that she was 'sitting around doing nothing at home…killing time… learning how to cook'. But then Amrita and Prasad decided that she should go back to school at ASU. She recently finished her Master's degree in business information management and got a job at a high-tech firm in the Valley. She is much more satisfied now that she is employed full-time.

Prasad and Amrita have very little free time because of their careers. They both work 12- to 14-hour days. So during those brief periods when they are not engaged in work-related activities, the couple spend time together. Amrita really enjoys taking her husband to the more exclusive malls in the area for shopping and restaurants. Otherwise, the couple stay at home. Prasad gets several computer magazines in the mail that he 'reads cover to cover' and Amrita enjoys 'American' television. The couple rent Hollywood-produced movies very often, though Amrita insists that they rent videos made in India every so often, too.

Prasad has a cousin that lives in the area that they see maybe once a month, but the couple do not have much other free time to spend meeting with friends.

Amrita maintains, 'We didn't make the time to keep in touch'. Neither partner is affiliated with any of the local Indian organisations. Prasad knows about one group of people who come from their home state in India. The Telugu Association meets quite frequently:

> P: I come from a state called Andhra Pradesh in India…and we speak a language called Telugu…so, each state, because they speak their own language, they have their own groups here. It's called the Telugu Association. So all of the people that come from that part of the country, most of them go to this. They usually have, once in a month they meet – kids, birthdays and stuff; sometimes they have formal association gatherings. So, the guys get to play volleyball, the girls chat and the kids play around. They have potlucks.

But Prasad and Amrita do not attend these gatherings; they remember going only once since Amrita arrived. They also receive, in Prasad's terms, 'unsolicited' mail from other Indian groups in Phoenix, but the couple just is not interested in getting involved in community-related activities.

When asked why not, both Prasad and Amrita suggest that Indian culture and customs are too restrictive and traditional. Amrita, especially, has come to enjoy her privacy and feels 'oppressed' by the local migrant community: 'Everyone is involved in everyone else's business, just like it was in India'. She wants to be left alone and avoid the gossip, social pressure, and public scrutiny that she perceives as overpowering within the community. Prasad also thinks it is because their view of life has been transformed considerably:

> P: I think the last 10 years, you change a lot…You absorb things. You develop new preferences, you develop new skills, you develop new ideas. You open up a lot. You relax a lot more. Probably, opening up is the big thing…You are more tolerant. How do I say, you are more of a liberal now.

In terms of the Internet as 'thirdspace', about once a month, Prasad reads online newspapers from India and visits websites dedicated to his home state. Amrita reads them more often. Amrita also peruses the Indian entertainment and fashion magazines every so often. But typically, both use email and online chats to stay in touch only with their pre-established circle of friends and family. It is therefore only as an interpersonal medium that the Internet supports their constructions of ethnic identity. Meanwhile, Amrita's engagement with the public side of the Internet focuses primarily on mainstream American or global culture rather than Indian culture(s).

Vignette 5: Rama and Alka

Rama, and Alka, 46, moved to the United States to improve the chances for their two daughters, who in India would not have been able to accomplish the goals that their parents hoped that they would achieve. When they first arrived they moved to a major metropolitan area, where their oldest daughter began her graduate studies at the local university. After two years, she finished her Master's degree and was offered a job at a major electronics manufacturer in another city.

Because Rama and Alka's younger daughter had just begun college when they decided to relocate, the couple insisted that she stay to finish her schooling. Once she graduated from college, she decided to continue on to medical school. She moved in with a group of students in an apartment near the university. Because Rama and Alka followed their eldest daughter to her new job, they had not seen the younger daughter in two years; the cost of the trip would have proved prohibitive given their current financial situation.

When the family moved, they wanted to live close to their daughter's work, so Rama and Alka rented an apartment in one of the more affordable complexes in the area. The apartment's location was extremely inconvenient for Rama, who was hired as a veterinary technician at a local clinic. When he first began the job, the couple could not afford a car, so Rama was forced to take public transportation for the more than 15-mile trip. It often required over an hour to get to work. It was only because of their daughter's frugality that the family was eventually able to purchase a used car. While she continued to ride her bike to work, Rama used his daughter's car to make his commute less cumbersome. Meanwhile, Alka was stuck at home because she was terrified to go out alone during the day.

Since they first arrived, Rama and Alka have had difficulty making friends. They concentrated all of their attention on their daughter. They very rarely socialised. Rama had nothing in common with his young, mostly female white co-workers although they were all very kind to him. Because Alka stayed at home, it was nearly impossible for her to meet anyone: 'I do not have friends', she confessed to me quietly in one conversation.

With the departure of their oldest child (and the car with her), the couple had yet to increase their social activities in any substantial way. In fact, their children continued to absorb most of their energies. Now separated by thousands of miles, Rama and Alka spent a good deal of their free time keeping in touch with the daughters that brought them to the United States in the first place. Rama wrote daily 'snail mail' letters to his children, and Alka relied on their frequent telephone calls to catch up on daily events: 'Every day they call'.

Even though they desired the companionship of other migrants from their home state, it was now extremely difficult for the couple to get around town because they had to rely on public transportation. Since Rama's job paid very little (less than $20,000 a year), the couple could not afford to belong to the local Tamil-speaking organisation. The membership fees, along with associated costs of participating in monthly events, proved to be too expensive for Rama and Alka to justify spending on their tight budget. Instead, in order to maintain a sense of belonging, the couple took a bus to a local Indian store once a week to buy groceries and rent the latest movies from India. They also purchased newspapers to keep up with events happening in their hometown.

Because of the expense involved, Rama and Alka had only returned to India once since arriving in the United States. The purpose of that trip was to attend their oldest daughter's wedding. In order to remain connected with friends and family in India, the couple relied on the telephone, typically spending a significant amount of their monthly allowance on this expense. Both spoke with their families in India once every fortnight, and usually phoned friends every couple of months. Unlike most other migrants I met from India, Rama and Alka did not own a computer, nor had either of them used the Internet or email site for social exchanges.

Even though several years had passed since they first arrived in the United States, when we first met, Alka seemed especially reluctant to let go of her traditions. Unlike the more affluent and educated women that I spent time with over the course of my research (most of whom dress in Western-style clothing except for special events and celebrations), Alka insisted on wearing a sari at all times, both inside and outside the home. During our meetings, she usually wore a shirt made of leotard material underneath a flowing, gossamer dress that effectively covered her whole body. She also wore a religious gold pendant. The fact that she spoke very limited English and prepared extravagant vegetarian dishes from 'home' every day also suggested that Alka's heart and soul remained in India. But while the Internet is one of many resources available to most Indian migrants for overcoming separation, in the case of Rama and Alka, who are stranded because of their social status, the 'thirdspace' is just another place where they do not belong.

A Continuum of 'Embeddedness'

From the preceding vignettes, it is tempting to point out the commonalities and emphasise a mutual process of how Indian migrants in the US utilise 'thirdspace' as a means for constructing identity. Yet this would not do justice to the migrants, who clearly sustain and assert their identities as 'Indians' in varying ways, using the Internet unevenly and differently. They employ varying strategies using a multiplicity of means, at a variety of scales. Kiran is fully committed to building a sense of solidarity amongst migrants from India, both through physical and hybrid interactions. Prasanna, too, has invested a considerable amount of time and effort in maintaining her ethnicity and 'Indian-ness'. Venu is less faithful in her attempts to (re)build her community linkages, primarily because she finds that with the demands of work and family, she has less time to concentrate on this project. Prasad and Amrita make very little effort to participate within the Indian community, whether in reality or in 'thirdspace'. Rama and Alka, on the other hand, desire some sort of attachment with other Indians, but their limited resources compel them instead to rely on each other to sustain a sense of solidarity.

Each migrant's stage in their life course marked some similarities and differences in experiences. The presence and age of children in the household are particularly important in understanding the formation and maintenance of ethnic identities. For example, Kiran has more time to commit to organisational efforts because he is more established in his career and family life, whereas Prasad and Amrita are recently married and just beginning their careers, and thus have very little free time. Prasanna, on the other hand, as a young, single female, enjoys the time she spends in maintaining her 'Indian-ness' and even acknowledges that her Internet involvement is in part due to her desire to find a partner. Venu is in a transitional phase; she is somewhat distanced from Indian organisational and digital life because of work and family demands, but at the same time she recognises how important their ethnic linkages can be both for themselves and their young son. And despite the fact that Rama and Alka are closer to retirement age, which for others would usually mean more free time to devote to online and organisational activities, this couple arrived in the United States rather late in life and with a limited amount of resources, which means that much of their energy is focused on everyday survival.

My conversations with these migrants (and the others with whom I extensively met during the course of my research) indicate that the formulation and meaning of 'Indian-ness' in different families is far from uniform. Instead, the above vignettes suggest a continuum of the ways in which migrants come to define themselves and their community. Below, I categorise the migrants according to their degree of embeddedness in the process of ethnic identity formation. The continuum ranges from the most engaged participants (whom I call *active* ethnics) to the moderately connected members (whom I label *enduring* ethnics) to the somewhat disinterested onlookers (whom I label *retiring* ethnics) to the most dissatisfied witnesses (whom I label *dissenting* ethnics), as well as the completely disconnected bystanders (whom I label *stranded* ethnics).

The *active* ethnic is dedicated to the sustenance and expansion of 'Indian-ness' in the context of a new setting. These are the visible leaders, like Kiran, that expend a great deal of energy in bringing together the Indian migrant population (and their own families), whether at the local metropolitan scale or through the broader national arena; they even work to build solidarity at the global level through the Internet. As activists, they are concerned with matters affecting the Indian community and work extremely hard to keep track of current issues. As organisers, the active ethnic takes the initiative to coordinate various cultural functions and to keep a current directory of migrants. They also employ all sorts of modern communication technologies to link members of the community together. These individuals are volunteers and they often hold their positions for many years because other individuals in the community are unwilling to serve as webmasters, board directors or committee members. The activists spend a significant amount of their free time (approaching 100 per cent in some cases) working on community-related concerns; this is a sacrifice many other Indian migrants are unwilling to make. Without their leadership and dedication, most local Indian organisations (whether big or small, online or offline) would not persist as sites for the cultivation of past heritage and future tradition.

The *enduring* ethnic becomes and remains connected with those of shared ethnic identity. Within the local community, these migrants maintain solidarity through participation in a wide variety of social and service associations, religious functions, business interactions, cultural festivities, and online activities. Unlike the activists, enduring ethnics like Prasanna rarely take leadership roles within community organisations; rather, they enjoy the more social aspects of involvement. They are persistent and purposeful in their face-to-face and digital efforts to preserve their cultural identity. These migrants typically socialise with a circle of friends and associates from within the ethnic group, although they may be exclusive in defining who should belong to that group (i.e., linguistic-regional and religious characteristics along with class and generational status may work to split the migrants into various subgroups within the larger migrant community). Contact with others outside the group is often limited to conventional or work-related interaction; most enduring ethnics spend their leisure time caught up in community-related activities. These migrants also utilise an assortment of communication technologies to affirm their ethnicity beyond the local. Enduring ethnics use traditional means of contact, including letter writing and the telephone; in addition, they regularly access all sorts of electronic communication technologies, including email and the Internet, to (re)connect with friends and family living abroad.

The *retiring* ethnic is still attached to others of shared ethnicity. But these migrants, including Venu, have begun to decrease their participation in local group get-togethers. The maintenance of the ethnic community takes second precedence to work and family. While retiring ethnics make efforts to gather with members of their ethnic group regularly, everyday life takes priority, and these migrants find themselves attending fewer and fewer social functions. As they become consumed with quotidian activities, the retiring ethnic curtails attempts to remain up-to-date on events happening locally, regionally, and globally. The Internet as 'thirdspace' becomes less and less important. The migrant's daily routine in the United States almost becomes a matter of habit, a pattern that, with more time, becomes tremendously difficult to break. While they continue to be self-conscious and proud of their ethnic identity, they become more passive than active in its preservation.

Dissenting ethnics are content in their isolation and make no effort to gain any sort of migrant group membership. In fact, these dissenters, such as Prasad and Amrita, may sometimes resist others' summons for their participation. These migrants have ready access to the variety of social activities taking place in all kinds of realms, yet they choose not to utilise these spaces as a means to maintain cohesiveness with other members. Even as they resist affiliation, dissenters are reluctant to surrender their ethnic identity completely and still identify themselves as members of the group to others outside the group, especially when confronted about their allegiance. For the dissenting ethnic, this decision to remain detached from the group can be reversed by increasing engagement with others of shared ethnicity. The arrival of children, particularly, may become a key motivator in reviving ethnic ties. This is unlikely to occur, however, since these migrants appear to be rather individualistic in their outlook.

While the above types of migrants choose to participate (or not) and remain cohesive (or not), the *stranded* ethnic is restricted in his ability to (re)create a sense of ethnicity with other members of the group. Circumstances surrounding migration and settlement force these migrants to become segregated from their own ethnic community. Because stranded ethnics such as Rama and Alka have limited human and social capital, or belong to an unrecognised sect within the community, their means for participation are curbed. As a result, they are unable to readily access their ethnic group at any geographical scale. Most have never participated in the activities organised by Indian associations. Nor have they accessed space-transcending technologies in constructing community and identity. Without the aid of compatriots, these migrants focus on maintaining their ethnicity within the confines of the home. Families turn to one another and utilise traditional devices – including food, language, religion, and dress – to (re)construct a feeling of ethnic membership and solidarity. Consequently, they remain isolated in their new surroundings.

Discussion and Conclusion

The proposed continuum marks some of the sites of multiplicity and contradiction within the migrant population. It is within the context of this scheme that I argue that the migrants transform, resist, maintain, and negotiate their identities. Yet the continuum is neither comprehensive, exhaustive, nor broad-based. Rather, it provides a partial outline of the ways in which migrants create and sustain ethnicity and community. Contrary to more static views of ethnic identity, the continuum embraces the current constructionist view of ethnicity. It considers ethnic identity as being composed of a complexity of lifestyles and worldviews, forged by individuals at various life stages, with varying levels of privilege in order to identify themselves in relation to the surrounding society. This continuum of embeddedness also recognises that the Internet as 'thirdspace' for cultural preservation, ethnic community organisation, maintaining ties to India, and mediating between Indian and US society is undeniable in some cases, but not in others. While some migrants devise ways to appropriate 'thirdspaces' to empower themselves, others are left isolated by its very existence. Indeed, while some migrants are able to renegotiate dominant social ideals through the construction of these 'thirdspaces', where they are able to temporarily escape the confines of the us vs. them hierarchy, others become more firmly ensconced in those oppressive structures because of their inability to access information technologies. In their use and colonisation of 'thirdspaces', some migrants can impute meanings to these spaces which differ from those inscribed by the dominant social order, but the less mobile are left feeling excluded and immobilised in these environments, and are rendered even more powerless as far as their 'thirdspace' geographies are concerned.

The challenge posed by the Internet is therefore to discover the ways in which social and cultural particularity is constructed and reinforced, and how this may occur across the grain of conventional geographies through the appropriation of technology to create and inhabit virtual places for particular groups. In focusing on the uses and users of the Internet, scholars can begin to outline ways in which the Internet is appropriated for the maintenance of difference rather than homogenisation. Crang *et al.* (1999: 4), for instance, suggest that to see online communication as a force for cultural homogenisation 'produces a bluntness of analytical judgement, fetishises and over-simplifies both the virtual and the non-virtual…and allows little room for expressing variations across virtual time and space'. They contend that technologies become bound to place through *transduction*, 'the constant making anew of a domain in reiterative and transformative practices' (Dodge and Kitchin 2005: 166). As Mackenzie argues, transduction is, in essence, the binding of technologies, practices, representations, and places in a relatively stable way (Mackenzie 2002). Thus, through transduction the Internet is woven into individual lives as a facet of late modernity, disembedding activities from their established places and distanciating various kinds of social links through space, even as place-based aspects of identity and community are reenacted.

In the case of Indian migrants and the Internet, such transduction has produced many different 'thirdspaces' corresponding to the intersections of culture in the lives of various migrant populations. As a virtual context of interaction, 'thirdspaces' are supported by specific appropriations of the Internet (and other media) through practice and representation, facilitating the preservation and selective adoption of certain cultural traits at the expense of others among the migrant population. Consciously or not, most upper-middle- and middle-class Indians tend to hang onto their privileged status, in the hope of maintaining their position within the ever-shifting milieu of the US's political, economic, social, and racial dynamics. As a result, particular identities become essentialised and important to individual migrants and thus heighten social segmentation and class stratification already present in the community both off- and online. While many Indian migrants enter these new spaces quite easily, others are more apathetic, and some are undeniably refused admittance because of their social status.

This version of the concept of virtual place enhances understandings of the Internet since place – as geographers and other social scientists often understand it – is the product of the active appropriation of space into the ongoing construction of personal and collective identity (Tuan 1977: 161–178). So thirdspace is a virtual place created by the transduction of information technologies by a particular group, defined by its involvement in two (or more) disparate places. Clearly, the role of space-transcending technologies in constructing community and identity is important, and illustrates how culture is spatialised through technology, and how spatialised technology is infused with cultural values.

References

Adams, P. 1997. Cyberspace and virtual places. *Geographical Review*, 87 (2), 155–171.

Adams, P. 1998. Network topologies and virtual place. *Annals of the Association of American Geographers*, 88 (1), 88–106.

Adams, P. and Ghose, R. 2003. India.com: the construction of a space between. *Progress in Human Geography*, 27 (4), 414–437.

Adams, P. and Skop, E. 2008. The gendering of Asian Indian transnationalism on the internet. *Journal of Cultural Geography*, 25 (2), 115–136.

Bhatia, S. 2007. *American karma: Race, culture, and identity in the Indian diaspora*. New York: New York University Press.

Bhattacharya, G. B. 2011. Is social capital portable? Acculturating experiences of Indian migrant men in New York City. *Journal of Intercultural Studies*, 32 (1), 75–90.

Castells, M. 1999. Grassrooting the space of flows. *Urban Geography*, 20 (4), 294–302.

Cornelius, W. A. and Espenshade, T. J. 2001. The international migration of the highly skilled: 'High-tech *Braceros*' in the global labour market. In: W. A. Cornelius, T. J. Espenshade and I. Salehyan (eds.), *The International Migration of the Highly Skilled: Demand, Supply, and Development Consequences in Sending and Receiving Countries*. La Jolla, CA: Centre for Comparative Immigration Studies, University of California, San Diego, CA, 3–19.

Crang, M., Crang, P. and May, J. 1999. Introduction. In: M. Crang, P. Crang and J. May (eds.), *Virtual Geographies: Bodies, Space and Relations*. New York: Routledge, 1–13.

Dhingra, P. 2007. *Managing multicultural lives: Asian American professionals and the challenge of multiple identities*. Stanford, CA: Stanford University Press.

Dodge, M. and Kitchin, R. 2005. Code and the transduction of space. *Annals of the Association of American Geographers*, 95 (1), 162–180.

Graham, S. and Marvin, S. 1996. *Telecommunications and the City: Electronic Spaces, Urban Places*. New York: Routledge.

Khilnani, S. 1999. *The idea of India*. New York: Farrar, Straus, and Giroux.

Lakha, S. 1992. The internationalisation of Indian computer professionals. *South Asia*, XV (2), 93–113.

Lal, V. 1999. The politics of history on the Internet: Cyber-diasporic Hinduism and the North American Hindu diaspora. *Diaspora*, 8 (2), 137–172.

Lal, V. 2003. North American Hindus, the sense of history, and the politics of Internet diasporism. In: R. C. Lee and S. C. Wong (eds.), *Asian America.Net: Ethnicity, Nationalism, and Cyberspace*. New York: Routledge, 98–138.

Lowell, B. L. 2000. The demand and new legislation for skilled temporary workers (H-1Bs) in the United States. *People and Place*, 8 (4), 29–35.

Mackenzie, A. 2002. *Transductions: Bodies and Machines at Speed.* London: Continuum.

Mathew, B. 2008. *Taxi cabs and capitalism in New York City.* Ithaca, NY: Cornell University Press.

Mathew, B. and Prashad, V. 1996. The saffron dollar: Pehla paisa, phir bhagwan. *Himal,* 9 (7), 211–225.

Montgomery, A. F. 2008. Virtual enclaves: The influence of alumni email lists on the workspaces of transnational software engineers. *Global Networks,* 8 (1), 71–93.

Price, M. and Whitworth, C. 2004. Soccer and Latino cultural space: Metropolitan Washington *fútbol* leagues. In: D. D. Arreola (ed.), *Hispanic spaces, Latino places: Community and cultural diversity in contemporary America.* Austin, TX: The University of Austin Press, 167–186.

Rudrappa, S. 2008. Braceros and techno-braceros: Foreign workers in the United States and the commodification of low wage and high wage labour. In: S. Koshy and R. Radhakrishnan (eds.), *Transnational South Asians: The making of a neo-diaspora.* New York: Oxford University Press, 291–324.

Sahoo, A. K., Sangha, D. and Kelly, M. 2010. From 'temporary migrants' to 'permanent residents': Indian H-1B visa holders in the United States. *Asian Ethnicity,* 11 (3), 293–309.

Sardar, Z. 1996. alt.civilizations.faq: Cyberspace as the Darker Side of the West. In: Z. Sardar and J. R. Ravetz (eds.), *Cyberfutures: Culture and Politics on the Information Superhighway.* London: Pluto Press, 14–41.

Saxenian, A. 2006. *The new Argonauts: Regional advantage in a global economy.* Cambridge, MA: Harvard University Press.

Sharma, N. T. 2010. *Hip Hop Desis: South Asian Americans, Blackness, and a global race consciousness.* Durham, NC: Duke University Press.

Sheth, A. 2010. Little India, next exit: Ethnic destinations in the city. *Ethnography,* 11 (1), 69–88.

Skop, E. 2002. *Saffron suburbs: Indian immigrant community formation in Phoenix.* Ph.D. Dissertation, Arizona State University.

Skop, E. 2012. *The Immigration and Settlement of Asian Indians in Phoenix, Arizona 1965–2011: Ethnic Pride vs. Racial Discrimination in the Suburbs.* New York: Edwin Mellen Press.

Skop, E. and Li, W. 2005. Asians in America's suburbs: Patterns and consequences of settlement. *Geographical Review,* 95 (2), 167–188.

Skop, E. and Altman, C. A. 2006. The invisible immigrants: Asian Indian settlement patterns and racial/ethnic identities. In: J. W. Frazier and E. Tettey-Fio (eds.), *Race, ethnicity and place in a Changing America.* Binghamton, NY: Global Academic Publishing, 309–316.

Skop, E. and Adams, P.C. 2009. Creating and inhabiting virtual places: Indian immigrants in cyberspace. *National Identities,* 11 (2), 127–47.

Staeheli, L. A., Ledwith, V., Ormond, M., Reed, K., Sumpter, A., and Trudeau, D. 2002. Immigration, the internet, and spaces of politics. *Political Geography*, 21 (8), 989–1012.

Tuan, Y. F. 1977. *Space and Place: The Perspectives of Experience*. Minneapolis, MN: University of Minnesota Press.

U.S. Bureau of the Census. 2009a. *American community survey 2009 1-year estimate*. Washington, D.C.: U.S. Government Printing Office.

U.S. Bureau of the Census. 2009b. *American community survey 2009 1-year estimate, PUMS 1% sample*. Washington, D.C.: U.S. Government Printing Office.

U.S. Citizenship and Immigration Services. 2010. *Characteristics of specialty occupation workers (H-1B): Fiscal year 2009*. Washington, D.C.: U.S. Government Printing Office.

U.S. Office of Immigration Statistics. 2011. *2010 statistical yearbook*. Washington, D.C.: U.S. Government Printing Office.

Varghese, L. 2003. Will the real Indian woman log-on? Diaspora, gender and comportment. In: R. C. Lee and S. C. Wong (eds.), *Asian America.Net: Ethnicity, nationalism, and cyberspace*. New York: Routledge, 235–248.

Xiang, B. 2004. Indian information technology professionals' world system: The nation and the transnation in individuals' migration strategies. In: B. S. A. Yeoh and K. Willis (eds.), *State/nation/transnation: Perspectives of transnationalism in the Asia-Pacific*. London: Routledge, 161–178.

Chapter 5

Online Connections, Online *Yatras*: The Role of the Internet in the Creation and Maintenance of Links between *Advaita Vedanta* Gurus in India and their Devotees in the Diaspora

Heinz Scheifinger

Introduction

Amongst others, Ananda Mitra (2000), Daniel Miller and Don Slater (2000), Christopher Helland (2007) and Phyllis Herman (2010) have all emphasised the importance of the Internet for Hindus in the diaspora. The Internet has been a boon in a number of ways – allowing for Hindus living outside of India to connect with sacred places and religious figures and to keep up-to-date with current developments concerning Hinduism in India. This use of the medium has particular salience for devotees of Jayendra Saraswathi (1935–), the 69th head or *Shankaracharya* of the religious institution known as the *Kanchi Kamakoti Peetham* (or *Kanchi math* [Hindu monastery]) based in the south Indian city of Kanchipuram. The reason for this is that Jayendra Saraswathi has never travelled overseas. Shandip Saha (2007: 493) points out that this is because of concerns regarding the loss of purity as a result of such an undertaking. Threats to purity are taken seriously because the *Shankaracharya* is an orthodox *Smarta Brahman*, a member of a class that follows the *Dharma Shastras* – texts which emphasise that *Brahmans* are 'the class with the highest status' and are required to be 'the upholders of...purity' (Flood 1996: 57). Saha (2007: 493) further adds that Jayendra Saraswathi does not even delegate authority to his Indian disciples to travel overseas and visit devotees in the diaspora. Therefore, unless devotees of the *Shankaracharya* who reside abroad travel to India, they are unable to have any direct interaction either with him or with his close associates.

Although there are other gurus in India with followers living overseas who have also never left the Indian subcontinent, this is still relatively uncommon in an era of transnational guru organisations (Warrier 2005) in which gurus traverse the globe giving talks and offering blessings. Indeed, over a decade ago Jayendra Saraswathi himself was willing to break with tradition and did intend to travel overseas. However, this was met with opposition and, as a result of this, the proposed trip was never undertaken (Nadar 2004). While appreciating that gurus who do travel outside of India also utilise the Internet (and television) in order to communicate with their devotees, Saha makes the point that the use of modern communications technologies is perhaps an especially good way for Indian gurus who do not visit devotees abroad to stay in touch with their followers, and he briefly mentions the website of the Kanchi *math* (Saha 2007: 493–494). Stephen Jacobs (2012) also mentions the importance of both television and, especially, the Internet, to Hindus living outside of India but his observation that these communications technologies 'preserve a real sense of rootedness' (Jacobs 2012: 142) means that his emphasis is upon the link from those in the diaspora to India and not the other way around as is emphasised by Saha.

In this chapter I will focus on the use of the Internet by both the Kanchi *math* and its devotees – especially those in the diaspora. I consider in relative detail the situation concerning the Kanchi *math* and the Internet because this case especially highlights the extent to which the Internet can play a role in allowing devotees abroad and a religious organisation in India to connect with one another. It does this in two main ways. Firstly, it can explicate the potential of the Internet in this regard as a result of the aforementioned fact that the Kanchi *Shankaracharya* has never travelled overseas. For example, if Hindus in the diaspora are able to stay in effective contact with the *Shankaracharya* and his activities despite this barrier, then it suggests that it can also be achieved in other cases in which periodic contact between gurus and devotees occurs in countries other than India. Secondly, an unexpected event detailed below which occurred in Kanchipuram in late 2004 led to an increase in the employment of the Internet by devotees of Jayendra Saraswathi in order to achieve aims regarding the *math*. What was made possible as a result of this increased engagement with the medium clearly shows the potential of the Internet for followers of the *math* living overseas – something which will be demonstrated as this chapter unfolds.

Furthermore, as a result of the fact that diasporic populations and advanced communications technologies such as the Internet are key features of globalisation (see e.g. Appadurai 2000: 95–97), the observations that I am able to make are also demonstrative of central themes of globalisation. This intersection of empirical observation and theory will be highlighted in this chapter and this shows that insights gained from this particular case study have yet wider applicability. In addition to showing this, I will also comment upon the online presence of another *math* – the Sringeri *math* that is also situated in south India and which belongs to the same tradition as the one in Kanchi. I do this in order to highlight interesting links between an integral aspect of the life of Adi Shankaracharya (also known as Adi Shankara) (788–820) who founded the *math* in the ninth century AD and an online initiative engendered by the institution in the twenty-first century, and I briefly consider the possible implications of this latter development.

Adi Shankara, the *Maths*, and Jayendra Saraswathi

The purpose of this section is to provide important context to that which follows by briefly detailing the activities of the Hindu philosopher and Saint Adi ('Original') Shankara and providing details as to the standing of the current Kanchi *Shankaracharya*, Jayendra Saraswathi. These two tasks are related since the details and achievements of Adi Shankara's life directly impact upon the high status which Jayendra Saraswathi enjoys. At the same time, providing details of some of the aims and important activities of Adi Shankara allows me to later highlight the aforementioned links between his innovations and current developments emanating from a *math* that was founded by him more than a millennium ago.

Adi Shankara was a reformist Hindu, who, according to most scholars, was born in south India towards the end of the eighth century AD. At this time, the expression of Hinduism that directly drew upon the non-dual philosophy of *Advaita Vedanta* which is revealed in the ancient sacred texts the *Upanishads* was under threat. A multitude of sects, each adhering to different scriptural interpretations, had arisen and a reliance on elaborate rituals had become commonplace. In addition, Buddhism and Jainism had become relatively strong. Adi Shankara was able to successfully counteract the threats to *Upanishadic* Hinduism through systematising, developing and advocating the already extant philosophy of *Advaita Vedanta*. This not only revitalised this philosophical system but also had the effect of uniting the various Hindu sects. In short, the latter was achieved through propounding a framework which advocated that the various Hindu paths were all valid ways of approaching the final realisation of absolute non-duality even if they were dualistic and promoted the worshipping of images of the divine. In other words, according to Adi Shankara's argument, the philosophy of *Advaita Vedanta* stood over and above all other forms of Hinduism and encapsulated them (Rao 2003; Rangaswami 2012). This, then, united Hinduism and the effects of this can still be seen today in the fact that what is commonly known as Hinduism incorporates an incredible amount of diverse groups, beliefs and practices.

In addition to his voluminous writings and the taking-on of disciples, one of the strategies employed by Adi Shankara in his successful quest to propagate *Vedantic* Hinduism and to unite the disparate sects was to tour the Indian subcontinent. On tour he would meet with religious personalities, engage them in debate, and win them over to *Advaita Vedanta* (Rao 2003: 54–55). Although he died at the age of 32, it is likely that he managed to complete three such tours of India (Rangaswami 2012: 11). Another of Adi Shankara's important undertakings which contributed to the unification of Hinduism was his founding of a number of monastic centres. It is clear that he founded four major *maths*, each with its own *Shankaracharya* chosen from amongst his closest disciples. Crucially, these *maths* were set up at the cardinal points of India which meant that all of India was linked with teachers of *Advaita Vedanta* (Cenkner 1995: 109). One was founded at Badrinath in the Himalayas in the far north of India, the afore-mentioned Sringeri *math* was created in the south, and two more were set up in the east (at Puri) and west (at Dwarka) of India. Ten Orders of ascetics attached to these *maths* were also created by Adi Shankara (Klostermaier 1998: 164). These *maths* and Orders still exist today and the importance of this development is highlighted by Gavin Flood, who believes that it was 'partly instrumental in eradicating Jainism and Buddhism from south India and also in giving coherence and a sense of pan-Indian identity to orthodox, vedic traditions' (Flood 1996: 92–93). It is clear then that Adi Shankara's influence upon contemporary Hinduism cannot be underestimated.

Although the Kanchi *math* itself claims a direct link to Adi Shankara, according to most accounts it cannot be said with certainty that this *math* was founded by him. Indeed, the common view is only that this fifth *math* 'may' have been set up by him or one of his disciples (Flood 1996: 92). William Cenkner, a leading authority on the *Advaita Vedanta* tradition, states that 'the controversy whether there were four or five major maths founded by [Adi Shankara] continues and does not appear near resolution' (Cenkner 1995: xii). However, he accepts the account given by the Kanchi *math* itself regarding its tradition 'and the judgement of several contemporary scholars who have researched the problem' – both convince him that the Kanchi *math* and the position of *Shankaracharya* are linked to Adi Shankara (Cenkner 1995: xii). Similarly, Christopher Fuller acknowledges the dispute but concludes that the Kanchi *Shankaracharyas* are the 'spiritual descendants' of Adi Shankara (Fuller 2004: 126). David Smith concurs when he notes that the Kanchi *Shankaracharyas* are 'in direct line of spiritual descent from the original Shankaracharya' (Smith 2003: 176).

In short, despite some counterclaims, it is safe to say that the Kanchi *math*'s claim that it is directly linked to Adi Shankara has been successful. Not only has this been achieved despite opposition from the four afore-mentioned *maths* that are firmly associated with Adi Shankara (see Cenkner 1995: 114), but it is now arguably the pre-eminent *math*. According to Fuller (2004: 127), its growth in power and influence was largely due to Jayendra Saraswathi's predecessor, the charismatic Chandrasekharendra Saraswathi (1894–1994). However, the influence of the *math* and of the position of *Shankaracharya* has been further consolidated and extended by Jayendra Saraswathi. This has been achieved not solely as a result of his religious personage but also through his extensive involvement in political issues, which has enabled him to forge alliances with powerful politicians (see Bhatt 2001: 183–185; Viswanathan 2004). Consequently, Jayendra Saraswathi's influence is such that it has led Smith to assert that he is 'widely respected, and a national figure' (Smith 2003: 177) while Cenkner (1996: 60–63) provides evidence which demonstrates that he is extremely popular and Saha emphasises that he 'wield[s] an enormous amount of religious and political influence across India' (Saha 2007: 493) – a point also made by Nathan (2004). The Kanchi *Shankaracharya* also has a significant number of followers amongst Indians living in the diaspora and there is a large organisation associated with the *math* in southern California (Rajeev 2004). Coupled with his devotees in India, his total number of followers runs into the millions (Indo-Asian News Service 2004).

The Arrest of Jayendra Saraswathi

The high standing of Jayendra Saraswathi and the *math* that he heads not only emphasises the importance of this chapter's case study: in the light of the significance of the position that he holds and his wide-ranging religious and political influence, it also demonstrates that what occurred on 11 November 2004 was extraordinary. On this date the *Shankaracharya* was sensationally arrested on murder charges and imprisoned. Although the details of the case and whether or not Jayendra Saraswathi is guilty of that which he is accused are not the concern of this chapter; in order to provide context to my later discussion, it is necessary to recount the accusations against him.

Jayendra Saraswathi was accused of being involved in the murder of a former associate of the Kanchi *math* who had been close to his predecessor but who he had had differences with. For some time this individual had stopped attending the *math* and had become the manager of a temple in Kanchipuram unassociated with the *math*. He then began to write letters to the *math* threatening to expose a number of wrongdoings which he alleged that Jayendra Saraswathi and his heir, the junior *Shankaracharya* Vijayendra Saraswathi, were guilty of. Some of these letters were also sent to the press. The final letter that he wrote on 30 August 2004 contained the threat that he was going to attempt to have Jayendra Saraswathi removed from his position and, a few days later, he was murdered by a gang who, it is claimed by the prosecution, were instructed by Jayendra Saraswathi to carry out this act and who were paid out of *math* funds (see Anand 2004). Later key developments in the case occurred in January 2005 when Vijayendra Saraswathi was also arrested in connection with the murder (Indo-Asian News Service 2005) and in 2011 when Jayendra Saraswathi was accused of attempting to influence the trial judge (Press Trust of India 2011).

The Online Presence of the Kanchi *Math* and its Supporters

Within a short period of time – and before Jayendra Saraswathi's bail was granted by the Indian Supreme Court on 10 January 2005 – devotees of the *math* began to take advantage of the opportunities afforded by the Internet in order to disseminate news regarding the latest developments concerning the case and to mobilise support. More than seven and a half years after the arrest of the *Shankaracharya*, the case is still ongoing at the time of writing (5 July 2012) and online activities relating to the case continue. It is important to note though that even if online activity associated with the arrest of the *Shankaracharya* is discounted, a reasonably strong online presence of the Kanchi *math* can still be discerned, and the already extant presence of the Kanchi Kamakoti Seva Foundation should also be recognised. The latter is a charitable organisation associated with the *math* that was set up in New York in 1990 following a meeting in India in 1989 between a group of devotees residing in North America and Jayendra Saraswathi, who informed them that there were many devotees in the USA and Canada who wished to donate to charitable projects instigated by the *math* (see kksfusa.org).

The regular online presence of the Kanchi *math* at the time of the *Shankaracharya*'s arrest was relatively strong in two key respects when compared to other Hindu organisations – its website was highly accessible to individuals seeking general information about Hinduism, and the website itself was of a high standard. As a result of the fact that there are a countless number of websites dealing with Hinduism, achieving the former is both important and difficult. The central characteristic of Hinduism on the World Wide Web is that there is a deep pattern of reciprocal links between certain websites which, for a number of reasons, are highly likely to be encountered by individuals seeking general information concerning Hinduism (Scheifinger 2008). What is extraordinary is that out of millions of websites dealing with Hinduism, there is a very small number of such websites. For example, at the time of the *Shankaracharya*'s arrest in November 2004, there were only five. Although the website of the Kanchi *math* was not one of these select websites – hardly surprising since it belongs to a single tradition within Hinduism – it was directly linked to one of these five prominent websites (bbc.co.uk/worldservice/Hinduism) with the result that it would be far more likely to be encountered by those seeking general information about Hinduism online than the websites of other Hindu organisations.

kamakoti.org

The prominent position of the Kanchi *math*'s website on the World Wide Web is complemented by the quality of the website itself. The *math*'s vast official website kamakoti.org, which has been created and is maintained by devotees, is simple but well designed and consists of over 2,000 Web pages. It has not fundamentally changed in the almost eight years in which I have been periodically visiting it. Along with details about Adi Shankara's life, the website contains information about, and the history of, the *math*, and a number of downloads are available consisting of audio, video and still images. The outstanding feature of the website is the vast amount of written material available on it. For example, the complete text of a book consisting of a number of speeches made by Chandrasekharendra Saraswathi is available as well as a large number of articles written about the *math* and the current and former *Shankaracharyas*.

There is a regularly updated announcements page and the facility to contact those responsible for the website is offered, as is the opportunity to be placed on various mailing lists which allow devotees to be sent material with a religious content and to be kept informed of *math* activities. However, this is the extent of the interactivity offered by the website. This low level of interactivity is not surprising since this is a common feature of websites belonging to established religious organisations (see Helland 2002: 294–295, 298). Such websites are likely to provide 'information concerning doctrine, dogmas, polity and organisation… but there is no avenue for the participants [i.e. visitors to the website] to contribute their beliefs and input into the site' (Helland 2002: 294) and this is certainly the case with kamakoti.org. A small number of links to websites that are not directly controlled by the institution which are likely to be of interest to devotees of the *math* are offered, however. This is unlike the case of those religious organisations mentioned by Helland (2002: 296) that give the impression that their websites link to external websites whereas in actual fact they only offer internal links to Web pages that the organisation itself has created. However, it is true that many of the 14 links that are offered on kamakoti.org are to websites of groups or organisations that are closely related to the Kanchi *math*. One of these links is to kanchi-sathya. org – a website that will be considered in due course.

The fact that the Kanchi *math* embraced the Internet and had a reasonably strong online presence even in 2004 is perhaps unsurprising. This is because Jayendra Saraswathi is open to the possible benefits offered by new technology. This is a point made by Smith who reveals that the *Shankaracharya* once stated that there should be an embracing of both the 'culture of one's own land and technology from abroad' (Smith 2003: 177). This also explains why Jayendra Saraswathi consented to attend the 2 August 2004 launch of the website of the aforementioned Kanchi Kamakoti Seva Foundation based in the USA. This website (kksfusa.org) allows devotees to keep up-to-date with news and events both in North America and India and, amongst other facilities, allows for the newsletter of the Kanchi *math* to be downloaded. It is now also available in a more advanced beta version (beta.kksfusa.org).

Although the Kanchi *math* and its supporters already had an online presence at the time of the *Shankaracharya*'s arrest, the value of the Internet to the institution and to its devotees was exemplified following this event. The sequence of developments concerning the official *math* website, which constitutes a noteworthy episode in the history of Hinduism on the World Wide Web, will first be detailed.

In the six days immediately after Jayendra Saraswathi's arrest on 11 November 2004, kamakoti.org continued as usual without any reference to this extraordinary happening. Then, without warning, on 18 November the website was removed. Instead of being able to access the website, visitors were now only able to see the following message which appeared on an empty background:

> Praying for the security, safety, health and immediate release of…Jayendra Saraswathi Sankaracharya…,various prayer meetings, mass chantings of Vishnu Sahasranama Parayanam, Hanuman Chalisa, Kanda Sashti Kavacham and Veda Parayanam [hymns and prayers] are being held in several places, under the guidance of…Vijayendra Saraswathi Sankaracharya…[who, as mentioned, was later also arrested]. All devotees are requested to participate and offer prayers. Our email: kanchimutt@kamakoti.org.

Just one day later, on 19 November, the website was available again and this was accessed via the Web page showing the above message. However, shortly afterwards, direct access was available again and there were some references to the current situation. On 23 November – only 12 days after the arrest of the *Shankaracharya* – an entirely new website became available which specifically dealt with the situation, and those who had previously signed up to be on a mailing list via the original website were alerted to this fact. Meanwhile, kamakoti.org carried on largely as it did before but with some references to the current situation and with the link to the new website on its homepage.

Other Websites

This new website, kanchi-sathya.org (*'sathya'* means 'truth' in Sanskrit), puts forward the view that the *Shankaracharya* has been unfairly treated and is concerned about the media attention surrounding the case, which is seen as propagating lies. Amongst other facilities, kanchi-sathya.org offers the opportunity to download all the documents that have been filed with the court regarding the case, gives access to various articles online, and provides an online petition asking for the release of the *Shankaracharya* and apologies from the officials responsible for his arrest. It is also possible to post questions in the expectation of receiving a personal response. In addition, an appeal for help is made by the devotees responsible for the website. On 4 December 2004, those individuals who had previously registered with this new website received an e-mail requesting a donation to help in the dissemination of truthful information concerning the situation and another e-mail containing an invitation to a meeting held in Chennai on the same day. This was organised by the trustees of a Chennai organisation associated with the *math*. Up until August 2011, kanchi-sathya.org continued to publish material regarding the ongoing case. In addition, a number of digests of early material have now been created and individuals are urged to distribute copies of these digests (see kanchi-sathya.org/kanchidigest). Furthermore, because of high legal costs, the Dharma Rakshana Trust, a Trust established by the Kanchi *math*, began to solicit donations from devotees and this appeal appears on the website.

On 17 January 2005, in addition to kanchi-sathya.org, another new website – kanchiforum.org – was set up. This website is hosted in North America and was created, and is maintained by, devotees living outside of India. As in the case of kanchi-sathya.org, the website was set up as a direct result of the arrest of Jayendra Saraswathi. Although those responsible for the website claim not to be associated with either kamakoti.org or kanchi-sathya.org, these websites are recommended on kanchiforum.org's homepage, and there is the comment that these websites 'have been our source of strength, inspiration and motivation'. Also listed on the homepage are the aims of the devotees responsible for the website. These aims, which are all directly related to the situation concerning the *Shankaracharya*'s arrest, are: to act as a support group and to channel the 'energy and force' of Hindus, 'to spread the real news to the anxious devotees around the world', to create awareness, and to link devotees. They are worth recounting because the website, as a result of being accessible to vast numbers of devotees around the world and allowing for almost instantaneous communication, has the potential to contribute to their realisation in a way that was not previously possible.

The website itself consists largely of a discussion board which allows interested parties to discuss issues concerning the case against the *Shankaracharyas* through the posting of messages. This website thus provides a level of interactivity that is absent from the *math*'s official website kamakoti.org. Due to the fact that the case against the *Shankaracharyas* is still ongoing, those interested in it are still posting news and opinions at the time of writing – seven and a half years after the website was created. As in the case of kanchi-sathya.org, those responsible for the website have also made a plea (in July 2011) on behalf of the Dharma Rakshana Trust for financial help in covering the mounting legal costs of a case that has dragged on for such a long time.

In addition to the new websites concerned with the arrest of the *Shankaracharyas*, existing websites which focus upon the Kanchi *math* also feature material regarding their arrests. For example, the afore-mentioned kksfusa.org, the website of the Kanchi Kamakoti Seva Foundation, runs a campaign to support Jayendra Saraswathi. Furthermore, this website links to the other three websites concerned with the Kanchi *math* that have been referred to in this chapter.

Discussion

Both the Kanchi *math* and its devotees utilise the Internet effectively. This was the case prior to the arrest of Jayendra Saraswathi but further potentialities of the Internet to the devotees in particular were exemplified following this event. Before the arrest the *math* used its website kamakoti.org to furnish devotees with information and current news and announcements and, like Saha (2007: 493–494), I suggested that this use of the Internet is of particular significance to the Kanchi *math* and its followers living abroad because of the fact that the *Shankaracharya* has never travelled beyond the Indian subcontinent. Through their website the *math* is able to reach out to devotees around the world in a way that was not possible before its introduction. In contrast, in the case of websites which are set up by devotees in the diaspora such as kksfusa.org, the connection is in the opposite direction – to the *math* in India. In both cases a link between the two parties is established and maintained. This link which is facilitated by the Internet is crucial because it allows the *math*'s devotees living abroad to connect with India which, as Jacobs argues, 'maintains an important role in the construction of identity amongst Hindus in diaspora' (Jacobs 2012: 142). This emphasises why the use of the Internet by the Kanchi *math* and its supporters is significant and explains why Jacobs further asserts that 'developments in communication technologies are important in understanding Hinduism today, and the way in which it has evolved in a global context' (Jacobs 2012: 136).

Far from the connection that overseas devotees are able to feel they have with the *math* in India as a result of the Internet, remaining abstract, their use of the medium following the arrest of Jayendra Saraswathi is able to demonstrate on a practical level how such a connection can be maintained and strengthened. For example, the Internet has been used by devotees to try to counteract what they see as the lies of the media and to provide a means to publicise the situation and propagate their point of view, and in this way they are forging a connection with events unfolding in India. The Internet has also been used to communicate with other devotees in an attempt to mobilise them. For example, the online petition that was set up demanding that the *Shankaracharya* be released has the potential both to enable the collection of signatures amongst devotees in the diaspora more quickly and in a far higher number than would be possible through a petition administered in any other way. As these devotees are widely dispersed in the USA, Canada and the rest of the world, it is even arguable that a petition could not have been successfully administered if it had not been for the employment of the Internet in this regard. Furthermore, requests for financial assistance are able to reach a wide audience.

Meanwhile, the discussion forum provided on kanchiforum.org allows devotees from around the world to keep up-to-date with the latest developments in the case and to discuss the matter in real time, and at any time, wherever they are in the world. The availability on kanchi-sathya.org of all the documents submitted to the court is also highly significant as these documents can furnish visitors to the website with facts concerning the case in a way that the media is unable to. Furthermore, prior to their availability online, the number of people who would be able to scrutinise the court documents would obviously be very small indeed and this undertaking would usually necessitate a trip to India.

In all of these ways, links both between devotees themselves and between devotees and the *math* are strengthened. Events unfolding in south India are quickly brought to the attention of devotees who may live thousands of miles away from the *math* and these devotees are able to experience an involvement in the situation as a result of their engagement with the Internet. Of course, there is a digital divide – uneven access to the Internet – which means that some supporters of the *math* cannot forge a connection in this way. However, the USA and Canada where many of the overseas devotees of the Kanchi *math* live have high Internet penetration rates. Nevertheless, as Pramod Nayar (2004: 280) points out, even in regions where Internet use is prevalent, there is still a digital divide. This reminds us that some overseas supporters of the *math* will not be Internet users but it does not negate the fact that the Internet is being used by diasporic Hindus in order to connect with each other and to India.

In the same way, the existence of the digital divide does not negate wider findings that emerge from this chapter's case study – that the online activities of the Kanchi *math* and its supporters in the diaspora provide a clear example of the extent to which the Internet can enable the crossing of traditional borders (and hence undermine their relevance) and bring about a compression of space and time as a result of the fact that it allows for information to travel vast distances almost instantaneously. These findings are clear because I have shown that the devotees of the Kanchi *math* have utilised the Internet to disseminate information across the globe regardless of national boundaries and to communicate in real time wherever they may be in the world which, effectively, results in 'time-space compression' (Harvey 1989, cited in Vásquez and Marquardt 2000: 124).

Although what is meant by the term 'globalisation' is contested (see e.g. Scholte 2000: 39), these developments constitute basic non-contentious core features of globalisation – as does the fact that the rise of modern communications technologies, especially the Internet, plays a key role in these developments (see e.g. Giddens 1990: 19–21; Apolito 2005: 152–155). Therefore, this case study, which features the use of the Internet by Hindus in the diaspora, gives further weight to the centrality of the Internet in theories of globalisation, exemplifies core themes of globalisation, and, in showing that the Internet can bring about a decline in the importance of traditional borders, supports a key aspect of the globalisation theories of Ulrich Beck (2000) and Jan Aart Scholte (2000). In addition, the fact that via the Internet devotees are able to stay in touch with the current situation concerning the *math* regardless of the country in which they live means that, in this regard, Manuel Castells's assertion that in a globalised world connection is more important than location (see Hine 2000: 61, 84) is vindicated. This is because it is possible that a devotee with Internet access living thousands of miles away from Kanchipuram could keep up-to-date and get involved with the situation to a greater extent than a devotee in India without Internet access. Furthermore, the case of the use of the Internet by the supporters of the Kanchi *math* particularly highlights processes that are occurring as a result of globalisation because the existence of diasporic populations is, in itself, another integral feature of globalisation (see e.g. Scholte 2000: 60).

Sringeri *Math* Websites

Although the Sringeri *math* is largely unaffected by the arrest of the Kanchi *Shankaracharya*, as in the case of the websites associated with the Kanchi *math*, a consideration of one of its official websites shows, albeit in a different way, how the use of the Internet can result in a new opportunity for its devotees – especially those living overseas. However, in contrast to my investigation of the use of the Internet by the Kanchi *math* and its overseas devotees, which constituted a specific case study that was subsequently shown to exemplify general themes of globalisation, a consideration of this website can also suggest ways in which globalisation as represented by the Internet may actually impact upon a central feature of Hinduism. This is achieved through an analysis of an online manifestation of an important practice undertaken by Adi Shankara – that of the *yatra* or religious tour – which has been emulated by subsequent *Shankaracharyas* including the current ones.

sringeri.net, the main website of the Sringeri *math*, was set up in 2003. In many ways, it is similar to the Kanchi *math*'s website. In addition to providing information about the *math*, the tradition and its *Shankaracharya*, it also features regularly updated announcements. As in the case of kamakoti.org, it offers almost no interactivity whatsoever – it is only possible to send the *math* a message. While it is claimed on the website that a devotee can request a ritual to be carried out on their behalf at the *math*'s temple complex through online channels if they are unable to attend, in effect this is of little significance because they are still required to fill in a form (which can be downloaded via the website) and send that to the *math* along with a cheque in order to facilitate the process. Furthermore, it is emphasised that it is better to actually visit the *math* in order that one can receive the *darshan* or divine glance of the goddess residing at the temple there and receive the blessings of the *Shankaracharya*. This view that despite the capabilities afforded by the Internet it is still preferable to visit the religious site in order to take *darshan* there is one which has also been expressed by other Hindu authorities (Scheifinger 2009, 2010: 333).

These characteristics of sringeri.net mean that the website does not particularly invite analysis in the light of globalisation. Although devotees abroad are able to access information and news through it, the website's low interactivity means that the instantaneous criss-crossing of information around the globe is not occurring as was the case as a result of the creation of the websites by the Kanchi *math* devotees following the arrest of their *Shankaracharya*. Furthermore, the fact that sringeri.net explicitly encourages devotees to visit the *math*, despite the fact that it is possible to request that a ritual be carried out at the temple there on one's behalf, does not demonstrate a further supposed effect of globalisation that is exacerbated by the Internet – that of the alteration of the status of physical sites (Castells 2000: 406; Apolito 2005: 152–155). However, an important offshoot of sringeri.net – the website vijayayatra.sringeri.net – does allow us to consider the validity of such a claim. This website, prominently linked to from the former's homepage, focuses specifically on the south Indian *yatra* that the *math*'s *Shankaracharya* Bharati Tirtha commenced in February 2012. It features information about the *yatra* along with regular updates consisting of text, images from the tour, and videos which capture the talks given by the *Shankaracharya* at his halts. It also includes a regularly updated interactive map where it is possible to track the *Shankaracharya*'s progress and access the afore-mentioned features which correspond to the various locations covered by the *yatra*.

Yatras

Despite the fact that the *Shankaracharyas* do not normally travel overseas, the undertaking of *yatras* within India is an important part of their role. This is following in the tradition of Adi Shankara himself who, it will be remembered, made three tours of the subcontinent in his short life in order to achieve his largely successful aim of linking the whole of India to the philosophy of *Advaita Vedanta*. For example, like Adi Shankara, Jayendra Saraswathi's predecessor

Chandrasekharendra Saraswathi 'spent most of his life on tour' (Cenkner 1995: 131). His first *yatra* alone, which covered the length and breadth of India and which was undertaken mostly by foot, lasted about 20 years (Cenkner 1995: 131). At the age of 73, the current Puri *Shankaracharya* Nischalananda Saraswathi tours regularly, so much so that on the homepage of that *math*'s official website govardhanpeeth.org there is the link 'Where is Guruji Now', which leads to his tour schedule and thus enables devotees to keep in touch with his current whereabouts.

The online manifestation of Bharati Tirtha's *yatra* is of particular interest because of the fact that, through his tours and the setting up of the *maths* at strategic places in India, Adi Shankara built up a network. It is now not only the case that the *Shankaracharyas* who have followed him have reinforced and expanded this network through their own tours. Instead, the network has been able to be further expanded as a result of the Internet allowing for connections overseas, and the various linked websites in the network are nodes that can be likened to the nodes consisting of the *maths* and the sacred sites associated with Adi Shankara that are the original nodes in a Hindu network that was set up in the ninth century AD. In addition, the simulacrum of part of the physical network in India which features the towns, cities and sacred sites visited by the Sringeri *Shankaracharya* on his 2012 *yatra* is made up of nodes within the single node of the website vijayayatra. sringeri.net. But the online manifestation of the *yatra* does not simply constitute a network within a network; it also means that the status of the physical geographical network has the potential to be altered when, through its online manifestation, it becomes subsumed within the network of the Internet. For example, Castells has argued that, as a result of the Internet, 'localities become disembodied from their cultural, historical geographical meaning' (Castells 2000: 406).

Despite Castells's claim, it is safe to say that the various physical sites visited by Bharati Tirtha are not declining in importance even though, through vijayayatra. sringeri.net, it is possible for a Hindu overseas to interactively follow online the *Shankaracharya*'s progress without being present at the locations that he visits. This is because, when partaking in this online simulated journey, unlike in the case of performing a 'virtual pilgrimage' (MacWilliams 2002) in which another party does not undertake the physical pilgrimage concurrently (see MacWilliams 2004), here the *Shankaracharya* is still physically carrying out the journey and visiting various locations – something which he must do in order for the interactive online map to have any relevance.[1] In other words, the online manifestation of the *yatra* is complementing the traditional form and is not replacing it. Hence, in this case the local sites retain their traditional meaning.

In addition, Jacobs (2010) points out that Hindu pilgrimage 'is arguably more widely practised than ever before' and that one of the reasons for this is that,

---

1   This is not to say that a virtual pilgrimage in which another party does not make the physical journey at the same time necessarily brings about a decline in the importance of the sacred site, but a consideration of this is beyond the purview of this chapter.

particularly because of television and the Internet, 'growing numbers of people know about various pilgrimage places' (Jacobs 2010: 33). Therefore, there is the strong suggestion that the existence of the interactive nodes representing the physical *yatra* locations on the Sringeri *math*'s website will lead to more Hindus visiting the various sites, and thus their importance will certainly not be undermined as a result of this online presence. Furthermore, Scholte (2000) has argued that those in the diaspora can 'feel transworld unity and at the same time forge their solidarity around a shared connection to a territorial homeland' (Scholte 2000: 60), and the website vijayayatra.sringeri.net can facilitate this. Devotees of the Sringeri *math* can access the website from disparate countries around the world and, through following the *Shankaracharya*'s *yatra* via the various features of the website, are able to connect with south India.

Conclusion

Various religions espouse universalistic notions such as the oneness of humankind, but, by virtue of the fact that the philosophy of *Advaita Vedanta* proclaims the idea of absolute non-duality; the message of the *Shankaracharyas* is completely universalistic. James Beckford, though, asserts that universalistic claims made by various religions can never be purely universalistic because they necessarily derive from a specific cultural viewpoint (Beckford 2000: 173, 181). Unlike the majority of religious worldviews which do not adhere to the notion of absolute non-duality, the *Advaita Vedantic* viewpoint itself is difficult to reconcile with this claim because of its assertion of absolute non-duality which therefore negates any notion of the existence of specific cultures. However, Beckford's idea is still certainly applicable in this case because, despite its absolute non-duality, the philosophy of *Advaita Vedanta* still emanates from a specific cultural milieu. For example, it derives from India and its exponents are influenced by specific Indian sociocultural norms. It is even said that, as per prevailing norms, Adi Shankara himself once asked a social outcast to make way for him and his entourage – before realising that such a request was incompatible with non-dualism (Rao 2003: 36–39).

As mentioned at the outset of this chapter, the Kanchi *Shankaracharya* is a *Smarta Brahman* and, furthermore, Rajeev (2004: online) reports that 'despite the fitful attempts to involve Dalits [those outside of the Hindu caste-system], the [Kanchi] math remains a largely Brahmin preserve' (see also Fuller 2004: 127– 128). Despite the universalism of *Advaita Vedanta*, the Kanchi *math* supporters, then, although dispersed around the world, primarily come from a social group that has a particular affinity to the *math* and south India – something which clearly shows the particularistic aspects of the tradition. This particularism means that it is especially significant that the opportunities afforded by the Internet enable these devotees to connect with the *math* in India and their *Shankaracharya* in a way that was not previously possible. On the other hand, as a result of the Internet allowing for the wide promotion of the philosophy and activities of the *Shankaracharyas* to those outside of India who do not have any prior sociocultural links to the *maths*, there is now the potential for the attainment of the full realisation of a title that each of the *Shankaracharyas* holds despite their reticence to travel abroad – that of '*Jagadguru*', meaning 'Guru of the World'. This possible transcendence of particularity is perhaps fitting for those who espouse the non-dual philosophy of *Advaita Vedanta*.

References

Anand, S. 2004. Swami and Fiends. *The Outlook*, 29 November. http://www. outlookindia.com/article.aspx?225795 [Accessed 6 July 2012].

Apolito, P. (trans. Shugaar, A.) 2005. *The Internet and the Madonna – Religious Visionary Experience on the Web*. Chicago, IL: The University of Chicago Press.

Appadurai, A. 2000. Disjuncture and Difference in the Global Cultural Economy. In: J. Beynon and D. Dunkerley (eds.), *Globalization – The Reader*. London: The Athlone Press, 92–100.

Beck, U. 2000. *What is Globalization?* Cambridge: Polity Press.

Beckford, J.A. 2000. Religious Movements and Globalization. In: R. Cohen and S. M. Rai (eds.), *Global Social Movements*. London: The Athlone Press, 165–183.

Bhatt, C. 2001. *Hindu Nationalism – Origins, Ideologies, and Modern Myths*. Oxford: Berg.

Castells, M. 2000. *The Rise of the Network Society*. Oxford: Blackwell.

Cenkner, W. 1995. *A Tradition of Teachers – Sankara and Jagadgurus Today*. Delhi: Motlilal Banarsidass.

Cenkner, W. 1996. The Sankaracarya of Kanchi and the Kamaksi Temple as Ritual Center. In: R. B. Williams (ed.), *A Sacred Thread – Modern Transmission of Hindu Traditions in India and Abroad*. New York: Columbia University Press, 52–67.

Flood, G. 1996. *An Introduction to Hinduism*. Cambridge: Cambridge University Press.

Fuller, C. J. 2004. *The Renewal of the Priesthood – Modernity and Traditionalism in a South Indian Temple*. New Delhi: Oxford University Press.

Giddens, A. 1990. *The Consequences of Modernity*. Cambridge: Polity.

Helland, C. 2002. Surfing for Salvation. *Religion*, 32, 293–302.

Helland, C. 2007. Diaspora on the Electronic Frontier: Developing Virtual Connections with Sacred Homelands. *Journal of Computer-Mediated Communication*, 12 (3), article 10. http://jcmc.indiana.edu/vol12/issue3/hell and.html [Accessed 6 July 2012].

Herman, P. 2010. Seeing the Divine Through Windows – Online Darshan and Virtual Religious Experience. *Online – Heidelberg Journal of Religions on*

the Internet, 4 (1), 151–177. http://archiv.ub.uniheidelberg.de/volltextserver/
   volltexte/2010/11303/pdf/09.pdf [Accessed 6 July 2012].
Hine, C. 2000. *Virtual Ethnography*. London: Sage.
Indo-Asian News Service. 2004. Shankaracharya in Jail – Shock, Anger Across
   Nation. *The Times of India Online*, 12 November. http://www1.timesofindia.
   indiatimes.com/articleshow/921199.cms. [Accessed 17 November 2004].
Indo-Asian News Service. 2005. Jayendra Out of Prison, Mutt Shifted. *Worldwide
   Religious News*, 11 January. http://wwrn.org/articles/13872/?&section=hindui
   sm [Accessed 1 July 2012].
Jacobs, S. 2010. *Hinduism Today*. London: Continuum.
Jacobs, S. 2012. Communicating Hinduism in a Changing Media Context. *Religion
   Compass*, 6 (2), 136–151.
Klostermaier, K. 1998. *A Concise Encyclopaedia of Hinduism*. Oxford: Oneworld
   Publications.
MacWilliams, M. W. 2002. Virtual Pilgrimages on the Internet. *Religion*, 32 (4),
   315–335.
MacWilliams, M. W. 2004. Virtual Pilgrimage to Ireland's Croagh Patrick. In:
   L. L. Dawson and D. E. Cowan (eds.), *Religion Online – Finding Faith on the
   Internet*. London: Routledge, 223–37.
Miller, D. and Slater, D. 2000. *The Internet – An Ethnographic Approach*. Oxford:
   Berg.
Mitra, A. 2000. Virtual Commonality – Looking for India on the Internet. In:
   D. Bell and B. M. Kennedy (eds.), *The Cybercultures Reader*. London:
   Routledge, 676–694.
Nadar, A. G. 2004. Who was Sankararaman?. *Rediff.com*, 13 November. http://
   www.rediff.com/news/2004/nov/13agn1.htm [Accessed 1 July 2012].
Nayar, P. K. 2004. *Virtual Worlds – Culture and Politics in the Age of Cyberspace*.
   New Delhi: Sage.
Press Trust of India. 2011. Shankaracharya Refutes Allegations of Influencing
   Judge. *OUTLOOKindia.com*, 26 April. http://news.outlookindia.com/items.
   aspx?artid=732625 [Accessed 1 July 2012].
Rajeev, P. I. 2004. Commotion in Kanchi. *expressindia.com*, 21 November. http://
   www.expressindia.com/news/fullstory.php?newsid=38670 [Accessed 6 July
   2012].
Rangaswami, S. (ed.) 2012. *The Roots of Vedanta – Selections from Sankara's
   Writings*. New Delhi: Penguin Books.
Rao, S. 2003. *Adi Shankaracharya – The Voice of Vedanta*. New Delhi: Rupa and
   Co.
Saha, S. 2007. Hinduism, Gurus, and Globalization. In: P. Beyer and L. Beaman
   (eds.), *Religion, Globalization, and Culture*. Boston, MA: Brill Academic
   Publishers, 485–502.
Scheifinger, H. 2008. Researching Religion on the WWW: Identifying an Object of
   Study for Hinduism. *Methodological Innovations Online*, 2 (3), 30–49. http://

www.pbs.plym.ac.uk/mi/pdf/Volume%202%20Issue%203/4.%20Scheifinger %2030-49.pdf [Accessed 6 July 2012].

Scheifinger, H. 2009. The *Jagannath* Temple and Online *Darshan. Journal of Contemporary Religion*, 24 (3), 277–290.

Scheifinger, H. 2010. *Om*-line Hinduism: World Wide Gods on the Web. *Australian Religion Studies Review*, 23 (3), 325–345.

Scholte, J. A. 2000. *Globalization – A Critical Introduction*. Basingstoke: MacMillan.

Smith, D. 2003. *Hinduism and Modernity*. Oxford: Blackwell.

Vásquez, M. A. and Marquardt, M. F. 2000. Globalizing the Rainbow Madonna: Old Time Religion in the Present Age, *Theory, Culture and Society*, 17 (4), 119–143.

Viswanathan, S. 2004. Controversial Career. *Frontline*, 21 (24). http://www. flonnet.com/fl2124/stories/20041203006300800.htm [Accessed 1 July 2012].

Warrier, M. 2005. *Hindu Selves in a Modern World: Guru Faith in the Mata Amritanandamayi Mission*. London: Routledge.

Websites Cited

bbc.co.uk/worldservice/Hinduism.http.//www.bbc.co.uk/worldservice/people/features/ world_religions/hinduism.shtml [Accessed 26 October 2005].

beta.kksfusa.org. [Accessed 6 July 2012].

govardhanpeeth.org. [Accessed 10 July 2012].

kamakoti.org. [Accessed 1 July 2012].

kanchi-sathya.org. [Accessed 1 July 2012].

kanchi-sathya.org/kanchidigest. www.kanchi-sathya.org/kanchidigest.htm [Accessed 1 July 2012].

kanchiforum.org. [Accessed 1 July 2012].

kksfusa.org. [Accessed 1 July 2012].

sringeri.net [Accessed 10 July 2012].

vijayayatra.sringeri.net. [Accessed 10 July 2012].

Chapter 6

Cyberspace, the Globalisation of Hinduism, and Protocols of Citizenship in the Digital Age

Vinay Lal

Prologue

Hinduism, unlike Islam and Christianity, has historically been confined largely to the Indian subcontinent. To be sure, substantial parts of Southeast Asia had been 'Indianised' by the first half of the first millennium of the Common Era, though there is a complex literature on just what it is that is to be understood when we speak of the Indianisation of the Malay Archipelago, the Mekong Delta, Java, Angkor, and other areas that fell under the sway of Hindu or Buddhist rulers. Some older theses about the spread of Hinduism and Indic culture, which represented Indian traders as constituting something of a cultural and religious advance force, or dwelled, far more improbably, on *kshatriyas* as carriers of Indian civilisation to Southeast Asia, have now been jettisoned or put into serious question. Nevertheless, there is still substantial agreement not only on the long history of the cultural and spiritual presence of Indian civilisation in Southeast Asia, but on the apparent fact that the artefacts of this civilisational presence, such as the Ramayana and Mahabharata, were not – unlike, say, Antonio de Nebrija's grammar of the Spanish language, which the author himself characterised as an instrument of empire and colonisation (Illich 1981) – mere foot soldiers of a greater military force. Indeed, the viewpoint of two German scholars who have long been scholars of Indian history may be considered quite representative in this respect: as they write, 'The transmission of Indian culture to distant parts of central Asia, China, Japan, and especially Southeast Asia is one of the greatest achievements of Indian history or even of the history of mankind. None of the other great civilisations – not even the Hellenic – had been able to achieve a similar success without military conquest' (Kulke and Rothermund 1998: 143).

What is equally certain is that over time Hinduism eventually survived, outside South Asia, only in Bali – before, that is, the diffusion of Hinduism in the nineteenth century under vastly different conditions. The system of indentured servitude, which dispersed Indians around the globe, to Trinidad, Guyana, Surinam, South Africa, Malaysia, Fiji, Mauritius, and elsewhere, constitutes one of several chapters in Hinduism's forays into the wider world in the modern era.

Hailing predominantly from either the Hindi heartland, or from Tamil country, indentured labourers took their gods, their *desi* traditions of worship, and (as was the case with migrants from the Gangetic plains) their beloved *Ramacaritmanas* to the scattered outposts of the British Empire and to far-flung islands which had now become cogs in the machinery of industrial production. Hinduism reached those corners of the world that it had never before breached, but neither scholarship nor popular memory has claimed these early migrants as the first emissaries of a new diasporic wave. Indeed, many of the migrants never returned to India, and over a couple of generations their descendants ceased to have any living contact with India at all.

In India itself, Hinduism would go through various dramatic transformations during the course of colonial rule. In the late nineteenth century, as Indian nationalists pondered over the fate of their country, they sought the revival of an ancient faith and cast it in a militant mode, partly on the assumption that the religion's supposed accent on nonviolence and pacifism had rendered it spectacularly vulnerable to the Semitic faiths (Lal 2008b). Bankimcandra Chatterjee, who pioneered the novel in Bengali with immense success and became a writer of great repute, was among those who argued that the Hindu's attachment to the philosophy of *bhakti* (devotion) had emasculated the once rigorous race of the Aryans and made them incapable of defending themselves against more the more militant and single-minded adherents of Islam and Christianity. His affirmation of a Hinduism that would at once be more masculine and possessed of a semblance to the Hebraic faiths did not go unheeded. By this time, as Tomoko Masuzawa (2005) has persuasively argued, the very idea of 'religion' was to be understood in the template of Protestant Christianity, and the endeavour in India would be to transform Hinduism, a religion sadly confined (as its more vocal followers claimed) to South Asia, into a proper 'world religion'.

The 'Worldliness' of Hinduism and the Swaminarayan Faith

Over the last three decades, Hinduism's followers in India and abroad have been aggressive in forging a new – more militant, global, and scientised – conception of their faith. There is, to begin with, the well-documented rise of Hindu nationalism in India: if the *Bharatiya Janata Party* represents the interests of Hindus in formal political institutions and political parties, the *Vishwa Hindu Parishad* [Global Hindu Network] does the cultural work of Hinduism just as the *Rashtriya Swayamsevak Sangh* [literally, National Volunteer Corps] provides Hinduism with its muscle power. This history, however, is well known and need not be rehearsed at this juncture. There is another part of this story that is less well understood, namely the unprecedented attempt to forge awareness of Hinduism as a 'world religion'. Hindu nationalists, often modelling themselves on Christian evangelical groups, have sought to link Hindus across the world and have argued that Hindus 'left behind', for example in relatively remote diasporic settings, must be embraced by 'Mother India'. Hinduism's mutation into a diasporic faith and a 'world religion' is now being writ large in the Indian diaspora of the North, and nowhere is its rapid ascendancy more marked than in the United States. Before the passage of sweeping immigration legislation in 1965, there were fewer than 10,000 Indians in the US; today, judging from the 2010 Census, Indian Americans number in the vicinity of three million, and of these the preponderant number are Hindus.

Hinduism's emergence in the United States (Lal 2008a), and as something of a 'world religion', can be marked by a wide array of socio-cultural phenomena, from the creation of Hindu student groups at virtually every major American college campus to the extraordinary proliferation of temples. Though I have written elsewhere about 'temple Hinduism', the prominent visibility of the BAPS [*Bochasanwasi Shri Akshar Purushottam Swaminarayan*] *Sanstha*, one of the three groups of the *Swaminarayan* sect, is illustrative of the tendencies that I wish to bring to the fore. Indeed, what is distinct about the *Swaminarayan* faith is that its leaders and adherents are determined to usher Hinduism into a new era of monumental architecture and what may reasonably be described as modernist achievement. The BAPS temples, which have sprung up not only in Gujarat but perhaps even more spectacularly so in the diasporic setting of North America, are a case in point. When the BAPS *Shri Swaminarayan* temple was inaugurated in Neasden, just outside London, in 1995, it was described as the world's largest Hindu temple outside India (except, however, for Angkor Wat, which is an archaeological site rather than a functioning temple). The temple website proudly states that '2,820 tonnes of Bulgarian limestone and 2,000 tonnes of Italian Carrara marble were shipped to India, carved by over 1,500 craftsmen and reshipped to London. In all, 236,300 carved pieces were assembled like a giant jigsaw puzzle in less than 3 years. It is a miracle of modern times worked by over a thousand volunteers' [www.mandir.org/introduction]. BAPS then broke its own record when, in quick succession, it opened, on each occasion, the world's largest temple — in Houston (2004), Chicago (2004), Toronto (2007), and Atlanta (2007). The $40 million *Shri Swaminarayan Mandir* in Bartlett, some 40 miles from downtown Chicago, is described on its website as a place of 'wonder': 'This masterpiece of ancient design and workmanship, which was put up in only 16 months, is testimony to the sheer dedication and devotion of over 1,700 volunteers' [www.chicago.baps. org.introduction]. The enchantment with numbers is visible throughout: as the website further informs its visitors, nearly 500 craftsmen in India laboured over the 108 marble pillars which support 15 domes. The Atlanta temple's introduction begins on a more innocuous note: 'A Mandir is a Hindu place of worship – a haven for spirituality and a place of paramount peace'. Apparently, to rehearse an old belief, places of worship should reflect the greatness of God; and so, effortlessly, the site goes on to rehearse nearly the same facts about yet another temple: 'The BAPS Shri Swaminarayan Mandir was inaugurated in August of 2007 after only 17 months of construction time utilising 1.3 million volunteer hours. The Mandir is comprised of 3 types of stone (Turkish limestone, Italian marble, and Indian pink sandstone). More than 34,000 individual pieces were carved by hand in India, shipped to the USA and assembled in Liburn like a giant 3-D puzzle' [http://atlanta.baps.org].

One should perhaps not be surprised that there has been little if any expression of discontent at such affluent displays of Hindu religiosity. The BAPS temple is an affirmation not only of community and ethnic pride, but also of the alleged values of Hinduism and the (Indic) civilisation with which it is indelibly linked. Recognising the supreme place of *the museum modality* in the culture of the modern West, the BAPS temple, in what might be called the 'Gallery of Indian Achievements', showcases the contributions of ancient India and purports to establish the persistent modernity of India. The permanent exhibition on 'Understanding Hinduism', divided into five sections, commences with 'Glorious India'. The remote ancestors of contemporary Hindus, the viewer is informed, were familiar with aviation, atomic energy, even aeronautic surveillance; indeed, in whatever domain of knowledge, the ancient Hindus not merely excelled but somehow anticipated the very scientific developments for which the modern West cavalierly takes credit.[1] India was the first to introduce the concept of 'Zero' to the world in 700 BCE: since this is one achievement that cannot be doubted, the reader is lulled into believing the rest, namely 'that the law of gravity was first discovered in 600 BCE, by Maharshi Kanad, an Indian Physicist'; and, furthermore, 'the first history book, the first university, the first Hospital — all founded in India, hundreds of years before any thought of [these arose] in countries across the world.'[2] The question is not whether some of these claims are fraudulent,[3] but what relationship achievements in surgery, physics, metallurgy, and mathematics have to Hinduism. Why should religion have to validate itself in the language of science? The

---

1   There is no gainsaying the fact that the history of science, much like other disciplines and areas of intellectual inquiry, has taken little cognisance of developments outside the West — notwithstanding, of course, such major research accomplishments as Joseph Needham's *Science and Civilisation in China* (1954–2008). What passes for 'history of science' has in general no time for developments outside 'the modern West'; it has also become extremely skilful in writing out the history of those viewed as interlopers, or otherwise construed as assistants or helpers to the white man. A case in point is the recent discovery of the Higgs boson particle, a critical development in particle physics. Higgs takes its name from Peter Higgs, a British physicist; boson, without the capital B, referring to the class of particles that follow the Bose-Einstein statistics, takes its name from the Indian physicist Satyendra Nath Bose, whose role in the Higgs boson has been minimised, if not elided, particularly by commentators in the West.

2   http://chicago.baps.org/Exhibition/Exhibition.htm.

3   I am certainly prepared to accept that Indian achievements in the sciences and mathematics were seldom recognised in the West, and that the conventional narrative, which, to simplify, equates modern science with the West, cannot withstand scrutiny. See, for example, C. K. Raju, *'Is Science Western in Origin?'* (Penang: Multiversity and Citizens International, 2008), and idem, *Cultural Foundations of Mathematics*, Vol. X Part 4 of the *History of Science, Philosophy and Culture in Indian Civilization*, ed. D. P. Chattopadhyaya (Delhi: Centre for Studies in Civilizations and Pearson Longman, 2007).

necessity of attempting to demonstrate the compatibility of modern science with the tenets of an ancient faith apart, what is just as striking is the effortless ease with which Hindu elides into India. There is, in the exhibition at the BAPS temple in Bartlett, the reassurance that it was *the Hindu mind* that discovered the law of gravity or wrote the first textbook of surgery.

Hinduism's Histories on the World Wide Web

Let me turn, then, to one of the most pronounced features of modern diasporic Hinduism. Among the world's principal religions, none appears to be so apposite for our digitally wired times as Hinduism. Only Hinduism, if one may put it so boldly, can match the internet's playfulness: the religion's proverbial '330 million' gods and goddesses, a testimony to the intrinsically decentred and polyphonic nature of the faith, find correspondence in the world wide web's multiple points of origin, intersection, and dispersal (Lal 1999). Hinduism has neither a historical founder, nor a text so supremely authoritative that all of the religion's adherents are enjoined to turn to it; and, similarly, it is distinct in that it has, rather than anything akin to a *Kaaba*, multiple pilgrimage sites. It will not do, by way of rejoinder, to consider the Vedas as occupying within Hinduism the same place that the Koran holds in Islam or that the New Testament occupies in Christianity, just as it is indubitably erroneous to suppose that Banaras is the Mecca of Hindus, even if it is nearly singular among the world's cities as a place to which the orthodox Hindu might retire on the eve of his or her life.[4] In all these respects, Hinduism has appeared to anticipate many of the internet's most characteristic features, from its lack of any central regulatory authority and anarchism to its alleged intrinsic spirit of free inquiry and abhorrence of censorship. What is certainly clear is that Hinduism's adherents, nowhere more so than in the United States, have displayed a marked tendency to turn towards various forms of digital media, and in particular the internet, to forge new forms of Hindu identity, furnish Hinduism with a purportedly more coherent and monotheistic form, engage in debates on American multiculturalism, and partake of the protocols of citizenship in the digital age. The aspiration to create linkages across Hindu groups worldwide, embrace Hindus in remoter diasporic settings who are viewed as having been severed from the motherland, and create something of global Hindu consciousness has a fundamental relationship to India's ascendancy as an 'emerging economy'

---

4   There are far too many Hindus who revere Puri, or Pushkar, more than Banaras, the city of Shiva. In common conversation, even among middle-class families in north India, no temple is spoken of with as much veneration as Tirupati, or, more formally, the Tirumala Venkateswara temple in Tirumala, a Vaishnava shrine near Tirupati – but this is in Andhra, not Banaras. One might still admit that an extraordinary literature has developed around Banaras: for a sampling, one could turn to Diana L. Eck, *Banaras: City of Light* (reprint ed., New York: Columbia University Press, 1998).

and the confidence with which its Hindu elites increasingly view the world and their prospects for prosperity and political gain.

Recent research on the internet that focuses on political mobilisation and activity has been directed largely to the study of how terrorist or extremist groups wage net wars, gain recruits and funding, and otherwise disseminate radical ideologies. For reasons that are not entirely surprising, scholars and public commentators have dwelled overwhelmingly on the place of Islam on the internet, the *jihadi* appropriation of cyberspace, and the radicalisation of Muslims by means of the internet (Bunt 2003; Hoskins 2011; Lappin 2010; Sageman 2008; Seib 2010; Weimann 2006), though there is ample evidence that Christian fundamentalists have been just as adept in their use of the internet to form new communities of believers committed to End Times ideology (Howard 2011). Much of the scholarly focus that was once riveted on the 'terror networks' said to have been generated in the Soviet Union's proxy wars on the United States and its allies has effortlessly shifted to Islam's 'terror networks',[5] and the supposition remains that Muslim terrorists, who have found themselves on the run, hounded from one continent to another, bereft of funds as a consequence of tighter controls over financial exchanges and money laundering, have naturally gravitated towards cyberspace as the most secure arena for their activities. Yaakov Lappin puts it cryptically apropos the American invasion of Afghanistan following the attacks of 11 September 2001: 'Jihadis had just lost their latest physical safe house in Afghanistan. Now, no country afforded them the freedom to openly recruit and train an army, conduct mass indoctrination, and plot to bring down governments in order to establish the caliphate. Al Qaeda loyalists quickly began seeking digital refuge' (2010: 25). The old dream for the establishment of an Islamic caliphate survives, contends Lappin, except that the jihadis are now bound together to create a 'Virtual Caliphate', an Islamic state on the internet.

It might well be argued that many scholars and commentators who have worked on 'terror networks' have allowed themselves to be guided by the idea, which has had an astonishingly – indeed alarmingly – long run in the last few years alone, that though not all Muslims are terrorists, all terrorists are Muslims. The very conception of 'Political Islam' has narrowed considerably, even if there is a parallel if less visible strand of scholarship that has valiantly sought to shift attention to the creative uses of digital media in fomenting democratic revolutions in the Islamic world (see, for example, Sreberny and Khiabany 2010; el-Nawawy and Khamis 2009). It is nevertheless a much wider expanse of 'Political Hinduism' that I propose to put into play in my consideration of the political engagement of Hindus with computer-mediated communications. While adherents of Hinduism are, as is now transparent, by no means singular in being predisposed towards digital media, and there are at present no quantitative studies that might enable us

---

5   The phrase 'terror network' first made an appearance in 1981 in a book with the same title. Claire Sterling argued that the then Soviet Union had deployed a large network of terrorists to conduct proxy wars against the United States and its allies.

to gauge internet usage among different religious communities, there is nonetheless an overwhelming amount of anecdotal and circumstantial evidence to suggest that Hindus have been particularly conscientious, if not innovative and aggressive, in mobilising members of the perceived Hindu community through the internet.

The rise of Hindu militancy in India since the late 1980s, signalled by the term Hindutva (the 'essence' of Hinduism), had its counterpart in the creation of new Hindutva histories on the internet. History is preeminently the terrain, as I have argued in several works over the course of the last 15 years (Lal 1999, 2003a, 2003b, 2005), on which disputes over religious identity and the constitution of the nation-state are waged; and these disputes are accentuated in the setting of the diaspora, where Hindus simultaneously might imagine themselves as the vanguard of an ancient faith and entertain an interpretation of their faith which has the effect of reifying what are believed to be Hindu practices, beliefs, and modes of worship. Hindus in North America have forged what I have previously characterised as *a postindustrial Vedic civilisation*, one in which what are represented as the practices of Hinduism can be followed in the US without hindrance from Muslims or the restraints imposed by the pseudo-secularism of the Indian state in the space of uninhibited technological freedom; moreover, in this postindustrial Vedic civilisation, the freedoms gained under the rubric of American democracy are conjoined to the inner freedoms which are represented as the supreme achievements of the spiritual practices that have evolved in India over the course of a few thousand years.

It is remarkable that, when the internet was in a relative state of infancy, a more aggressive and even militant conception of Hinduism had already secured its place on the internet. In the early 1990s, Ajay Shah, who had arrived in the US as a doctoral student in chemistry at the University of Mississippi in 1989, set about creating on the net what became known as the Global Hindu Electronic Network (GHEN). When he was interviewed by Jeff Zaleski a few years later, Shah admitted that email presented virtually unprecedented possibilities for collaboration among immigrants from India who were otherwise scattered around the US and had done precious little to establish communication networks. 'That's how we ended up using electronic email', Shah says, 'because it was virtually free for all the people who went to universities. It was a quick and easy way of communication' (Zaleski 1997: 220). Within a few years, Shah had developed an email list of over 30,000 subscribers, and GHEN was, so to speak, absorbed into the Hindu Students Council. In 1996, IWAY, then one of the leading internet magazines, recognised GHEN with its 'Best Web Page Award' in the religion category, and one of GHEN's members described the pleasure that he and his friends experienced at the thought that the world was finally 'taking cognizance of the most important movement in this century, "The Hindutva Movement"'.[6]

Even a cursory glance at what were then the web pages of GHEN would suggest how Hinduism and Hindutva were sought to be fused into a single entity. GHEN's

---

6   See 'Award Recipient', *India-West* [Los Angeles: 15 March 1996], C20.

home page took one to predictable categories such as 'Scriptures', 'Temples', and 'Organisations', and the page that opened up to the 'Hindu Universe' was graced by the sign of 'Aum'. But what is striking is how the home page for 'Hindu Universe' in turn led to other pages,[7] designated as follows: 'Latest News from Bharat (India)'; 'Kashmir'; 'Terrorism in Bharat (India)'; 'Hindutva Nationalist Ideology'; and 'Shri Ramjanmabhoomi Movement'. Though it is, of course, true that Kashmir has been the traditional homeland of Kashmiri Pandits, it is also indisputably the site of an even more extensive culture of Islam. The creators of the 'Hindu Universe' do not appear to have been burdened by any reflections that might necessitate a reconsideration of the effortless ease with which the complex and disputed history of Kashmir is assimilated into a general narrative framework on what is termed the 'Hindu' universe. There are similar, indeed far more pressing, questions that might be posed about the purported relationship of the discourse of Islamic terrorism to the Hindu worldview. Have Hindus been reduced to such insecurity that they can no longer comprehend their own history and culture except through references to those who are represented as the lethal enemies of Hinduism?

Throughout the 1990s, there would be a proliferation of sites resolutely devoted to a reinterpretation of Indian history. One could point to many such endeavours which strain the limits of credulity, among them the virtual Hindu Holocaust Museum,[8] but what should not be obscured is that the very proclivity to argue in the language of the historian shows how far the diasporic proponents of Hindutva have abandoned the language of Hinduism for the epistemological imperatives of

---

7   The idea of a 'home page' on the internet is not without its ironies. The home and the world have long stood in opposition, as in Rabindranath Tagore's novel, *Ghaire Bhaire* ('The Home and the World'), by the same name. The home signifies interiority, the space of domesticity, the female sphere; the world, by contrast, suggests exteriority and the sphere of masculinity. The world wide web takes us on a tour of the world, but the intent of the traveling is to return to where one started from, namely the home. It is as if the intent is to reinforce the idea that, after all our travelling – whether to remote places, or in the most radical of ideas – we must be rooted at home: the technology is not without some degree of self-reflexivity, holding up the idea that ceaseless wandering around the world wide web may not be without its perils if one does not, from time to time, return home. There is an equally significant play on the idea of domesticity: the world wide web may make it possible to evade a crushing domesticity, but one doesn't have to leave one's home at all. It remains to be said that a 'home' for the 'Hindu Universe' is a strikingly anomalous idea, more so than it might be for the Hebraic faiths. As I have argued above (see, in particular, note 4), Hinduism has nothing strictly analogous to Mecca or to Jerusalem; with respect to texts, as well, there is nothing in Hinduism that resembles the place – let us call it 'home' – that the Koran or the Bible occupy within Islam and Christianity.

8   There are, however, plans to build a Hindu Holocaust Museum, and at a fundraiser in New Jersey in 2009, $50,000 was raised to this end. See the discussion online at: http://facttruth.wordpress.com/2010/01/19/hindu-holocaust-museum/ (accessed 15 September 2012).

modernity and the nation-state. What is of equally critical importance is the fact that Hindus settled in the United States have nonetheless received these public histories, the vast majority of which have been greatly discredited by scholars of Indian history, with wide approbation. A fuller sociological understanding of this phenomenon is still awaited: what is certain is that Indian American Silicon Valley engineers, and hundreds if not thousands of Indian male graduate students in the computer sciences, laboured over these web sites, list serves and bulletin boards dedicated to revisionist and Hindu nationalist accounts of Indian history and culture (Lal 1999, 2003a).

Let me turn, however, to rather more recent phenomena which suggest the emergence of what I would term *aggressive internet Hinduism*. To understand the politics of the internet's deployment by nationalist Hindus who are fully cognisant of the discourses of multiculturalism, and the opposition they have aroused among secular and avowedly progressive Hindus, the fierce controversy that arose in California in 2005 over the content of school history textbooks serves as a poignant case in point. California state law mandates a review of textbooks every six years, and in 2005 history and social science textbooks for sixth- and seventh-graders were up for review. The occasion furnished certain Hindus with the opportunity to petition for over 200 changes to the content on ancient India and Hinduism found in such textbooks. Many of the changes they proposed were altogether unobjectionable, and no one cared to dispute them: as an illustration, one textbook stated, altogether erroneously, that Hindi is written in the Arabic script, and 'concerned Hindus' demanded that this mistake be rectified. But they advanced many other claims that cannot withstand scrutiny and which, if accepted, would furnish a view of Hinduism that has little relation to the religion on the ground. They argued, for instance, that Hinduism is incorrectly represented in the school texts as a polytheistic religion, and that Hinduism is as much a monotheistic religion, if different in other crucial respects, as Islam or Christianity. In putting forward this argument, these aggrieved and self-appointed representatives of the Hindu faith show little awareness that neither 'monotheism' nor 'polytheism' are intrinsic to any indigenous understanding of 'Hinduism': these are categories derived from the study of something called 'religion' in the West. They similarly averred, to take another example, that in ancient India men had not more rights than women, a claim encountered in these texts, but rather that men and women had 'different' rights. The proponents of the changes advanced no substantive argument about what it would mean to speak of 'different' rights for men and women, though there are clearly situations where, in principle, an argument to this effect could be countenanced. The law might stipulate, for example, that a woman has a right to breast-feed her infant in public without being hauled into jail on charges of obscenity or indecent exposure: such a law, quite obviously, cannot be gender neutral, and would not confer a similar immunity on men. But ancient Hindu law books have nothing to say on these matters, and this is evidently not what 'concerned Hindus' had in mind.

One suspects that these diasporic Hindus are classic illustrations of the phenomenon expressed in the proverb, 'once bitten, twice shy'. Led by the Hindu Education Foundation and the Vedic Foundation, both organisations based in the United States, Indian American Hindus waged, predominantly over the internet, a relentless campaign to energise the Hindu community into action. The Hindu Education Fund is affiliated to the Hindu Swayamsevak Sangh, an American chapter of the RSS; the Vedic Foundation, meanwhile, is parented by Barsana Dham, also known as Radha Madhav Dham, a large temple complex in Austin, Texas, which hosts meetings of the VHP, RSS, and the Hindu Students Council [http://www.radhamadhavdham.org/]. The California State Board of Education reported, throughout late 2005 and early 2006, being flooded with emails, faxes, letters, and phone calls from irate Hindus who claimed that textbook representations of Hinduism and the caste system were calculated to make Indian American school-children feel ashamed about their faith and heritage, and that in multicultural America Hindus were entitled to as much respect as adherents of any other religion or community. Thus, for instance, an organisation known by its acronym CAPEEM – California Parents for the Equalization of Educational Materials – objected that 'Hinduism is **not** treated on par with other religions in these textbooks. Positive aspects of ancient India and Hinduism are ignored, while Eurocentric, colonial and Biblical views are given prominence in the textbooks' (www.capeem.org; emphasis in original).

CAPEEM's marketing and rhetorical strategies are not without some subtlety: the very name of the organisation obscures the fact that its membership is confined to Indian Americans, and that they are concerned solely with representations of Hinduism and ancient India, not with material that might be objectionable to anyone. There are, indeed, some further elements in the strategies deployed by CAPEEM and its partner organisations that merit mention. First, by describing itself as an organisation of 'California Parents', CAPEEM highlights the entitlements that Hindu Americans have as Americans and Californians, and the effrontery they feel not only as Hindus and Indians but also as American citizens and as tax-paying residents of California. Secondly, the critique of the textbooks as 'Eurocentric' has the advantage of appealing to all right-minded people, particularly to those who might describe themselves as left-of-centre, and it attempts to preempt the charge that the objections to the textbooks are being fuelled by mere nationalism. Thirdly, and in a rather similar vein, it is striking that the demand for the radical changes to the textbooks is accompanied by the plea, 'Let India Develop'. An internet site by this name, www.letindiadevelop.org, describes opponents to the changes as 'miscreants' who are determined to prevent India from developing. To suggest that one's opponents are anti-national is, of course, the oldest canard; and that opponents of the textbooks are fundamentally of the same ilk as Naxalite revolutionaries and Pakistani terrorists, both allegedly determined to prevent the emergence of India as a developed nation, is suggested by the fact that the 'California Hindu Textbook Controversy' is featured prominently on the site's home page. Moreover, it is the specificity of the charge, namely that opponents stand in the way of India's development, that points to the relative sophistication of the strategy: though there may be in some academic and NGO circles a resounding critique of the ideology of development, the Hindu American activists act with the confidence that in common parlance the idea of development is still prized. Who would not want to be part of a developed state? To be opposed to 'development' is to open oneself to the charge that one is nothing but an obdurate primitive or, at best, a misguided Gandhian idealist out of touch with reality [see Nandy 1984 and 1987; Lal 1995b; Roy 1999]. The supposed singularity of Indian academics in opposing the proposed changes is highlighted in a table on 'how the California public process has worked' that appears in the article, 'What is the Hindu Textbook Controversy About': here it is argued that only with respect to Hinduism – as distinguished from Islam, Judaism, and Christianity – were the community's activists opposed by academics. One could go on in this vein, parsing exactly what it is that the members of CAPEEM, the Hindu Education Foundation, letindiadevelop.org, and other Hindu advocates understand by terms such as 'colonial' or 'biblical', or why opponents should be branded as 'people [who] actually hate Hinduism' [http://www.letindiadevelop.org/irochtc/].

The proposed alterations to the textbooks would have been implemented but for the last-minute 'awakening' of scholars of Indian history, of Indian origin and otherwise, who were in agreement that many, though not all, of the proposed changes could not be justified. Several internet campaigns – one among 50 well-known scholars of Indology from around the world, the other among South Asian scholars in the humanities and social sciences at leading American universities, and yet another waged by secular activists, progressives, and Hindus who disputed that the advocates of Hindutva could speak for all Hindus, not to mention other Indians – eventually led the State Board, at two contentious meetings, to reject the most controversial of the alterations proposed by those acting in the name of the Hindu community. Nevertheless, CAPEEM represented the efforts of the Hindu Education Foundation and Vedic Foundation as victories for Hindu parents and their wards. Though that claim does not appear to be very credible, it is not altogether hollow, insofar as some within the community had taken a gigantic step in overcoming what many Hindu Americans have long viewed as the greatest liability afflicting the community, namely the invisibility of Hindu Americans in the United States.

'Mr. Patel', American Hindus against Defamation, and Other Artefacts of an 'Invisible' Community

The name Patel, as of this writing, is not one without some familiarity to many Americans. Telephone white pages have become nearly obsolete with rapid advancements in cell phone and digital technologies, but a few years ago the Patel surname would have surfaced at least as often in the telephone directories of the Greater Los Angeles area as the name Singh in the telephone directories for Greater London. Some Americans associate the name Patel with motel, even if they are unaware of the circumstances under which this linkage came to be established, and there are even those who suppose that Patel is the Indian word for motel. The Indian journalist Tunku Varadarajan wrote with some provocation about the 'Patel motel cartel' for the *New York Times* in 1999, but as far back as 1978–79 the *Washington Post* had reported at length on growing Indian, and especially Gujarati, ownership of motels. The Gujaratis are at once grounded and diasporic, and equally renowned for their entrepreneurial spirit; and it is in the fitness of things that they should have cornered the motel business, which has been captured in a number of books and even films.

The Gujaratis might have brought some visibility to the Indian community in the United States, though many Indian Americans, particularly those who think of themselves as Hindus before counting their membership in other groups that confer identity, may not be keen on such visibility at all. It is certainly true that the vast majority of Americans have little awareness that many diasporic Hindus hold to the view that the obscurity surrounding Hinduism leaves it without protections available to more organised religions. Hinduism's adherents in the US are certain that their religion is least understood among all the major faiths; it is also the faith most likely to be exoticised and, before the events of the last decade which have made Americans view Islam with deepening suspicion, the faith most likely to be demonised. For all the virulent criticism levelled at Islam, it is still a monotheistic faith and thus within the circle of reason; but Hinduism, by contrast, remains beyond understanding. Hindu Americans view their faith with pride, as is to be expected, but equally with some trepidation, fearful that Hinduism has, for a variety of reasons, left itself vulnerable to the more self-aggrandising ambitions of the Semitic faiths. Since Hinduism was, in their view, trampled upon by hordes of invaders and colonisers over centuries, the religion remains unusually vulnerable and its adherents are called upon to exercise vigilance in defending Hinduism not only from the zealots and guardians of other faiths but from those who ironically have done it harm by assuming that Hinduism's vast universe can be mined at will and without hindrance in the era of globalisation.

Among the most prominent organisations now in the vanguard to safeguard Hinduism against the depredations of fanatics and corporate interests is one that styles itself 'American Hindu Against Defamation' (AHAD). More information has become available about AHAD in recent years. It appears to be the brainwave of Ajay Shah, the same Indian graduate student in chemistry who in the 1990s set up GHEN, the Global Hindu Electronic Network, though Shah has evidently found a cohort of sympathisers who are animated by the same concerns which impelled him to set up AHAD, which on the internet is housed under 'the Hindu Universe' [www.hindunet.org/ahad/]. Some ten years ago, AHAD's attraction was drawn to 'Mr. Patel', one of a series of 'Trash Talker Dolls' created by a Florida toy company that, in its own way, cashed in on the rage for multiculturalism. AdultDolls.net, the company that manufactures these dolls, is clearly ecumenical in its choice of targets, including gays, Jews, Hindus, Chinese, and white trailer trash. Each of the dolls, which are described as 'adult party sensations', is programmed to utter five phrases on demand: the Chinese one, called Lee Chan Li, speaks the following phrases in a Chinese accent: 'Ahhh...you bang my head? I bang your wife! Ha ha ha!'; 'Oh don't worry, peanut oil let me slide in very easy'; 'Confucius say: Time for you to bend over' [www.adultdolls.net/003_Lee_Chan.html].

While Mr. Patel's pronouncements are not focused exclusively on sex, the doll doubtless sets new standards for political incorrectness – which, surely, must have been among the objectives being aimed at by the manufacturers. Mr. Patel commences with the following hugely offensive remark: 'What are you doing, you dirty piece of fecal matter?' The Indian's supposed unease with the idioms of English, and more generally the immigrant's struggle with a new language, is attempted to be captured in two of Mr. Patel's remarks: 'Don't talk like that in front of my back' and 'In my country, we would've already killed you already'. The customer is asked to imagine what a Hindu might say upon entering McDonald's or Burger King: 'Hamburger. Everything on it please, but no beef', a stereotype that feeds on the vaguely understood sentiment among Americans that Hindus hold the cow in veneration and abjure the consumption of beef. The pièce de résistance may well be Mr. Patel's declamation, in the tone of a husband accustomed to acting with imperious authority towards his wife, 'I am needing to want sex with you now' [http://www.adultdolls.net/sounds/Patel_1.mp3]. 'Mr. Patel', alarmingly, also sports a turban, which to AHAD suggests that Hindus are being conflated with Muslims, and most particularly with terrorists of the Osama bin Laden variety. It is not surprising, then, that AHAD would go on to warn that the Mr. Patel doll could incite anti-Indian and anti-Hindu sentiments.[9]

For all of AHAD's protestations, however, it did not succeed in having the dolls removed from the market. 'Mr. Patel', as of September 2012, is still featured on the company's website, though it is one of several dolls that is described as 'sold out'. AHAD has had much else to keep its members occupied through the last decade, as the organisation conducts vigorous campaigns against a number of companies charged with the exploitation of Hindu deities and the profanation of the Hindu faith. AHAD's wrath has fallen upon the kitchen and bath appliances company Kohler, which released a glossy advertisement of a scantily clad woman with four arms and a raised right leg who is clearly a representation of Nataraja, the dancing Shiva,[10] the West Coast microbrewery Lost Coast which produced an Indian pale ale that carried Ganesh's picture on the front,[11] American Eagle

9   Lisa Tsering, 'Maker of "Mr. Patel" Doll Laughs at Racist Allegations', *India-West* (6 December 2002), p. C1. See also the discussion on www.redhotcurry.com/views/trash_talker.htm.

10   See Ashfaque Swapan, 'Hindu Group Lambastes Kohler Ad', *India-West* (25 October 2002), p. B1.

11   See http://ratebeer.com/ShowBeer.asp?BeerID=5556.

Outfitters for the manufacturing of flip-flops with images of Ganesh on the sole,[12] and Fortune Dynamic for its marketing of footwear with 'pictures of Hindu Gods and Goddesses imprinted on them' [http://www.hindunet.org/anti_defamation/shoes/]. The AHAD website explains that 'Hindus consider shoes to be "dirty" and do not wear them at home or temples. It is a common Hindu practice to remove shoes before entering homes or temples. This is why, putting pictures of Hindu God and Goddesses on shoes is particularly offensive and outrageous to Hindus'. One might well agree that a foot placed on a sole bearing the image of a deity represents a gross insult to Hinduism, but since when did Hindu deities become so fragile? One suspects that Indian American Hindus are not familiar with the large canvas of Indian literature known as the Puranas, which ought to be the heritage of everyone who purports to describe himself or herself as a Hindu, and which are ecumenical enough to entertain conceptions of Hindu deities who are often given over to erotic, playful, and even perverse activities.

AHAD's most spectacular campaign to date has been against the toilet seat manufacturer Sittin' Pretty, which placed images of Shiva, Kali, and Ganesh on toilet seat covers.[13] AHAD contends, not unreasonably, that Hindu images, which are 'cool' and popular among followers of Semitic faiths who may well be starved of images of the divine, are assumed to be public property,[14] and that the reverence extended to other religions is entirely wanting in the American experience of Hinduism. AHAD's convener, Ajay Shah, described the toilet seat covers in a letter to the company's head as 'an outrageously insensitive use of Hindu symbolism', and he asserted that 'sacred Seats with Christian, Jewish or Islamic symbols would have evoked a much [more] vigorous outcry'.[15] Hindu images may be 'cool', but, evidently, one can also, so to speak, shit on them. 'Little did we know', AHAD's website states apropos of the toilet seats planted with images of Hindu deities, 'that there is no limit to how low can one sink when it comes to the depiction of revered Hindu images'.[16]

---

12   'Trampling on Hindu Sentiments: Footwear with Ganesh Images', *India-West* (2 May 2003), p. A37.

13   Viji Sundaram, 'Hindus Incensed Over "Sacred" Toilet Seats', *India-West* (24 November 2000), p. A1, 40.

14   Sittin' Pretty's activities were brought to the attention of the Rajya Sabha, the Upper House of the Indian Parliament, where a demand was voiced that the Indian government should pressurise the US government to take legal action against the Seattle-based firm. Vijay Singh Yadav of the Rashtriya Janata Dal is reported to have said that 'there was a current craze in the U.S. about Hindu gods and firms were exploiting it by painting figures of Hindu gods on toilet covers'. See anon., 'Parliament Slams Hindu Gods on Sanitaryware', *India-West* (1 December 2000), p. A28.

15   Ibid., p. 40. See also http://hinduism.about.com/library/weekly/aa111900a.htm (in 3 parts, accessed 1 September 2012).

16   See http://hinduism.about.com/library/weekly/aa111900a.htm (accessed 1 September 2012) and http://www.hindunet.org/anti_defamation/sittinpretty (cached). However 'cool' the images, I suspect that Hindu Gods leave some of us hot, some of us cold: the Japanese,

AHAD is at a loss to explain why, if Hinduism appears to bear the burden of commercial obscenities, Sittin' Pretty should also have placed the Holy Mary on one of its toilet seat covers. True, the manufacturer appears not to have placed an image of the Holy Mary cover on its website, but it can also be argued that to the manufacturer all divine images are fair game. What could have been a critique of the relentless logic of the market becomes, in AHAD's hands, resentment over the base treatment that is apparently reserved only for Hindus and their faith. That Sittin' Pretty can so casually place Hindu deities on its toilet seat covers is an expression not necessarily of contempt for Hinduism, but more so of the fact that categories such as 'reverence' and 'sacred' have lost much of their purchase under conditions of modernity. What AHAD needs to be engaged with here is a critique of modernity and market-place morality, but this is much too difficult: its own frame of reference is furnished by the very institutions and cultural practices that devolve from modernity, such as the idea of demanding a political apology. AHAD demanded, and received, an apology from Sittin' Pretty, whose co-owner, Lamar van Dyke, described 'our beloved Goddess Kali' and 'Lord Ganesha' as deities to whom 'we feel personally close', adding: 'We meant neither harm nor insult, and apologise to the Hindus of the world for unintentionally upsetting them'.[17] Little does AHAD realise that an epidemic of apologies has engulfed us, and that 'apology' itself has become a category of market-place morality.[18]

It is perfectly reasonable for people to become agitated if they believe that their religious sentiments have been violated or profaned, and crass commercial exploitation of religious icons and beliefs is to be at least as much deplored as the naked use of religion in the service of political extremism. Doubtless, some absurd defence of Sittin' Pretty's rights of free expression of speech and artistic license is not inconceivable, but Sittin' Pretty will find few defenders. Still, one must ask how 'defamation' came to be an operative category for Hindus, just as one must probe those to whom the category of 'blasphemy' to describe offences committed against Hinduism apparently presents no problems. Whatever moral charge there may be in the term 'defamation', it is today preeminently a legal category, and Hinduism's defenders have consistently maintained that matters of religious belief are outside the purview of the legal system. Can religions at all be defamed, or in the eyes of the law is it only individuals who may be wrongfully subjected to slander and thus entitled to protection against defamation?

---

who have invented toilet seats that can be heated with the press of a button, would doubtless have put a different spin on the whole affair.

17 Viji Sundaram, '"Sacred Toilet" Seat Maker Apologises to Community', *India-West* (1 December 2000), p. A28.

18 For a more extended discussion, see Vinay Lal, 'An Epidemic of Apologies', *Humanscape*, 6 (4), (April 1999), 38–41.

Digital Hinduism and the Protocols of Citizenship

For all their veneration of Swami Vivekananda, often characterised as a vigorous defender of the faith who urged Hindus to march onwards and usher India into modernity, Hindu nationalists have been little attentive to what is unquestionably one of the more compelling stories from his life. Vivekananda himself has reported that, on a trip to Kashmir, he experienced a deep sense of anguish at seeing broken images of Hindu gods and goddesses, the evidence of countless acts of the invaders' disdain for Hindu idolatry. Filled with rage at 'this humiliating testimony of history', Vivekananda fell at the feet of the Divine Mother in a Kali temple and asked her, 'How could you let this happen, Mother, why did you permit this desecration?' Vivekananda reports that her retort came swiftly, 'What is it to you, Vivekananda, if the invader breaks my images. Do you protect me, or do I protect you?' (Gandhi 1992: 10).

The notion that Hinduism has to be defended vigorously against its detractors and nowhere more so than on the internet, as I have hitherto argued and will demonstrate at greater length in this concluding section, has taken deep roots among Hindus worldwide. At the World Hindu Conference in South Africa in 1995, which brought together Hindus from 38 countries, delegates resolved that they would 'ask governments to outlaw blasphemy and violations of religious rights': while committing themselves to 'inter-religious dialog', the delegates also cautioned 'all other religious groups that Hinduism will not necessarily accept with simple magnanimity all their attacks and affronts on Hinduism. We will resist vigorously attempts at conversion'.[19] But just who are the detractors of Hinduism? Are they within the community, or without, or both? Do the detractors launch frontal attacks on Hinduism and its adherents, or do they just as effectively succeed in rendering Hindus, and their achievements, all but invisible to the wider community? Why, nationalist Hindus ask, are Hindus in the United States so reluctant to concede the Hindu origins of many practices that have taken hold in the US? And how, the question that is most germane to this paper, might the internet be used to advance the interests of Hindus and ensure that Hinduism receives the same protections and entitlements which the Abrahamic faiths claim for themselves?

Insofar as Indian American Hindus, whose share in the American population has been rapidly increasing and has now reached the three million benchmark, approximating more than 0.75 per cent, have been most aggressive in their deployment of the internet and even see themselves as the vanguard of the faith, a recent episode from that community's public profile will serve productively as the starting point of this discussion. The community, let us say, has more than once in recent years been up in arms. Two years ago, the object of their rage was the *Time* columnist Joel Stein, who, they complained, had the audacity to write a piece called 'My Own Private India' [after 'My Own Private Idaho'] which begins

---

19   See http://www.hindunet.org/alt_hindu/1995_Jul_2/msg00088.html (accessed 20 September 2012).

thus: 'I am very much in favor of immigration everywhere in the U.S. except Edison, N.J. The mostly white suburban town I left when I graduated from high school in 1989—the town that was called Menlo Park when Thomas Ava Edison set up shop there and was later renamed in his honor—has become home to one of the biggest Indian communities in the U.S...'[20] And he adds: 'The town is [now] totally unfamiliar to me'. When Stein writes that he is 'very much in favor of immigration', he seems to want to signal his distance from those bigots, in Arizona and elsewhere in the US, who have declared their determination to keep the US as free of immigrants as possible; but the qualifier, 'except Edison, N.J.', was bound not to go down well with Indian Americans who feel outraged that *Time*'s columnist should have marked Indian Americans, who have become the dominant ethnic group in Edison, as the undesirable immigrant community.

What follows in Stein's piece is not surprising. The sparkling town where Stein grew up is unrecognisable though, if anyone knows America, it is doubtful in the extreme that it was recognisable in the first instance. Main Street, Anytown, America, is just that: a stretch of stores that appear with predictable tedium all over the country, signalling a mind-numbing homogeneity in the land of what purports to be the bastion of individualism. Stein complains that the Pizza Hut outlet – one of thousands in the country, which along with Burger King, McDonald's, KFC, Jack in the Box, Taco Bell, Carl's Jr., and Dunkin' Donuts have succeeded remarkably well in making every American town look like any other – has been replaced by an Indian sweet shop; the local A & P – never mind that this chain is a shadow of its former self, having filed for bankruptcy in 2010 – has given way to an Indian grocery store; the Italian restaurant 'is now Moghul' (by which our enlightened writer means not that it has become a movie palace or an icon of a movie Moghul but rather that it serves Mughlai food); and the local multiplex, where Stein and boys of his ilk once gyrated their loins to the music of R-rated films, now screens Bollywood films with their buxom belles and serves samosas during the 'intermission'. Stein and his friends, modern-day Huckleberry Finns, shoplifted, raided the cash drawers, and sneaked into places where they did not belong. But those days belong to the past: 'There is an entire generation of white children in Edison', Stein bemoans, 'who have nowhere to learn crime'. The place of those delightful pranksters was taken by nerds from India, who all seemed adept at computers and to the white boys appeared nothing short of 'geniuses'. At this point, one almost expects to read a comment pointing to the winning streak of Indians in the national spelling bee over the last decade and more, but Stein departs from that script only to adopt another predictable point of view. Over time, he says, that first generation of educated and professional Indians gave way to a motley crowd of relatives who would run Dunkin' Donut shops, 7–11 franchises, and gas stations. Some years later, the not so dazzling 'merchant cousins brought

---

20   The article was first published on 5 July 2010, and appeared in both the print and internet editions of *Time*; see http://www.time.com/time/magazine/article/0,9171, 1999416,00.html (accessed 1 September 2012).

[over] their even-less-bright cousins, and we started to understand why India is so damn poor'. And, luckily for the white man, he could once again begin to feel like he was on the top of the world.

Stein's attempt at humour, for that is evidently what he had in mind, appears not to have succeeded. Following the publication of his column, Indian Americans conducted an intensive internet campaign to have his column removed, and to have Stein censured for his 'racist' comments. Some in the Indian American community have been outraged that as prestigious a journal as *Time*, for that is how this long-standing conduit of mediocrity is imagined, should have allowed the expression of the most tiresome stereotypes: perhaps all that is missing from Stein's piece is a comment about the smell of curry taking over the town. As I have argued in the preceding section, ours is a culture of apologies, and it is not surprising that the Indian American community should immediately have striven to exact an apology from *Time* and Joel Stein. 'We sincerely regret', responded *Time*, 'that any of our readers were upset by this humor column of Joel Stein's. It was in no way intended to cause offense'. Poor Stein followed suit, though his apology deviates from the standard form: 'I truly feel stomach-sick that I hurt so many people. I was trying to explain how, as someone who believes that immigration has enriched American life and my hometown in particular, I was shocked that I could feel a tiny bit uncomfortable with my changing town when I went to visit it'.

One of the least commonly explored facets of Americanisation is how immigrant communities embrace the dominant idiom of literal-mindedness that pervades American society, and the irony and ambivalence of Stein's remarks was certainly lost on Indian Americans. A place that he associated with his childhood had irretrievably changed, and Stein found himself outside, so to speak, his comfort zone. The small town seems remote, perhaps even an ungainly sight, after the dizzy pace of life in the metropolis; in Stein's case, the sense of alienation he may have experienced upon his return to Edison was compounded by the fact that even the intimacy and familiarity promised by the town had disappeared. In the internet exchange that followed the publication of Joel Stein's essay, neither Stein nor Indian Americans were to come across as impressive figures. Some commentators have deplored the absence of humour among Indian Americans, to which of course they have responded with the observation that they have for long been the target of insults and jokes and have had enough of 'humour'. In India, on the other hand, some writers and media broadcasters have not fully understood the emotions that are understandably aroused when Stein, adverting to the fact that townsfolk started referring to the Indians as 'dot heads', adds by way of trying to be ironical: 'In retrospect, I question just how good our schools were if "dot heads" was the best racist insult we could come up with for a group of people whose gods have multiple arms and an elephant nose'. Caricatures of a religion never go down too well with its adherents; moreover, there is a lasting memory, especially in New Jersey, of a previous chapter of racial history when the 'dot busters' went around assaulting Indians and even murdered a young Indian professional, Navroze Mody (Misir 1996; Anand 2006).

Judging from the response to Stein, we can infer that Indian Americans have become increasingly vigilant, a reflection in part of the fact that the community has become more visible and affluent over the years. A more unusual instance of their confidence and assertiveness surfaced in 2008, when in early January of that year Arun Gandhi, co-founder and President of the University of Rochester's M.K. Gandhi Institute for Nonviolence, penned a short blog for the *Washington Post* entitled 'Jewish Identity Can't Depend on Violence'. Arun Gandhi described the future of Jewish identity as 'bleak': even as many Jews remain 'locked into the holocaust experience', not merely convinced of the absolute exceptionality of the Holocaust but firm in their view that their victimhood gives them unique entitlements, the state of Israel, which is the guarantor of Jewish life, history and culture, remains unapologetically tethered to the view that it has every right to exercise unquestioning dominance over its neighbours and its own Palestinian subjects besides having a monopoly over the legitimate use of violence. If, as Gandhi suggested in his blog, even the peace activists he met in Israel are committed to the Wall and an arms build-up, what hope is there that Israel will ever come around to the view that its existence cannot be secured by 'bombs and weapons'? Jewish people, Gandhi argued, had furnished a 'very good example of [how] a community can overplay a historic experience to the point that it begins to repulse friends'.

Israel is, of course, far from being the only purveyor of violence in its immediate neighbourhood, and the rockets launched into Israel by Palestinian extremists as well as the suicide bombings of recent years are grim testimony to the fact that violence is widely pervasive in this area torn apart by war, resistance movements, and perhaps even more so the oppressions of everyday life. However, in describing 'Israel and the Jews' as the 'biggest players' in this 'culture of violence', Gandhi undoubtedly erred – insofar as he failed to make a distinction between Jews, not all of whom are by any means Zionists, and the state of Israel. The response was fast and furious, nearly all on the internet; and he graciously responded with – what else? – an apology, stating unequivocally that he does 'not believe and should not have implied that the policies of the Israeli government are reflective of the views of all Jewish people', while reaffirming his conviction that the policies of the state of Israel remain inexcusable.

There is much in Arun Gandhi's comments, and the heat generated by them, that is worthy of interpretation; but what is even more intriguing is the cavalier position adopted by the Hindu American Foundation (HAF), which cannot be described as a party to the controversy as such. On 27 January the Hindu American Foundation issued a press release, prominently displayed on its website, where it described itself as 'disturbed' by Gandhi's comments on the Jews.[21] The

---

21   The press release can still, as of late September 2012, be accessed online at: http://www.hafsite.org/issues/interfaith?q=/media/pr/20080127_disturbed_by_comments_

Foundation noted that it 'absolutely rejects an entry by Arun Gandhi, a grandson of Mahatma Gandhi', which had lambasted the Jews, and it affirmed that, in view of Gandhi's unwillingness 'to categorically disown his remarks', his resignation was the only fitting if 'rather unhappy end to his controversial career as director of the M.K. Gandhi Institute'. Speaking as a member of the Foundation's Board of Directors, attorney Nikhil Joshi characterised Gandhi's comments as 'simplistic and biased' and not only 'unbecoming of one who presumes to lead a conflict resolution institute, but dangerously misguided'. HAF condemned Gandhi's comments for his 'sweeping attacks on Jews as a people, rather than focusing an argument against specific policies of Israel in response to the daily threats against and attacks on Israel'. One can understand why HAF might have been agitated by Gandhi's suggestion that 'Israel and Jews are the biggest players' in the global culture of violence, but the precise wording of the rest of the statement leaves no doubt that Israel is cast as the victim rather than as the perpetrator of acts of aggression.

A number of important issues thus come to the fore as we attempt to understand the rules of civic engagement and the protocols of citizenship in the digital age. Hinduism has, as many besides myself have argued as well, no common 'church', no historical founder, and no singular authoritative text to which all Hindus subscribe, and one cannot speak of any medium, axis, or contrivance through which all Hindus have been bound in conversation with each other. This is not to say that there may not be some notions – among them the idea of Hinduism as *sanatan dharma*, the concept of *varnasrama dharma*, and the belief in the ritual superiority of Brahmins as the conveyors and interpreters of the scriptural authority of the Vedas – which have the assent of a considerable number of Hindus and might have had a significant place in determining the course of Hinduism's evolution over three to four millennia. Nevertheless, it is useful to recall that the religion's most famous practitioner of the twentieth century, Mohandas Gandhi, pointed to what might be called the anarchic nature of the faith when he even declared that 'a man could call himself a Hindu and yet not believe in God' (see Sharma 1996).

Hinduism's vociferous adherents of our times, none more so than the cyber-inclined Hindus of the United States, have consequently been riddled by an 'anxiety of influence' (Lal 2003b), an anxiety that Hinduism is not taken seriously as a religion, and that, ironically, translates into the belief that Hinduism would be best served by transforming it into something akin to the very Abrahamic faiths that Hindu nationalists profess to abhor. I have argued that they see the internet – along with a renewed form of temple Hinduism, though that is treated only marginally in this chapter – as the medium through which Hinduism can be forged into a worldwide religion, and pliant Hindus, both in India and in the older Indian diasporas of the nineteenth century, should be brought to an awareness of the global strengths of a 'modern' Hindu community. It is not surprising that,

about_jews.

as India slowly begins to imagine itself as an emergent world or at least Asian power, the Hindu community in the United States, which contributes substantially more to direct foreign investment in India than Hindus elsewhere, should begin to feel emboldened, mindful of its 'rights' and prerogatives; in a similar vein, not unexpectedly these Hindus view themselves as the vanguard of *internet Hinduism*.

At the same time, these new forms of political participation give rise to considerations which call for greater deliberation, as my discussion of the interventionist strategies of 'American Hindus Against Defamation' and the Hindu American Foundation has sought to establish. One should be wary of dismissing these considerations on the specious grounds, frequently encountered in everyday conversation and often in scholarly literature, that internet technologies, much like other applications of science, can be used either for good or bad. Increased internet mobilisation of Gujarati Hindus, for example, played a not insubstantial role in communalising Gujarati Hindus living in the United States. The interviews that I conduced among Gujarati Hindus in California showed that a preponderant number of them gave their tacit approval to the Narendra Modi government's complicity in the pogrom carried out against Muslims in early 2002: if most of the interviewees were careful not to suggest that the 'Muslims had it coming', they were nonetheless wholly inclined to adopt the view that, in Modi's words, every action has a reaction.[22] The argument that Indian Muslims regrettably owe their first loyalty to the *ummah*, to some notion of universal Muslim brotherhood, rather than to the Indian nation is one that I heard frequently expressed and that has become, in India itself, a way of justifying second-class citizenship for Muslims. On the other hand, it may not be too much to ask whether increased internet mobilisation of the Indian American Muslim community might not have done something to mitigate the pogrom against Muslims in the Indian state of Gujarat in 2002. There is growing awareness of the power of diasporic communities, and nowhere more so than in the state of Gujarat, where the appellation 'non-resident Gujarati' has a standing all of its own besides the more familiar idea of the non-resident Indian.

There are also more abiding considerations of how a community, in this case Indian Americans, deploys certain categories of interpretation and protocols of citizenship without accepting its ethical responsibilities. Nationalist Hindus in the United States have become wise to the advantages that are to be gained in taking recourse to arguments about multiculturalism and diversity. When it serves the community, it flaunts its minority status, and is extraordinarily adept and versatile in suggesting that Indian Americans as Hindus lend something unique to the mosaic of American society. But it is not at all clear that nationalist Hindus in the United

---

22 Twenty interviews were carried out, in the spring of 2003, among Gujaratis in Southern California: there were an equal number of men and women, and interviewees included shopkeepers, motel owners, professionals, and homemakers. The majority of the interviewees had been living in the United States for at least ten years, nearly half of them for over 20 years; a few had spent less than five years in America.

States, largely drawn from the ranks of the upper castes and professional classes, have at all been hospitable to multiculturalism, or Indian variants of pluralism, in India itself. It seems that multiculturalism is all but necessary and certainly desirable in the United States, but that India can clearly do without such imports. Digital media technologies have thus created new interfaces for articulations of citizenship in a world where rules of civic engagement are evidently still under negotiation. Just how far internet Hinduism will proceed in helping us understand changing protocols of citizenship in a transnational world remains to be seen.

Acknowledgments

The author would like to acknowledge that much of the research for this article was made possible by grants from the Academic Senate, and the Asian American Studies Center, both at UCLA.

References

Anand, V. Z. J. 2006. The Dotbuster Effect on Indo-American Immigrants. *Journal of Immigrant and Refugee Studies*, 4 (1), 111–113.

Brasher, B. E. 2001. *Give Me That Religion Online*. San Francisco, CA: Jossey-Bass Inc.

Bunt, G. R. 2003. *Islam in the Digital Age: E-Jihad, Online Fatwas, and Cyber Islamic Environments*. London: Pluto Press.

el-Nawawy, M. and Khamis, S. 2009. *Islam Dot Com: Contemporary Islamic Discourses in Cyberspace*. London: Palgrave Macmillan.

Finger, S. 2001. *Origins of Neuroscience: History of Explorations into Brain Function*. New York: Oxford UP.

Gandhi, R. 1992. *Sita's Kitchen: A Testimony of Faith and Inquiry*. New Delhi: Penguin Books.

Hoskins, A., Awan, A. and O'Loughlin, B. 2011. *Radicalisation and Media: Connectivity and Terrorism in the New Media Ecology*. New York: Routledge.

Howard, R. G. 2011. *Digital Jesus: The Making of a New Christian Fundamentalist Community on the Internet*. New York: New York University Press.

Illich, I. 1981. *Shadow Work*. London: Marion Boyars.

Kulke, H. and Rothermund, D. 1998. *A History of India*. 3rd ed. London: Routledge.

Lal, V. 1999. The Politics of History on the Internet: Cyber-Diasporic Hinduism and the North American Hindu Diaspora. *Diaspora*, 8 (2), 137–172.

Lal, V. 2003a. North American Hindus, the Sense of History, and the Politics of Internet Diasporism. In: R. C. Lee and Sau-ling C. Wong (eds.), *AsianAmerica. Net: Ethnicity, Nationalism, and Cyberspace*. London: Routledge, 98–138.

Lal, V. 2003b. India in the World: Hinduism, the Diaspora and the Anxiety of Influence. *Australian Religion Studies Review*, 16 (2), 19–37.

Lal, V. 2005a. *The History of History: Politics and Scholarship in Modern India.* 2nd enlarged ed. Delhi: Oxford University Press.

Lal, V. 2005b. The Concentration Camp and Development: The Pasts and Future of Genocide. *Patterns of Prejudice*, 39 (2), 220–243.

Lal, V. 2008a. *The Other Indians: A Political and Cultural History of South Asian Americans.* Los Angeles, CA: Asian American Studies Center Press/UCLA; New Delhi: HarperCollins.

Lal, V. 2008b. Hinduism, in *Oxford Encyclopaedia of the Modern World*, IV, edited by P. N. Stearns. Oxford: Oxford University Press, 10–16.

Lal, V. (ed.) 2009. *Political Hinduism: The Religious Imagination in Public Spheres.* Delhi: Oxford University Press.

Lappin, Y. 2010. *Virtual Caliphate: Exposing the Islamist State on the Internet.* Washington, DC: Potomac Books.

Masuzawa, T. 2005. *The Invention of World Religions: Or, how European Universalism was Preserved in the Language of Pluralism.* Chicago, IL: University of Chicago Press.

Misir, D. 1996. The Murder of Navroze Mody. *Amerasia Journal*, 22 (2), 55–75.

Nandy, A. 1987. Development and Authoritarianism: An Epitaph on Social Engineering. *Lokayan Bulletin*, 5 (1), 39–50.

Nandy, A. 1994. Culture, Voice and Development. A Primer for the Unsuspecting. *Thesis Eleven*, 39, 1–18.

Roy, A. 1999. *The Cost of Living.* New York: Modern Library.

Sageman, M. 2008. *Leaderless Jihad: Terror Networks in the Twenty-First Century.* Philadelphia, PA: University of Pennsylvania Press.

Seib, P. and Janbek, D. M. 2010. *Global Terrorism and New Media: The Post-Al Qaeda Generation.* New York: Routledge.

Sharma, A. 1996. *Hinduism for Our Times.* Delhi: Oxford University Press.

Sreberny, A. and Khiabany, G. 2010. *Blogistan: The Internet and Politics in Iran.* London: I.B. Tauris.

Varadarajan, T. 1999. A Patel Motel Cartel? *The New York Times* (July 4), online: http://www.nytimes.com/1999/07/04/magazine/a-patel-motel-cartel. html?pagewanted=all&src=pm (accessed 17 August 2012)

Vertovec, S. 2009. *Transnationalism.* London: Routledge.

Weimann, G. 2006. *Terror on the Internet: The New Arena, the New Challenges.* Washington, DC: United States Institute of Peace Press.

Zaleski, J. 1997. *The Soul of Cyberspace: How New Technology is Changing Our Spiritual Lives.* San Francisco, CA: HarperCollins.

SECTION II:
Power

Chapter 7

(Re-)connecting with the Indian Diaspora from the 'Homeland': Diaspora Conferences and the Construction of Online Linkages with Non-Resident Indians

Mirian Santos Ribeiro de Oliveira

This chapter examines the (re)construction of transnational linkages between non-state actors based in India and emigrants through online communities. Activities of participant observation at the conference Pravasi Bharatiya Divas 2011 in New Delhi, internet resources related to the event every PBD delegate eventually comes across (from brochures, business networks and newsletters, to sponsored and sponsors' links, to mention just a few), and personal online networks built in the course of such diaspora conferences (which rendered the author an invitation to vote for one NRI Power Podium 2012 contestant and, therefore, allowed observation of virtual transnational interactions) provided the primary sources analysed.

In order to discuss the formation of an internet community by non-state actors intending to connect Indian 'homeland' and its emigrants, namely NRI Matters web portal sponsors, I focus on the web portal content as well as on online interactions related to the NRI Power Podium contest, an event aimed at electing emigrant 'representatives' to attend the Pravasi Bharatiya Divas conference. The interplay of governmental and non-governmental initiatives with the purpose of (re)connecting emigrants with their sending-country through the internet is addressed first. The role played by online events and diaspora conferences in the (re)interpretation of transnational identifications, mainly as regards the conception of Overseas Indian and its subcategories Non-Resident Indians (NRI) and Persons of Indian Origin (PIO), is approached in the following section. Finally, I highlight convergences between NRI Power Podium and Pravasi Bharatiya Divas practices and discourses, giving special attention to: the construction of a positive homogenous image of the Indian emigrant (depicted as powerful and successful); the dynamics of celebration established by online interactions furthered by both events; and the stress on seasonal activation of transnational networks.

Emigration and Transnationalism

Research on Indian transnationalism has so far produced relevant and insightful analyses on Indian migrants and their connections with the homeland mainly from the perspective of immigration – that is, from the point of view of the (re)construction of linkages with their sending-country by Indians or persons of Indian origin living in their countries of adoption. This chapter focuses instead on Indian transnationalism from the perspective of emigration, looking into the engagement of social actors within India in the (re)construction of ties with Indians or persons of Indian origin based abroad. It is important to acknowledge first of all the increasing complexity of human migration flows, and, therefore, the simultaneity of processes of immigration and emigration in most societies around the world (Castles and Miller 2009; Koser 2007; Peralva 2008). Secondly, although simultaneous and interrelated in many senses, immigration and emigration understood as 'social problems' make up significantly distinct areas from the point of view of public policies or academic research (Sayad 1998). On the one hand, immigration policies and studies have been concerned mainly with the challenges of the *presence* of non-nationals in 'national communities' they originally do not belong to and, in this connection, with the subjects of control/management of migration inflows and incorporation of immigrants to social institutions and processes of the receiving-country. On the other hand, emigration policies and studies, considerably less developed so far, while dealing with the *absence* of nationals from the sending-country, have focused primarily on the relationship between emigration and development (the influence of underdevelopment on emigration or the effects of emigration on homeland development) and, increasingly, on the (re)construction of (economic, political and cultural) linkages between sending-countries and emigrants (Castles and Miller 2009; Koser 2007; Østergaard-Nielsen 2003; Vertovec 2009).

Thirdly, it must be considered that the categories 'emigrants' and 'sending-countries' or 'sending-societies' are not monolithic, comprehending numerous social actors and their diverse interests, perceptions and action modalities. As far as the (re)construction of ties between sending-societies and emigrants is concerned, it can be conceived from the point of view of emigrants (as individuals, hometown associations, diaspora organisations, political and/or religious organisations) and their growing participation in 'homeland' processes through investment or philanthropy, for instance. It can also be considered from the perspective of the sending-society, whose outreach strategies are devised by governmental organisations – ministries or (national or sub-national) departments for overseas nationals – and non-governmental organisations – political parties, religious and human rights organisations, transnational mass media, private companies etc. (Mármora 1999; Østergaard-Nielsen 2003; Vertovec 2009). I focus on non-state actors within the sending-society engaged in the construction of online communities intending to connect the 'homeland' and its emigrants. Hence the choice of presenting a case study on the website 'NRI Matters' and, more specifically, on its contest 'NRI Power Podium', aimed at electing emigrant 'representatives' to attend the diaspora conference Pravasi Bharatiya Divas (PBD).

Online Linkages between Sending-Society and Emigrants

Since the PBD is organised by the Ministry of Overseas Indian Affairs (MOIA), I start from a brief discussion of governmental policies for the (re)construction of linkages between sending-society and emigrants, mainly as regards the process of 'symbolic nation-building', in order to understand the interaction between Indian governmental and non-governmental organisations surrounding the formation of online emigrant communities. Comparative studies have shown that 'homeland' governmental policies for the diaspora are comprehensive, ranging from symbolic and institutional initiatives to political and financial measures, and employed in varying degrees by different sending-societies (Gamlen 2006). As far as governmental initiatives for the Indian diaspora are concerned, the most visible are probably investment policies – focused on attraction of remittances and foreign direct investment and aimed primarily at the highly qualified emigrants settled in the North, deemed the third largest highly skilled diaspora in the world (Beine *et al* 2009). However, institutional and symbolic capacity-building measures have received significant attention in the last decade too. The constitution of the Ministry of Overseas Indian Affairs (2004) and related entities, as the Overseas Indian Facilitation Centre (2007), a partnership with the Confederation of Indian Industry (CII), must be taken into account as institutional capacity-building. Amongst symbolic nation-building policies, one can point out the construction of an inclusive rhetoric which represents India as the 'homeland' of residents *and* emigrants, continuously stressed during the PBD, the annual diaspora conference held since 2003, a highly visible symbolic policy itself (Gamlen 2006; Khadria 2009; Raj 2003).

Nevertheless, the development of media channels connecting India and emigrants, a relevant tool for the making of online transnational networks, has not been significantly advanced as a governmental policy so far. As regards the internet, more specifically, the institutional core dedicated to 'homeland' – diaspora relations created websites (and linked existent ones to the newly created) providing 'official' information on India and on legitimate and/or desired forms of engagement of emigrants with the 'motherland' (see the Ministry of Overseas Indian Affairs and the Pravasi Bharatiya Divas websites, for instance). Some of them are highly economic-oriented – as the Overseas Indian Facilitation Centre website, whose section 'Network' intends to construct an online community focused on business partnerships/interactions – whereas others seek to 'connect India with its diaspora' in a broader sense (as the Overseas Indians website, which hosts MOIA e-magazine, Pravasi Bharatiya, and news and opinions' sections – both written by the website content producers and closed to users' posts). Yet one must consider that none of these web portals was devised with the purpose of providing a platform for the construction of online transnational communities. Such institutional websites are neither interactive nor open to multiple discourses on emigration and related subjects as social networks or non-institutional websites potentially are. In fact, they reinforce the dynamics observed in many instances of the relationship between sending-country institutions and overseas nationals: emigrants' participation is expected to conform to or, at least consider as a starting point, the official governmental discourse on emigration and its related guidelines for the (re)construction of linkages between the parts.

However incipient the aforementioned internet resources may be, they interact with and are supplemented by non-governmental initiatives aimed at the 'diasporic audience' in many ways, leading to a profusion of internet content somehow connected to the subject of Indian emigration. Web portals created and managed by media and corporate groups based in India such as 'India Empire', 'Pravasi Today' and 'NRI Matters' bring together magazines, discussion groups and blogs approaching several issues considered relevant for India-diaspora relations on the one hand, and for Indian emigrants' lives in their countries of adoption on the other. Most of such websites dialogue with governmental policies for the Indian diaspora through articles, links, advertisements, comments and (less often) criticisms posted on their websites. Yet they can be said to take their purpose one step further once the combination of thematic diversity, employment of interactive tools and relative openness to content production (registered users are usually allowed to express their views) makes these websites potential platforms for the construction of online transnational communities organised around the subject of Indian migration.

NRI Matters distinguishes itself amongst the aforementioned web portals because of its explicit focus on the formation of an online diasporic community, described as a 'powerful NRI community', allegedly numbering more than 14,000 emigrants who 'share their experiences and celebrate their achievements on NRI Matters'. The idea of an online NRI community is furthered in this case by a stress on common interests, histories and symbols. Emigrants' well-being and Indian national growth and development are depicted as interconnected causes and reciprocal interests. Migration trajectories are mostly described as success stories (see 'NRI of the fortnight' section, for example). Economic issues are naturally emphasised on a web portal sponsored by a financial group (Kotak Mahindra), in a special section – 'Question and Answers', a sort of online consultancy that gathers experts on finance, real state, investment, citizen law and tax – as well as throughout the website, mixed with subjects of a more sociocultural tone in sections as 'Power NRIs' (the expression 'Power NRIs' being a reference to the guest bloggers in this window), 'Debates' and 'NRI Life'. The latter highlights 'national symbols' such as cricket – featured in an electronic book and object of an online contest, 'Golden Memories of cricket' – and Indian 'national' festivals – Diwali or Holi are represented as transnational events with the aid of software applications allowing emigrants a virtual participation in such festivities (see 'Light a Diya' and 'Rang De Holi' applications, for instance). Interestingly enough, one can find amongst the peculiar internet representations of 'national symbols' the advertisement for the 'NRI Power Podium' contest, quite literally the link between the web portal and the annual diaspora conference Pravasi Bharatiya Divas (in its second edition, NRI Power Podium was advertised on the PBD website itself).

Although debates, polls and blogs do not seem to be particularly appealing to most of the web portal members (the number of users' posts is low in absolute and relative terms), the NRI Power Podium contest displays a greater capacity of mobilisation. Held for two consecutive years, 2011 and 2012, each one of its editions involved more than 13,000 participants from 60 countries and awarded its sponsors a mention on the Indian book of records for 'biggest NRI sign-up campaign'. Candidates aspiring to represent the 'global NRI community' at Pravasi Bharatiya Divas 2012 created profiles in a dedicated section of the web portal, introducing themselves through answers on questions about: their migration journeys; their business ideas and projects for 'cohesive growth' (that is, growth benefitting both emigrants and India, according to the contest theme and in tune with the PBD 2012 main topic, 'Global Indian: Inclusive Growth'); the influential NRIs or Indian leaders they would like to meet during the event; the reasons why they would be the best representatives of their 'NRI fellows' at the diaspora conference. Taking into account the number of indirect participants or observers made aware of this online event by the significant advertising on media channels aimed at the Indian 'diasporic audience' (websites, social networks, and partner radio stations like Hum Desi, for example), as well as by the own applicants canvassing for the first place in the podium, the contest's reach could be considered even greater in the candidature stage. However, after the nomination of the winners, depicted as 'leaders who [would] represent the Indian diaspora' at the conference, besides blog-like posts on the NRI Matters web portal and one inexpressive debate on PBD effectiveness as regards the improvement of Indian economy through 'homeland'-diaspora relations, activities surrounding the event are hardly identifiable. Such dynamics are quite telling of the peaks and troughs of internet interactions surrounding online or face-to-face events: high levels of activities follow the preparation and the realisation of the event but rarely last more than a short period of time after its conclusion. Thus, seasonal activation is the marker of continuity of online connections initiated or furthered through such happenings.

Online Events, Diaspora Conferences and Transnational Identifications

The stress placed by the NRI Matters web portal on the construction and strengthening of economic linkages between emigrants and sending-society became once more evident with the contest, described in a press release as intended to 'sensitise Overseas Indians on issues concerning Indian economy' (*Indo-Asian News Service* 2011). Nevertheless, symbolic ties were also evoked throughout the online event, namely the nomenclature 'Non-Resident Indian' conceived as a transnational identification and the emotional attachment to the 'motherland' it supposedly implies. What I would like to highlight in this case is the underlying assumption that symbolic linkages between the sending-country and emigrants not only go hand in hand with the construction or strengthening of transnational economic bonds with India but, more fundamentally, they would be crucial for the very decision of 'connecting' with the homeland. However questionable this conception may be, once investment decisions are very probably the most rationally oriented decision-making processes known (Prashad 2004), it brings to light the importance given by state and non-state actors to the (re)construction of a sense of belonging to the sending-society. In fact, outreach strategies devised by social actors within the 'homeland' intend to attract resources *and* to encompass geographical, economic, political and cultural spaces placed beyond the national territory. Such a process is an attempt to expand symbolic national borders which implies the broadening of norms and senses of belonging to the 'national community' and, therefore, the (re)construction of national identities and perceptions on emigration in order to include absent nationals, the emigrants, in this larger community whose core is considered to be the sending-society (Vertovec 2009). According to this perspective, India is depicted as the 'homeland' of resident *and* Non-Resident Indians (Raj 2003) on the one hand, and the centre of transnational relations/transactions stretching out beyond the scope of Indian society on the other.

Diaspora conferences as the *Pravasi Bharatiya Divas* are particularly important for such attempts to reinforce the centrality of the sending-country within transnational networks once they provide a privileged space for the enunciation of the 'homeland' official discourse on emigration. Such conferences disclose not only perceptions on emigrants and the very process of migration (mostly positive images, highlighting emigrants' achievements, besides emphasising the sense of belonging to India as the 'homeland', the notion of emigrants' responsibility for Indian development and their potential to constitute an expatriate lobby) but also policies aimed at the diaspora – increasingly resembling an 'agenda for the diaspora' which points out areas of concern and interest that should be regarded as priorities by emigrants in their relations with the 'motherland' (consider the seminars on specific topics preceding the conference as well as the state partners featured as suitable investment destinations in exhibition areas, for instance) (MOIA and CII 2011). Diaspora conferences have also become an arena where 'official' transnational identifications are (re)defined and represented as a prerogative of governmental institutions based in the sending-country. 'Indian diaspora' and 'Overseas Indian' (with its subcategories 'Person of Indian Origin' and 'Non-Resident Indian'), quite common expressions in the political vocabulary of the sending-country and among emigrants themselves, are not self-identifications constructed by emigrants dealing with the challenges of adaptation to the new environment and preservation of cultural traditions and identities (Koser 1997; Vertovec 2009). On the contrary, they refer to nomenclatures created within the sending-country: NRI, which sought to address the *absence* of Indian citizens from the 'homeland' since the 1960s, initially focusing on tax law norms and gradually incorporating regulations on investment, real estate acquisition and education in India; PIO, made official in 1999 by the creation of the PIO Card, which extended the aforementioned regulations to descendants of Indians; Overseas Indian, consolidated in 2005, when the *Overseas Indian Citizenship* was put into effect (Khadria 2009; Raj 2003). Although the term Indian diaspora has not been created by governmental institutions, it was appropriated and given an official tone by them with the establishment of the High Level Committee on the Indian Diaspora in 2000 and the definition of Indian diaspora presented in its 2002 report (High Level Committee on the Indian Diaspora 2002).

Increased interest in emigration issues from the late 1980s on was followed by popularisation of such expressions in the sending-country itself and, as a result, by greater flexibility as regards its uses. On the internet, and more specifically, on websites aimed at the 'diasporic audience' such as NRI Matters, usages of the aforementioned nomenclatures are even more flexible. New perceptions or appropriations, reinterpretations and dialogues with the 'official discourses' on emigration are primarily made visible by online recorded interactions – very often short-length blog posts and comments, as well as quicker and non-discursive opinion markers as 'likes' or 'dislikes', 'for' or 'against' etc. – rather than by elaborated discourses on the topics proposed. NRI Power Podium candidates' profiles follow this pattern, showing that eloquence does not necessarily win points – at least no more points than applicants' ability to create good slogans and activate their own online networks. This does not mean, however, that the web portal content is irrelevant for analysis purposes. Since the content and dynamics of online interactions are closely related, perceptions of emigration, broadly speaking, and of transnational identifications, more specifically, can be accessed by the researcher attentive to recorded interactions between the community members. Such a process is not altogether distinct from face-to-face interactions and conversations the social scientist engages in, for interviewees or observed groups' impressions are very often fragmentary and/or display low levels of reflexivity, construction of meaning being a task largely undertaken by the social researcher him/herself.

Although the construction of the nomenclature NRI as a new sense of belonging to India as the 'homeland' and/or to a transnational entity as the 'Indian diaspora' or an 'NRI community' is not easily identifiable on the NRI Matters web portal, its usage throughout the website emphasises images and perceptions of emigrants in many senses convergent with the 'official discourse' on Indian diaspora. No matter how diverse they might be (as regards their backgrounds, migration journeys and potential economic, political or cultural contributions to the 'homeland'), NRIs are depicted as successful individuals whose achievements must be acknowledged and celebrated by Indians settled in the sending-country and by the very emigrants. Within such virtual environment, 'NRI Life' is put in motion by online events supposedly strengthening emigrants' connection with their 'desi roots' (like virtual festivals celebrations and contests awarding trips to India) and made significant by the exemplary character of the experiences shared. 'Power' is a notion highly stressed by the online community members. The 'Powerful NRI community' is made up of 'Power NRIs' who create blogs and special sections of the website as well as of NRIs who aspire to be powerful – either nominated 'NRIs of the Fortnight' or first place winners of the 'NRI Power Podium' contest. The meanings of power in this context are broad, referring not only to status (the prestige of being an NRI) but to capacity too. Emigrants would be able to contribute to development in receiving-countries and, more importantly, in the sending-country due to the economic and social resources they are endowed with. In this connection, the notion of social remittances, increasingly discussed in policy-making processes, generally speaking (Castles and Miller 2009), and implicit in mass media perceptions of emigration, more specifically, makes ordinary online activities highly valued practices as sharing experiences and networking. Duty is also related to power in these representations. Emigrants are considered responsible for uplifting Indian society, a perception summed up in the NRI Power Podium slogan 'Can you lead the change?', evocative of the traditional association of power and philanthropy existent in India on the one hand, and of emotional attachment to the 'homeland' that would have provided the primary resources for their achievements on the other.

NRI Matters web portal content production is undoubtedly a process of construction of power and success as values continuously reinforced by the dynamics of ongoing celebration of achievements, which has as its higher point the NRI Power Podium contest. In addition to creating intelligent, persuasive and appropriate profiles (according to the theme established by the contest managers and sponsors), applicants are expected to be 'achievers in their own right' and potential leaders, individuals that 'people will want to follow' (NRI Matters TV 2011). The prize – attending the 'prestigious Pravasi Bharatiya Divas' – is described as an opportunity to 'stand up for the cause of NRI community' and a chance for 'making your voice heard' and 'making a difference' (Hum Desi Radio 2011). The connection between emigrants and the 'homeland' is thus depicted as a two-way relationship. As 'representatives' of a transnational community, the 'NRI community', emigrants would be given the chance of delivering 'Indian diaspora' demands during the conference and, in this sense, of making outreach policies more than investment attractions. It is important to note the underlying conception, similarly stressed by the governmental discourse on the Indian diaspora, that after a long period of neglect, the 'motherland' would be attentive to emigrants' needs. Also, emigrants would have the opportunity to contribute to the sending-country growth and development, to 'lead the change'. Perhaps the most significant opportunity given by the contest, from its sponsors' point of view, would be face-to-face interactions with 'prominent political and economic leaders' of India, deemed incomparable possibilities of networking as well as symbols of distinction and prestige (NRI Matters TV 2011). Celebration of power and success by NRI Power Podium participants and managers is therefore a process initiated by candidature, enacted by winners' attendance at PBD in India and fed by online interactions following the event – on the very web portal (through blog posts, debates, comments etc.) or through institutional and personal networks built during the conference (institutional websites such as the one managed by the Overseas Indian Facilitation Centre, which also intends to create an online business community, are an important complement to business meetings held during the PBD).

NRI Power Podium Affinities with PBD

The NRI Power Podium contest displays great affinity with PBD as regards the emphasis on status and achievement. Both events construct and reinforce an ideal image of the emigrant: successful, powerful and benevolent (devoted to the 'homeland'). However, Indian emigrants can hardly be described as a cohesive community. There are quite diverse regional, religious, linguistic and professional groups of Indian origin. Different migration trajectories and settlement experiences in receiving-societies must also be taken into account and are somehow acknowledged in the subcategories NRI and PIO that make up the concept 'Overseas Indian'. Levels of achievement, success and power are significantly distinct too. Non-Resident Indians, participants of more recent emigration flows towards North America, Oceania and Europe – very often described as the 'new diaspora' – are the ones depicted as powerful, successful and resourceful, whereas Persons of Indian Origin – the 'old diaspora' mostly composed of descendants of Indians settled in Asian, African and Caribbean societies – are neglected or marginalised in discourses and policies aimed at the emigrants conceived as a community. Divisions within the 'new diaspora' are also left aside. The existence of low-skilled workers among Indian emigrants is frequently omitted (as regards Indian emigrants living in developed countries) or addressed as a problem (Indian workers in the Gulf, for instance, are said to require the sending-country protection and, hence, the making of specific policies of emigration regulation) (Brown 2007; Prashad 2004). Despite conveying an intentionally homogenous and apparently comprehensive image of NRIs, the emigrant celebrated by the web portal NRI Matters (and to a great extent by the Pravasi Bharatiya Divas) is clearly the high-skilled professional settled in the North, mainly in the United States if one considers the massive advertisement of the contest undertaken by Hum Desi Radio in that country.

Furthermore, emigrants' attachment to India as a *national* community is disputable because of the strength of kinship ties and regional identifications, for instance, that channel symbolic and material linkages to a sub-national level – hence the combination of national and sub-national outreach initiatives existent within the sending-society. The very conception of an Indian 'homeland' is questionable, once transnational linkages with the sending-country are weakened, interrupted, and/or supplanted by senses of belonging to receiving-societies, mainly as regards the 'old diaspora' (Raj 2003; Vertovec 2009). Also, emigrants' capacity and willingness of (re)connecting with India as expected by social actors within the sending-society must not be overestimated. Actual participation in Indian national affairs as a cohesive transnational entity is unlikely since the incipient (although apparently fast-developing) levels of organisation of the diverse emigrant groups and associations are a hindrance to the construction of a sense of belonging to a transnational entity such as the 'Indian diaspora' and, more immediately, of an identification with 'Indian diasporic fellows'. Moreover, emigrants' individual contributions through remittances, for example, are hard to assess. Amounts received by and invested in India are rough estimates – 55 billion dollars in 2010 (World Bank Data 2011) – and their uses and impacts on local development have not been looked into thoroughly so far (Castles and Miller 2009; Khadria 2009). On the other hand, investment decisions made by Indian emigrants as individuals or representatives of international corporations take emotional attachment to India into account as one amongst several factors to be considered, very often as a secondary factor, as discussed earlier (Prashad 2004).

Online contests and diaspora conferences in India examined in this chapter also share the concern with seasonal activation of transnational linkages. Long-distance connections and interactions made feasible by technological developments in the last decades challenged the assumption that co-presence is a requisite for maintenance or construction of social relationships. Actually, one must consider that society

> can also 'bear' absence or even define itself by it significantly. Social relationships extend beyond the immediate link to location and to presence, because the social character of a relationship – for example of friendship or family relations – is not exhausted by the termination of physical presence, but instead continues. The confirmation of such relationships, however, requires encounters once in a while. Moreover, family or friendship relationships weaken if they are not kept alive by visits, meetings and shared experiences. (Mau 2010: 33)

Once absence has been constant in social relationships, changes brought about by mass media developments meant primarily new ways of experiencing and perceiving the interplay of absence and presence in daily life. In addition to overcoming distance, internet was undoubtedly significant to furthering new modalities of co-presence. Live chats and the use of webcams allow instant interactions while social networks create a sense of presence even when users are gone – there is at least an illusion of presence, since friends and acquaintances' profiles are visible in each individual network and potentially accessible at any time. Sharing experiences through recorded interactions (debates, comments, testimonials, etc.) is equally relevant to the preservation or strengthening of online connections established through such social networks. Online communities follow the same pattern, providing a virtual space for instantaneous and non-instantaneous communication. As far as NRI Matters is concerned, the web portal itself provides for recorded interactions between registered users (mostly emigrants and resident

Indians interested in connecting with NRIs), whereas instant communication surrounding the online community is left to Facebook and Twitter, networks the website is linked with.

Although efforts required for the maintenance of long-distance relationships have been considerably reduced by the use of the internet, interactions between individuals or groups situated in distant geographical locations still have to be provoked once such social actors cannot count on casual or spontaneous encounters allowed by contiguity (Mau 2010). Because linkages between social actors within the sending-society and emigrants may have been lost or weakened, as discussed earlier, intentional construction or (re)construction of ties with emigrants is an important characteristic of the very process of creation of institutional or non-institutional outreach mechanisms as diaspora conferences or websites aimed at a 'diasporic audience'. Longing for periodical meetings also persists despite all the changes brought about by technological developments. Seasonal face-to-face encounters are valued by social actors engaged in transnational relations, for they provide an opportunity to reinvigorate and/or start long-distance relationships. In other words, such meetings are important mechanisms of activation of transnational networks (Mau 2010). Distinct transnational groups naturally engage in diverse modalities of seasonal encounters. Meetings gathering highly mobile businessmen from all around the world (the very prototypes of 'transmigrants') are considerably different from migrant workers family visits as concerns motivations, frequency, nature of interactions and exchanges etc.

Diaspora conferences as the PBD have been depicted as privileged spaces of interaction between emigrants and sending-society representatives, as a valuable tool for (re)constructing economic, political and symbolic linkages between the parts. More importantly, they have been conceived as reminders of the relevance of periodically returning to the 'motherland' in order to keep alive such transnational ties. Diaspora conferences are in this sense transnational rituals furthering cohesion among peers (Ribeiro 1997) on the one hand, and generating the longing for seasonal returns to the sending-country on the other. NRI Power Podium could be described as an online transnational ritual. As far as online interactions are concerned, the contest forges a sense of belonging to an 'NRI community' through the reinforcement of particular images of emigrants in the course of the selection of 'NRI representatives'. Competition for a prize described as a unique opportunity for meeting powerful and resourceful social actors and for strengthening one's cultural identity enhances the longing for periodical and temporary returns to India. Thereby transnational online interactions and linkages, instead of replacing physical presence, make up new patterns of interplay of absence and presence as well as of online and face-to-face relations.

Conclusion

Looking at transnational relations from the perspective of emigration is quite revealing of the complexity and the diversity of contemporary migration processes. Thereby I would like to acknowledge that, although emigration and immigration can be constructed as distinct 'social problems' and topics of investigation, these are closely related processes as far as migrants' experiences or intergovernmental relations are concerned, for instance. Migrants may start their journeys as emigrants but will definitely settle down, either temporarily or permanently, becoming immigrants (Sayad 1998). Living and reflecting upon whatever is peculiar to each stage – emigration or immigration – Indian migrants tend to create associations situated in receiving-countries that are in constant dialogue with emigration-oriented organisations in the 'homeland' (GOPIO is a case in point). This brings me to the second point: diaspora conferences and online communities and contests discussed in this chapter, different from most immigrant associations, are not a result of spontaneous association of emigrants. It would be reasonable to ponder, in this connection, whether and to what extent the events examined, deliberately created by non-migrants, are representative of emigrants' aspirations and perceptions – a topic for further research.

Similarly important is the questioning of the emigrant stereotype constructed and reinforced by perceptions conveyed in and dynamics created by the NRI Matters web portal and governmental institutions' internet resources. While this point has already been addressed in the chapter, I would like to underline that positive images of emigrants are constructions related to changes in perceptions of transnational identifications, broadly speaking, and of emigration as a process, more specifically. In a nutshell, negative images of transnational senses of belonging and of emigration – deemed as disloyalty or treason and looked at with suspicion – were gradually supplanted by positive representations – transnational identifications were then 'celebrated' due to their supposed flexibility, and openness to intercultural dialogue and emigration was considered a potential gain to emigrants themselves, to sending-countries eager of capitalising on migrants' resources, and even to receiving-countries willing to attract high-skilled professionals (Castles and Miller 2009; Khadria 1999; Khadria 2009; Østergaard-Nielsen 2003; Peralva 2008; Schnapper 2001). In India, such changes of perception were closely related to the institutional and symbolic capacity-building policies discussed earlier. The concern with national sovereignty and with the effects of 'brain drain' on the homeland development, prevalent from the 1950s to the 1980s (Dubey 2003; Prashad 2004; Raj 2003), was gradually replaced by the praise of Indian emigrants' achievements and the stress on the whole new set of opportunities brought about by 'brain circulation' and monetary or social remittances (Castles and Miller 2009; Khadria 2009). However widespread positive images of emigration, emigrants and transnational identifications may be, coexistence of positive and negative perceptions of the topics concerned within India must be pointed out. An interesting example is an article published by *Hindustan Times* in printed and electronic versions, presenting a negative image of emigrants. Besides depicting NRIs as consumerist and ultraconservative, text and cartoons produced by the newspaper refer to a sort of uneasiness (if not despair) felt by resident Indians at the very thought of receiving emigrant relatives (D'Souza 2010).

Finally, I suggest that the interplay of absence and presence addressed in the paper can also be interpreted as a dynamics of deterritorialisation and reterritorialisation of transnational relations. Diaspora conferences and online contests here considered stress the centrality of India within transnational networks. While regional Pravasi Bharatiya Divas meetings held in countries with significant numbers of Indian emigrants since 2007 focus on linkages between emigrants themselves, the annual conference in India – which significantly celebrates the date of the return of M. K. Gandhi to the sending-society – emphasises the relationship between 'homeland' and emigrants. It must be considered, however, that as conference delegates very often share ethnic or geographical origins but have different nationalities (descendants of Indians and Non-residents Indians who took dual citizenship being a case in point), both PBD versions seek to strengthen a transnational identification based on Indian nationality, as the expressions 'Indian Diaspora' or 'Overseas Indian' reveal. Advancement of interactions between individuals described as *Indians* in the sending-country at regular intervals through PBD conferences is therefore connected to a broader process of construction of identifications which intends to position India, perceived as the 'homeland' of migrants and non-migrants, at the core of transnational networks. The NRI Power Podium, by following the dynamics established by PBD (that also implies the creation of a longing for physical seasonal return to the sending-country by the virtual contest) and in many senses dialoguing with the 'official' discourse on emigration, reinforces such a conception of centrality of the 'motherland' in online interactions that otherwise would be considered deterritorialised. Emphasis on *Indian* (trans)national identification as a symbolic linkage on the one hand, and on *India* as the national territory capable of strengthening the connection between the parts on the other, placed by a deterritorialised space of online interactions – the NRI Matters web portal – points to the reterritorialisation of such virtual relationships once they become attached to a specific geographical location and to its related identifications.

References

Beine, M., Docquier, F. and Özden, Ç. 2009. Diasporas. *The World Bank Development Research Group – Trade and Integration Team*. Policy Research Working Paper 4984 [online]. Available from: http://econ.worldbank.org [Accessed 30 July 2009].

Brown, J. 2007. *Global South Asians: Introducing the modern diaspora*. New Delhi: Cambridge University Press.

Castles, S. and Miller, M. 2009. *The Age of Migration: International Population Movements in the Modern World*. New York: Palgrave Macmillan.

D'souza, M. 2010. Oh, my god! NRIs are here again! *Hindustan Times*. Saturday, 11 December.

Dubey, A. 2003. Indian Diaspora in Africa and changing policies of India. In: S. D. Singh and M. Singh (eds.), *Indians Abroad*. Kolkata: Maulana Abul Kalam Azad Institute of Asian Studies, 153–171.

Gamlen, A. 2006. Diaspora engagement policies: what are they, and what kind of states use them?' ESRC Centre on Migration, Policy and Society (COMPAS) *Working Paper No. WP-06–32* [online]. Available from: http://www.compas. ox.ac.uk/publications/working-papers/wp-06-32/ [Accessed: 16 June 2011].

High Level Committee on the Indian Diaspora. 2002. *Report of the High Level Committee on the Indian Diaspora* [online]. Available from: http:// indiandiaspora.nic.in [Accessed 30 October 2006].

Hum Desi Radio. 2011. NRI Power Podium Radio Spot [online]. Available from: http://www.youtube.com/watch?v=ShrDpLF2nIs [Accessed 09 February 2012].

Hum Desi Radio. 2012. Available from: http://www.humdesiradio.com/ [Accessed 08 February 2012].

India Empire. 2012. Available from: http://www.indiaempire.com [Accessed 28 January 2012].

Indo-Asian News Service. 2011. Contest for NRIs to attend Pravasi Bharatiya Divas. *Indo-Asian News Service*, Friday, 16 December. Available from: http://in.omg. yahoo.com/news/contest-nris-attend-pravasi-bharatiya-divas-095952104.html [Accessed 08 February 2012].

Khadria, B. 1999. *The migration of knowledge workers: Second-generation effects of India's Brain Drain*. New Delhi: Sage Publications.

Khadria, B. (ed.) 2009. *India Migration Report 2009: Past, present and future outlook*. New Delhi: International Migration and Diaspora Studies Project.

Koser, K. 2007. *International Migration: A very short introduction*. Oxford: Oxford University Press.

Mármora, L. 1999. Perception of International Movements. In: L. Mármora, *International Migration Policies and Programmes*. Geneva: United Nations and the International Organisation for Migration, 27–43.

Mau, S. 2010. *Social Transnationalism: Lifeworlds beyond the nation-state*. New York: Routledge.

Ministry of Overseas Indian Affairs. 2009. Available from: http://www.moia.gov. in [Accessed 08 February 2012].

Ministry of Overseas Indian Affairs and Confederation of Indian Industry. 2011. *Ninth Pravasi Bharatiya Divas Theme Paper: 'Engaging the Global Indian'*. New Delhi: MOIA.

NRI Matters. 2010. Available from: http://www.nrimatters.com [Accessed 26 December 2011].

NRI Matters TV. 2011. Mr. K. V. S. Manian on Power Podium 2011 [online]. Available from: http://www.youtube.com/user/NRIMattersTv?feature=watch [Accessed 09 February 2012].

Østergaard-Nielsen, E. 2003. International migration and sending countries: key issues and themes. In: E. Østergaard-Nielsen (ed.), *International Migration and Sending Countries: Perception, policies and transnational relations*. New York: Palgrave Macmillan, 3–30.

Østergaard-Nielsen, E. 2003. Continuities and changes in sending country perceptions, policies and transnational relations with nationals abroad. In: E. Østergaard-Nielsen (ed.), *International Migration and Sending Countries: Perception, policies and transnational relations*. New York: Palgrave Macmillan, 209–224.

Overseas Indian. 2011. Available from: http://www.overseasindian.in [Accessed 09 February 2012].

Overseas Indian Facilitation Centre. 2009. Available from: http://www.oifc.in [Accessed 09 February 2012].

Peralva, A. 2008. Globalização, migrações transnacionais e identidades nacionais. *Coesão Social na América Latina: bases para uma nova agenda democrática*. São Paulo: Instituto Fernando Henrique Cardoso [online]. Available from: http://www.plataformademocratica.org [Accessed 31 January 2009].

Prashad, V. 2004. Dusra Hindustan. *Seminar*, n. 538, June [online]. Available from: www.india-seminar.com [Accessed 7 November 2006].

Pravasi Bharatiya Divas. Available from: http://pbdindia.org/ [Accessed 09 February 2012].

Pravasi Today. 2006. Available from: http://www.pravasitoday.com [Accessed 09 February 2012].

Raj, D. 2003. Being British, becoming a Person of Indian Origin. In: D. Raj, *Where are you from? Middle-Class Migrants in the Modern World*. Berkeley, CA: University of California Press, 165–183.

Ribeiro, G. 1997. A condição da transnacionalidade: *Série Antropologia*. Brasília: Departamento de Antropologia da Universidade de Brasília.

Sayad, A. 1998. *A imigração: Ou os paradoxos da alteridade*. São Paulo: Editora da Universidade de São Paulo.

Schnapper, D. 2001. De l'État-nation au monde transnational. Du sens et de l'utilité du concept de diaspora. *Revue Européenne de Migrations Internationales*, 17 (2), 9–36. Available from: http://www.persee.fr [Accessed 28 June 2009].

Vertovec, S. 2009. *Transnationalism: Key Ideas*. London: Routledge.

World Bank. 2011. Migration and Remittances Factbook [online]. Available from: http://econ.worldbank.org [Accessed 05 October 2011].

Chapter 8

Is Guruji Online? Internet Advice Forums and Transnational Encounters in a Vaishnav Sectarian Community

Emilia Bachrach

I

While in the process of preparing this chapter, I happened to read a provocative *New York Times* op-ed piece entitled, 'How India Became America' (Kapur 2012a). In the article, writer Akash Kapur – also the author of the recently published book *India Becoming: A Portrait of Life in Modern India* (Kapur 2012b) – discusses the social, aesthetic, and economic changes that he has experienced in India post-economic liberalisation in the early 1990s. Unlike his childhood experiences of growing up in what seemed like two very different worlds – rural Minnesota and rural India (he does not tell us where), Kapur writes that he now feels that his two homes are 'no longer so far apart' (Kapur 2012a: 1). According to Kapur, 'India has been Americanized' (2012a: 1). While Kapur's sentiments are likely shared by other individuals who have lived through post-liberalisation India and likewise have experienced living in the Indian diaspora, the everyday realities that one encounters in India and abroad are, for countless individuals, very far apart indeed. While one can cruise shopping malls offering the same name-brand clothing or electronics in Ahmedabad or in Atlanta, in Bangalore or Brighton, Hyderabad or Houston, there are still, of course, infinite aspects of everyday life that remain in constant need of negotiation for many members of the Indian diaspora – both for those who do have the opportunity to return to India and for those who, for whatever reasons, do not.

This brief chapter will consider some of the ways in which the Internet plays a role in negotiating differences between religious practices and experiences in India and abroad. Specifically, I will be addressing how followers of the Vallabh Sampraday, a Vaishnav sectarian tradition with a majority Gujarati following both in India and in the diaspora, use the Internet as a way to maintain relationships between followers of the sect abroad and their counterparts and gurus in India. Over the past decade numerous websites managed by religious leaders and lay members of the Vallabh Sampraday have emerged, providing regular updates about rituals and festivals in the sectarian calendar as well as links to sectarian literature, history, and images of deities, gurus, and pilgrimage places. Another common feature of such sites is the advice forum, on which religious leaders, and sometimes lay followers, respond to devotees' inquiries on matters ranging from how to interpret scripture in terms of contemporary concerns to how to maintain prescribed dietary restrictions while on vacation. While devotees in India are increasingly patronising such advice forums (which also appear on popular social-networking sites, such as Facebook), the most regular users of these forums are still those who have recently joined the diaspora (namely in North America and the United Kingdom) or those who were born abroad and are actively seeking to learn about their families' religious tradition – sometimes for the first time. Thus, these advice forums are primarily filled with discussions about how to enter into or maintain a sectarian lifestyle while living away from one's guru and Indian-based community. This chapter will suggest that the online forums in question not only provide a welcome space for communication between members of the Vallabh sect in the diaspora and their gurus and fellow devotees in India, but also how such online relationships may be beginning to alter the offline demographic of active followers abroad as well as on the subcontinent.

II

According to tradition, the Vallabh Sampraday was founded during the early 16th century in today's north Indian state of Uttar Pradesh by a Hindu theologian known as Vallabhacharya (1479–1530) (hereafter Vallabh). Vallabh, accompanied by his son and spiritual successor Vitthalnath (1515–1585), developed a non-dualistic philosophical system called *Shuddhadvait* ('Pure non-dualism') and a devotional and ritual system called the *Pushtimarg* ('The Path of Nourishment').[1] Central to the teachings of Vallabh and Vitthalnath, and still considered fundamental for most followers of the tradition are the following beliefs and practices: singular devotion to the Hindu deity Krishna as Supreme Being, elaborate worship called *seva* ('service') of manifestations of Krishna in devotees' homes and in sectarian temples,[2] the mandate to lead a householder life – that is, the rejection of traditional forms of renunciation in one's spiritual practice – and finally a mandatory form of initiation into the sect, called the *brahmsambandh*, which is to be performed by a direct male descendent of Vallabh.

It is said that Vitthalnath passed on leadership of the sect equally to all of his seven sons, each of whom established a separate Seat (*gaddi*), or House (*ghar*), and in turn continued to pass on leadership of each House according to male primogeniture. Accordingly, while there has been considerable dispute over the control of various lineages, today there are still seven formally recognised

---

1   The standard text on the social and theological history and literature of the sect is Barz's (1992) *The Bhakti Sect of Vallabhacarya*.

2   Further discussion of the practice of *seva* in the Pushtimarg can be found in Peter Bennett's (1993) *The Path of Grace*.

Houses of the sect, each with one primary living guru who is often referred to in the community as *maharaj* ('king') or *goswami*.[3] As a group, the descendants of Vallabh are known as the 'Vallabh Kul', or the 'Vallabh Dynasty', and male members of the family continue to perform sectarian initiations and maintain an elevated (and sometimes what is considered to be divine or semi-divine) status as religious leaders. Women of the family also maintain elevated status and, like their male counterparts, may choose to establish themselves as public religious figures and teachers within the tradition. Since the late 17th century, the locus of sectarian activity has been western India, namely Rajasthan and Gujarat, and most lay followers (including those in the sectarian diaspora) have ties to these western states. The majority of the Vallabh Kul are also based in urban Gujarat (namely Ahmedabad, Baroda, and Surat) as well as in the city of Mumbai.

Since the early 19th century lay members of the Vallabh Sampraday, who hail largely from wealthy trading and business classes, have maintained a strong presence outside of the subcontinent (see Simpson 2008). In his Introduction to *Gujaratis in the West: Evolving Identities in Contemporary Society*, Bhikhu Parekh (2007) writes that in the 21st century, Gujaratis account for just over one third of the global Indian diaspora. Parekh suggests, at risk of oversimplification, that Gujaratis of various religions display certain similar behaviours in their diasporic lives: they tend, Parekh writes, to be flexible, tolerant, enterprising, family-oriented, and with a distinct preference for an opportunity to enter into business, commerce and the legal and medical professions. Further, while 'religious', Gujaratis seem to 'carry their religion rather lightly' and are prepared to make changes whenever necessary (Parekh 2007: xi).

The emerging results of my data collection from and observation of over a dozen Internet sites specific to the Vallabh Sampraday over the past several years complicate Parekh's simple stereotype about Gujaratis in the diaspora and their religious tendencies. Rather than giving up or compromising religious attitudes or practices, my nascent research suggests that members of the Vallabh Sampraday in the diaspora who are active in local sectarian activities and on sectarian websites are equally if not more eager than certain segments of their Indian-based counterparts to enter into or maintain a sectarian-specific lifestyle. Such a lifestyle can refer to engaging in daily *seva*, keeping a strict vegetarian diet, and participating in regular religious discussions and meetings (*satsang* and *sabha*). These diasporic devotees active online, however, represent a rather distinct demographic from the majority of active devotees offline both in India and abroad.

---

3   'Goswami' is a common epithet for a religious leader in Vaishnav sectarian traditions, which literally means 'master of the cows'. Cows are not only generically considered sacred animals in most Hindu religious traditions, but are also specifically associated with the pastoral mythology that surrounds Krishna, who in some narratives was said to have been a cow-herder himself. See Vaudeville (1996) for further on this mythology in relation to the Vallabh Sampraday.

While it was not within the scope of this project to accurately determine the average age of online forum users, the questions that are posted (when taken at face value), which often refer specifically to being overseas for studies, travelling with young children, or helping elderly parents, indicate that the majority of people using the forums are at least college-aged and under the age of 60. Further, based on names provided by forum users (again, taken at face value), there seem to be more male than female users across the sites that I am familiar with (roughly 25 per cent more men than women). Accordingly, this group of diasporic Internet users, actively seeking religious advice from their gurus and fellow members of the Vallabh Sampraday, is quite distinct from the demographic of devotees who regularly discuss religious issues with their gurus and fellow devotees offline in India. Based on over three years of ethnographic research among Vallabhite communities in the Gujarati cities of Ahmedabad and Baroda, several cities and towns in Rajasthan (including Jaipur, Jodhpur, Udaipur, Nathdwara, and Kankroli), and the city of Mumbai, I have observed that the vast majority of individuals who regularly (on a daily or weekly basis) perform *seva*, attend sectarian sermons (*pravachan*s), or join fellow devotees and gurus to sing devotional songs (*kirtan, bhajan,* and *dhol*) and to gather in *satsang* or *sabha* to discuss and ask questions about religious texts, theology, and other sectarian matters, are at least middle-aged, but often elderly. Furthermore, this demographic is predominantly female. Many male and female informants have explained to me that the reason for greater participation among elderly women than other demographics has to do with the fact that older women tend to have less domestic and/or occupational duties than other groups and therefore have more time to engage in 'religious activities'.

According to Lily Kong's article 'Religion and Technology: Refiguring Place, Space, Identity and Community', this contrast in the demographics of members of the Vallabh sect participating in religious dialogue online and those participating offline should not be surprising. According to Kong, access to 'techno-religious space' is expectedly dependent on the politics age, class, and language (Kong 2001: 406). Further, while techno-religious space cannot be considered to be an 'isotropic surface', 'most current Internet traffic, which is text-based, uses English as the *de facto* language of choice (Kinney 1995: 770), and the technology appeals to and is best negotiated by a younger and economically more advanced and better educated group' (Kong 2001: 406). Kong's comment not only confirms that the difference in demographics between online and offline participants in religious dialogue specific to the Vallabh sect is common across other religious communities, it also points us to another distinct way in which online and offline devotees often differ: language preference. The demographic of Vallabhite devotees actively engaging in religious activities including regular discussions with fellow devotees and gurus in India primarily rely on Gujarati and Hindi, while their online counterparts will almost always rely on English or code-switching between English, Gujarati, and Hindi. Online users also normally use the roman rather than the Hindi or Gujarati scripts. As I will discuss further below, this distinction in demographics between online and offline devotees in the Vallabh Sampraday plays a significant role in determining the ongoing changes in the demographics of active participants in the sectarian community and communication between Indian-based gurus and their followers both in the diaspora and in India.

III

During an early springtime visit in 2012 to Nathdwara, Rajasthan, the primary pilgrimage centre for the Vallabh Sampraday,[4] I had the pleasure of meeting with a popular religious figure and member of the Vallabh Kul in his early thirties.[5] I had gone to visit the goswami in order to discuss his knowledge of the Vallabh Sampraday's 17th century hagiographical literature (known as *Varta Sahitya*, or Chronicle Literature), which is one of the focal points of my ongoing research.[6] The goswami began to explain his approach to the literature but then stopped mid-sentence and asked if we were friends on Facebook. 'No', I answered, 'I don't believe that we are'. 'Add me as a friend', he said, 'that's where I keep my writing on the literature you are asking about. You can view my comments and see the questions and conversations that Vaishnavs had there. We have links to translations of the *varta*s and downloads too'. Indeed the goswami's Facebook page – like many other blogs, forums, chat-rooms, and social-networking sites run by members of the Vallabh Kul, temple administrators, or disciples – functions not only as a site for personal updates, but also as a place for religious instruction, textual commentary, reminders regarding the sectarian calendar, guru-devotee communication, and links to other websites in the Vallabhite world online. When I told the goswami that his Facebook page seemed like a useful source of information and communication for Vaishnavs not living in India, he replied in Hindi as follows: 'Oh, it's absolutely necessary, this is the digital age and if we want to keep things alive, then we have to catch onto current forms of communication. We have to recognise the changes but maintain tradition at the same time'.[7, 8]

Later the same day, one of the goswami's disciples – an American who was visiting her guru in India for several weeks – described to me in Hindi what she believed the goswami was getting at. 'These days there is a great concern about

---

4　See Amit Ambalal's (1987) *Krishna as Shrinathji: Rajasthani Paintings from Nathdvara* for a basic introduction to Nathdwara and the sectarian deity, Shrinathji, a local form of Krishna, who resides there.

5　I have chosen to omit names of the majority of the informants cited in this essay in order to protect their identities.

6　The working title of my forthcoming dissertation is, 'The Living Tradition of Hagiography in the Vallabh Sect of Contemporary Gujarat'.

7　Discussion on March 8th 2012: Nathdwara Rajasthan.

8　All translations are my own unless otherwise noted.

the lack of interest or initiative in our Sampraday – especially among youth and men. People are beginning to feel like, *Oh, that is what my grandmother did – the Pushtimarg is a religion for little old ladies*. So, people don't participate and now some of us are worried about the future'. This disciple is referring to a widespread stereotype amongst members of the Vallabh Sampraday that younger generations are intimidated by and fearful of the life-styles of older women in their families – those who most frequently visit sectarian temples in India for worship and *satsang*, most dutifully practice *seva* of Krishna in their homes, and most strictly adhere to dietary restrictions and other observances of ritual purity. 'The Web certainly provides a new space and new interest is growing', the disciple continued – 'it allows people who prefer the anonymity or convenience of the Internet to learn about their religion and not be scared of it. Look at my guruji, he is of the Vallabh Kul and he uses the Internet – he is not your grandmother, he is your guru and he will teach you in the way that you want to learn'.[9] Indeed, many sectarian websites that feature advice forums reveal that the majority of online communication between gurus based in India and their followers (specifically in the diaspora) focus on negotiating between scripturally prescribed forms of ritual practice and worship inherited from the past and the everyday demands and realities of life in the modern world. In other words, the principal aim of such sites is to both encourage participation and learning for youth and those outside of India, but also to effectively negotiate between perceived social norms and religious practices according to individuals' everyday life circumstances.

The following descriptions of two Vallabhite websites will provide the reader with a preliminary guide to understanding the phenomena of the sectarian advice forum. The first site I will discuss is Pushtimarg.net. Pushtimarg.net has been an active sectarian website with a steadily increasing number of users for nearly a decade. Like other sectarian sites with interactive features, Pushtimarg.net requires registration to use the site's forum. However, unlike many other sectarian forums, Pushtimarg.net's webmasters do not ask that participants cite affiliation with one particular guru in India. In fact, the site is run by three different goswamis of the Vallabh Kul, each of whom feature their own writing and *pravachan*s on the site, which are available for free download to any user or visitor without registration. All three goswamis affiliated with the site are primarily based out of Mumbai and are among the more powerful and popular religious leaders in the Vallabh Sampraday – including Shyam Manohar Goswami, a goswami of the sect's First House, who is considered to be one of the community's most learned living theologians and an active reformer.[10]

---

9   Conversation March 8th, 2012: Nathdwara Rajasthan.

10   See Frederick Smith's (2012) paper, 'Pilgrimage and *haveli seva*: A Pustimargi reformist current of the late 20th century', presented at the 11th annual conference on Early Modern Literature in North India.

Pushtimarg.net states its mission as follows on its 'About Us' portion of the site:

> 1) To revive the glorious portrait of Pushtimarg; 2) To create encyclopaedia (complete) information of Pushtimarg [sic]; 3) Son: Why Seva? Why Pushtimarg?? Why no Anyashray [the transgression of having faith in a religious tradition, deity, or guru that is not one's own]??? Father: Dear, lets visit http://www.pushtimarg.net & solve our queries; 4) Conceptual understanding of philosophy of Pushtimarg.[11]

Following the four mission statements are comments on the site's 'objectives', 'growth plans', and 'expansion'. Also included in the list is 'Why.net?', which explains that it is 'Our duty is to reconvey [sic]' the message of Vallabh, who in his time was said to have spread the word of the Pushtimarg by doing religious pilgrimages around India, through the 'fastest' and most 'penetrating' media available to the 'religious world'.[12] This self-conscious portrayal of the site as media savvy and as a contemporary continuation of the sect's 'traditional' forms of proselytisation (such as Vallabh's pilgrimages around India to 'spread the word' of the Pushtimarg) highlights a common goal of many of the sectarian websites that are occupied by advice forums.

On Pushtimarg.net's forum any registered user can pose or respond to a question or start a new forum thread. While a wide range of questions arise on the forum – ranging from inquiries about basic sectarian terminology and sectarian philosophy to questions regarding ideal conduct with respect to daily and seasonal ritual practices – the majority of inquiries coming from diasporic users (users routinely provide first names and locations, which have been taken at face value for the purposes of this chapter) are related specifically to negotiating sectarian thought and practice in the context of living outside of India. Normally one of the three goswamis associated with the site replies directly to users' questions (questions and answers are primarily given in English, with occasional code-switching between English, Hindi and Gujarati). When one of the goswamis does not provide a response to a question, other users often engage in dialogue with the inquirer and suggest possible answers to the stated inquiry. Periodically, the webmasters will provide answers to 'frequently asked questions', which are downloadable in a PDF format.

As suggested above, the demographic of forum users, including those who frequent Pushtimarg.net, is dominated by young, often college-going devotees, who are new to the diaspora and discovering what it means to identify as a member of the Vallabh Sampraday in the absence of older family members and

---

11   http://pushtimarg.net/pushti/index.php?option=com_content&view=article&id=3 74&Itemid=69 (accessed January 2012).

12   http://pushtimarg.net/pushti/index.php?option=com_content&view=article&id=3 74&Itemid=69 (accessed January 2012).

a community who would customarily guide daily rituals. Here is one example of a question posed by a young woman who tells us that she is in college in Richmond, Virginia:

> Question: I would like to know what daily prayers we have to say and when we have to say them and what scriptures we have to read. Because in college I have a roommate who is a Swaminarayan[13] and she does Pooja [ritual worship] every morning and she read [sic] their holy scripture, the Vachnamrat and she has certain things in her pooja that she has to do. I was wondering if we have something like that.[14]

One of the three goswamis replies with a detailed answer to the young woman's question. He tells her, according to his approach to the Pushtimarg, which texts to read in the morning, afternoon, and evening and how to start the day with a particular kind of attitude. The goswami recognises that the young woman probably does not actively practice seva – that is, ritual worship of a svarup, or embodied image of Krishna – and says as much in his reply. He writes: 'It is very difficult to carry out Seva in board [that is, while in college]. So it is preferable to do Paath [reading theological treatises], Jap [reciting the name of God etc.], reading, and Kirtan [that is, devotional singing specific to the Vallabh Sampraday]'.

In the aforementioned exchange, it is clear that the young woman who poses the simple inquiry about daily ritual has become self-aware of her religious practice and identity in the face of being separated from her family and community. She notices that her college roommate follows a daily ritual practice and she too wants to express herself according to her inherited religious tradition. While this particular young woman does not state that she is, likely for the first time, seeking help to understand her community while away from home, many other queries posted by forum users on Pusthimarg.net complete her narrative of discovering one's own religious heritage online while in the diaspora. Also from Pushtimarg.net we find the following question:

> Question: I have just come to the U.S.A. My parents are in India. I want to do something for my Lalan [an epithet that refers to svarups of Krishna cared for by devotees in the home]. What should I do?[15]

Once again, one of the three gurus associated with the site provides a lengthy answer explaining that since it seems that the inquirer's family's deity is at home in India,

---

13   The Swaminarayan Sampraday is a sectarian community founded in the 19th century with a majority Gujarati following and some philosophical and ritual similarities to the Vallabh Sampraday. Even more than the Vallabh Sampraday, the Swaminarayan Sampraday has a large presence in the Diaspora. See Kim (2001).
14   http://pushtimarg.net/newPushti/forum.php?page_nm=forum/forum.
15   http://pushtimarg.net/newPushti/forum (accessed on October 11th 2011).

there is nothing that can be done directly for the deity, only indirectly. The inquirer, the answering guru continues, should adopt a course of study similar to the one that was prescribed for the young college-going woman whose question we previously considered. Included in this course of study is satsang – that is, discussion on religious topics with 'other members of the sect'. If this is not possible where the inquirer is living then, of course, there is always the Internet. Online satsang can refer to recalling the sacred pastimes of Krishna, narrating the hagiographies of the founders and early followers of the sect, as well as discussing, as the inquirer is with his guru, potentially acceptable modes of worship based on one's worldly situation. If the inquirer plans on returning to India and wishes to deepen his own practice enough to bring a personal Krishna svarup to be worshipped in the USA, then he would be able to perform seva directly (all svarups that people bring into devotees' homes for worship must be directly bestowed upon the devotee by a guru in India or in the Diaspora, if the guru is able to travel abroad).

The young people's inquiries that we have briefly encountered here are only two examples of countless related questions that regularly appear on Pushtimarg.net's and other sectarian forums. As the Pushtimarg.net's mission statement itself suggests, the site's forum functions not only as a place for transnational encounters between India-based gurus and their diasporic followers, but also as an example of how the Internet itself makes such encounters, and therefore maintaining a sectarian lifestyle in the diaspora, possible in the first place. The second site I will address, Pushtimarg.info.com, further highlights the ways in which the medium of the Internet provides Vallabhite devotees online with practical and creative ways to preserve sectarian practices.

Pushtimarg.info.com's forum, in this case called an interactive 'blog', is run independently by a goswami in his late twenties who is based in the small city of Bhavnagar, Gujarat. The blog specifically states that it is related to 'discussions on *prabhu* [the Lord's] *seva, kirtan, smaran* [remembering the Lord] & *satsang*'.[16] The goswami's forum seems to attract a smaller and more intimate crowd than Pushtimarg.net's site, which has hundreds of users who have not necessarily been initiated into the sect by one of three gurus associated with the site. Rather, Pushtimarg.info.com's forum appears to be used primarily by those members of the community who have either been initiated by the site's managing goswami or another goswami in his immediate family, or at the very least have previously met with the site's goswami offline. Because of the relative intimacy between the online devotees and their guru, the kinds of questions that are posed on the blog are distinct from those posed on Purshimarg.net's forum. For example, many of the inquiries on Pushtimarg.info.com are directly related to caring for Krishna *svarup*s in the diaspora and are often concerned with the question of how to travel with these deities to and from India. Such questions indicate that forum users on Pusthimarg.info.com are generally more familiar with the prescriptions for

---

16 http://www.pushtimarg.info/blog/?page_id=43.

seva than users on Pushtimarg.net. Here is an example of a common inquiry on Pushtimarg.info.com.

The inquirer begins by saying 'Dandwat Jeje', which literally means, 'I prostrate myself before you, Jeje' (Jeje is an affectionate form of address to the Guru). This online introduction mimics what devotees are physically expected to do when they meet a member of the Vallabh Kul in person – that is, physically prostrate themselves before the guru by bowing down and often touching the feet of the goswami. The writer continues, the 'blog is very informative & resourceful. While travelling for more than 24 hours with Thakorji [a common epithet for a Krishna *svarup*]...What are the things needed...?' Signing off, the writer again writes, 'Dandwat', and then 'yours, very respectfully, Sanjay Mehta – Tampa, Florida'. Pushtimarg.info.com's managing goswami responds by first saying, 'Ashirwad', or 'auspicious blessings', and then continues to thank the inquirer Sanjay Mehta for his question. Just as the online 'prostration' performed by the inquirer mimics the standard offline performance of respect by a devotee for his or her guru, the word 'Ashirwad' is normally spoken by a guru after his disciple prostrates him or herself in person. After giving blessings, Pushtimarg.info.com's goswami provides a list, in short hand, explaining what should be done for the travelling *svarup* and assures the devotee that his need to travel with his Krishna *svarup* is perfectly acceptable and can be carried out according to sectarian protocol. The goswami tells Mehta that he should stay in contact via the 'blog' should there ever be any further doubts. Mehta replies with 'hearty thanks', and another 'Dandwat'. This kind of exchange between guru and devotee is, in fact, not remarkably different from the kinds of offline interactions between gurus and disciples in India: it is very common, both in the contemporary community and historically, for religious leaders of the Sampraday to offer regular advice on the nuances of *seva*, other ritual practices, and sectarian philosophy to doubtful disciples or those in need of basic guidance. In this sense, the Internet simply makes the continuation of the traditional guru-devotee relationship possible for diasporic devotees.

Another visitor to Pushtimarg.info.com's blog, Upendra Rajpura, writes the following: 'Since long I am away from Bhavnagar...As soon as I come to Bhavnagar from USA [sic], I will come to have my Hearty Dandwat to you'. The inquirer goes on to state that his time in the USA, apart from the guru, is akin to the feeling of *viraha*, a term which describes the pain of separation from a lover or from God and is key to the Krishna-specific theology of the sect. But, Rajpura continues, the guru is always present within his disciples, not to mention virtually available! 'Guruji is Online', after all.[17]

My suggestion that online forums specific to the Vallabh Sampraday provide space for guru-devotee communication transnationally and support creative ways of managing protocol for worship in the diaspora is clearly demonstrated by the aforementioned examples from Pushtimarg.net and Pushtimarg.info.com. What remains to be discussed is my contention that the activity of these diasporic online

---

17   http://www.pushtimarg.info/blog/?page_id=43 (accessed October 2010).

devotees is related more generally to shifts in the demographic of online and offline active devotees both in India and abroad.

IV

As expressed by the American devotee who was visiting her guru in Nathdwara, Rajasthan, there is a great deal of concern among older members of the Vallabh Kul and senior devotees about how appealing and practical certain ritual practices and modes of living are to younger generations – both in India and abroad. In the words of one senior goswami in his seventies:

> …today the new generation wants everything fast: fast food, fast love, and fast religion. What can we do? If we don't want to lose we have to accommodate the youth and give them tools to learn on the Internet – that's why we have more active youth in America, Canada, and Briton than we do here at home [in India]! We can learn something from our Vaishnavs abroad and get local youth involved on the Internet as well.[18]

According to one senior administrator at a temple that was established 13 years ago in Ahmedabad, Gujarat, the goswami's comment about use of the Internet as an indicator of the level of knowledge, interest, and community participation in the Pushtimarg for the 'new generation' is accurate:

> When I was posted at a temple in Canada for four years in the 1990s I couldn't believe that so many young men – even those in University – would come in daily to take darshan [an auspicious exchange of sight between deity and devotee] or to participate in satsang or sabha. Here [in Ahmedabad], it just wasn't like that – mostly senior ladies were coming and men and youth would only appear for special functions, to prostrate to a visiting goswami, or to donate money. How could they even know the timings of daily darshan or how to participate in satsang when they just go to the office or to school without asking or talking to anyone [about the goings-on of the local sectarian community] or bothering to read our [sectarian] literature? But now that they [men and youth] are on Facebook, along with all of the young goswamis, they can so easily see what is happening daily and they don't need to be scared to learn about our Pushtimarg because it's so easy now – you can read our philosophy in any language and in any place. Even we at our temple are developing a blog that provides updates on temple timings and the Pushtimargi calendar – this can be delivered by email or through mobile phone applications very easily.[19]

---

18   Conversation with goswami in Ahmedabad, Gujarat: June 2012.
19   Conversation with male temple administrator in Ahmedabad, Gujarat: October 2011.

However anecdotal, I have witnessed at least 12 such conversations and many more passing comments from goswamis, temple administrators and staff, and devotees in Gujarati in which people attribute the increasing involvement of young people in temple activities etc. to the opportunity to learn about the sect on the Internet as well as to the inspiration of seeing young people from the diaspora learning online. 'Look', one elderly woman exclaimed at one of the weekly sectarian satsangs in an Ahmedabad temple, 'Look at how many youths there are here today!' 'That one has come here from America', the woman's friend says, pointing to a young woman sitting in a group with about six other young men and women. 'She is going to take her brahmasambandh [sectarian initiation] tomorrow – she has learned all about it from Maharaj's [referring to a senior goswami] Internet vachanamrut [nectar-like speech]...maybe the other youngsters will also do as the NRI [non-resident Indian] is doing'. Both women look at one another, nodding and smiling.

V

In order to analyse the translational encounters and online and offline relationships that have been considered in this chapter, it will be helpful to refer to and challenge a theoretical framework that Warner (2002) has called 'publics' and 'counter publics'. According to Warner, publics are a necessary part of democratic life, vital for both understanding the self as well as the politics of social space. For Warner, publics can be imagined entities with 'real' consequences, which are varied in practice, and always products of some sort of social or, in the case of the Vallabh Sampraday Online, socio-religious negotiation or struggle. While the definition of a particular public is always distinct, a common factor underlying the power of most modern publics, argues Warner, is intelligibility across various landscapes of everyday living. In this case, the public in question – that is, the online sectarian advice forum – is what Warner might call a 'kind of engine of translatability, putting down new roots wherever it goes' (Warner 2002: 11). The new roots put down via sectarian forums not only seem to inspire what I would call a more committed, willing, and less anxious community of diasporic *and* Indian devotees, but also, in return, a gradual change in the way in which religion is understood, presented, and practised offline. In other words, I contend that there is active continuity between the online and offline in the transnational sectarian community.

Here the 'public' 'counter public' framework contradicts my observations. Warner defines a public as a space of discourse that differs from a live audience because it is constituted specifically through a text-based (audio, visual, or print) field of circulation. But, for Warner, the Internet yields distinct kinds of publics, which cannot function in the same ways as other mediums (Warner 2002: 97–98). The Internet, Warner continues, does not have the capacity to perform what he calls the 'counterpublic function' – that is, the Internet *cannot* actually produce changes in the 'real' (that is, offline) world because it does not have the ability to produce a social space of circulation over time. While it is true, of course, that some of the sectarian sites and forums that I have studied disappear after some time or do not care to maintain archives etc., I argue that the Internet forums that *do* remain in active use over time constitute a network of individuals (not mere strangers, as Warner might argue), whose relationality, even when predominantly virtual, does generate new forms of embodied sociality. That is, the virtual spaces and publics that I have referred to in this chapter do share a continuum with 'real' spaces (temples and community centres both in the diaspora and in India) and are actively becoming channels through which interest in sectarian-specific knowledge and practice has the opportunity to both increase and, at the same time, change with the tides of contemporary living around the world.

References

Ambalal, A. 1987. *Krishna as Shrinathji: Rajasthani Paintings from Nathdvara.* Ahmedabad: Mapin Publishing.

Barz, R. 1992. *The Bhakti Sect of Vallabhacarya.* New Delhi: Mushiram Manoharlal.

Bennett, P. 1993. *The Path of Grace: Social Organisation and Temple Worship in a Vaishnava Sect.* Delhi: Hindustan Publishing.

Kapur, A. 2012a. How India Became America. *The New York Times*, Op-ed, (9 March).

Kapur, A. 2012b. *India Becoming: A Portrait of Life in Modern India.* New York: Riverhead Books.

Kim, H. H-S. 2001. Being Swaminarayan: The ontology and significance of belief in the construction of a Gujarati Diaspora. Ph.D. Dissertation, Columbia University.

Kinney, J. 1995. Religion, cyberspace and the future. *Futures*, 27(7), 763–776.

Kong, L. 2001. Religion and Technology: Refiguring Place, Space, Identity and Community. *Area*, 33 (4), 404–413.

Mukadam, A. and Sharmina, M. (ed.) 2007. Introduction. In: *Gujaratis in the West: Evolving Identities in Contemporary Society.* Newcastle: Cambridge Scholars Publishing.

Simpson, E. 2008. Why Bhatiyas are not 'Banias' and why this matters: Economic Success and Religious Worldview among a Mercantile Community of Western India. In: P. Lachaier and C. Clémentin-Ojha (eds.), *Divine richesses: religion et économie en monde marchand indien.* Paris: École français d'Extrême-Orient, 91–111.

Vaudeville, C. 1996. *Myths, Saints and Legends in Medieval India.* Delhi: Oxford University Press.

Warner, M. 2002. *Publics and Counterpublics.* New York: Zone Books.

Internet Sources

Pushtimarg.net
Pushtimarg.info.com

Chapter 9

Globalisation and the Transnationalism of 'Dalit' Identity: Probings from Modern India

Ashish Saxena

Introduction

The revolution of information technology, multimedia and internet has facilitated the rapid emergence of online interactions of dispersed groups and communities having shared interests. These online groups with different compositions exhibit a wide range of characteristics and functionally serve a variety of purposes, from small groups engaged in focused discussions of specific topics, to complex created worlds with hundreds of simultaneous participants, to millions of users linked by an interest in markets or exchange networks for goods and information. These new media collectives might be mobilised to further particular political agendas or to bring together dispersed members of familial or ethnic groups. The new socio-metrics having the ability for groups and individuals to interact at great distances raises interesting insights for those investigating the construction of identity across territory, new forms of social interactions, and collective mobilisation or otherwise. No doubt, the new web-technology has created a new arena for group and individual self-representation, changing the power dynamics of representation for traditionally marginalised groups, especially in developing and under-developed nations.

Apart from web-related networking, modern society is also marked by civil society networks referring to the amorphous intermediate space represented by institutions between family and the state and acting as an agency for change. It is a space which is free of both kinship relations and those determined by the state. It may be constituted by formal organisations or informal networks; it may be characterised by high intensity interactions of a transitory nature or by intermittent short-duration interactions, or by relations of varying degree of permanence, clubs, associations, unions, movements and action groups (Young 1999). At this juncture, it is interesting to note that transnationalism as a phenomenon across nations focuses on citizens who, though migrating from poor to rich countries, manage to construct and nurture social fields that intimately link their respective homelands and their new diasporic locations. Thus, when citizens of the global South, with advanced human capital, migrate to a rich Western society such as the

United States and they maintain strategic dialectical interplay between the old and new locations, brain circulation occurs (see Patterson 2006: 1891). Precisely, Faist (2000: 189–222) rightly defines transnationalism as the 'sustained ties of persons, networks and organisations across the borders, across multiple nation-states, ranging from little to highly institutionalised forms'. He takes a cautious position, arguing that the effects of transnationalism on cultural identity and citizenship have not been adequately studied. He encourages scholars to consider three main mechanisms of transnationalism (reciprocity, solidarity, and exchange), and the correspondence of these mechanisms to three types of transnational social spaces (kinship ties, group ties based on solidarity, and the circulation of goods, people, and information).

Apparently, transnationalism is an efficient means of transferring knowledge, skills and wealth from core nations to those in the semi-periphery and the periphery. Transnational activism networks are defined as including 'those actors working internationally on an issue, who are bound together by shared values, a common discourse and dense exchanges of information and services' (Keck and Sikkink 1999: 89). Transnational networks may include national and global NGOs, foundations, advocacy or research organisations, media, intellectuals, and such others. The growing visibility of transnational networks in the international arena, it is argued, may point towards the emergence of a 'global civil society' (Clark *et al.* 1998). Thus, the phenomenon of 'transnational' can be equated with the relocation of geopolitical formations and as a tool towards political metaphoric against the rigid exploitative territoriality. As a perspective, the 'transnationalist' view clearly holds that there is a progressive and humane international current in contrast to the backward and reactionary domestic one.

Adding to the above discussion, one even observes the extension of the 'citizenship'. As rightly pointed out by Soysal (1994), in the new global context we see not just different sets of rights, but radical transformations in the very concept of citizenship. From being organised and legitimated by nation-state belonging, citizenship is shifting toward a post-national concept that is legitimated by deterritorialised universal principles of human rights and personhood, enforced by international organisations. Thus, the interconnectedness among societies and the rise of transnational processes, including global contingencies, which heighten the urgency of a global democracy, has gone hand in hand with the evolution of social systems in the advanced industrial societies. The agenda of democracy is an agenda of freedom. The spiritual challenge of freedom is one of transcending the opposition between self and other, and creating communities of discourse and practice where both can live as seekers of freedom. With the growing liberal democracy, the contemporary societies are increasingly confronted with minority and 'marginal' groups demanding recognition of their identity and accommodation of their cultural differences. Consensus seems to be emerging that a commitment to liberal democratic principles is compatible with and does require support and public recognition of different cultures and identities. The reverberations of this 'politics of recognition' have reached academia and in recent times, issues concerning multiculturalism and minority rights are at the forefront of debates in political and social theory. It is also observed that the resilience of cultural, linguistic, and religious differences among populations has led to a new search for understanding – not only the resurgence of ancient differences among peoples, but also the emergence of historically new ethnic groups. The issue has further led to increasing identity politics and is now mobilised and projected by the indigenous people, the icons of the historically marginalised groups, with a hope that their identities will be acknowledged and accommodated by wider society in a new fashion. No doubt the catalyst to this phenomenon is the twin processes of democracy and globalisation, which are providing more political space for protest and a new network of alliances respectively. In such a global era, the already declining role of the nation-state becomes crucial to accommodate the recognition of various identities vis-à-vis representation on the lines of multiculturalism, and simultaneously to maintain harmony in society. It thus becomes a vital issue to recognise and analyse the survival, development and mobilisation of the historically marginal communities by 'self' and by 'others'.

Owing to the neo-agenda of development i.e. inclusive development, even complex processes and procedures of institutional changes and the redistribution of economic and political power are made for attaining egalitarian society. It must be broadly conceived as the expansion of opportunities, enhancement of human capacities and universalism. Also the debate on colonial history has metamorphosed into post-colonial politics, and a 'marginals' life world and its understanding have also become central to new forms of contradiction. The 'subaltern studies' school of historiography has made a great contribution to retrieving the agency of the past, focusing on the 'politics of the people', the activities of subordinate groups in resisting colonial and elite domination. Most recent writings by postmodernists assume that cultural hegemony is both constituted and contested in relation to a fractured but powerful colonial history. They question the whole notion of dominance and the problem of centre constructed by colonial and elite categories, which attempts to marginalise and exclude 'others' (all 'marginal' categories including 'scheduled castes'). Finally, the quest for indigenous discourse and indigenisation has started exploring tradition and culture in a new way and re-deployed in both popular and more scholarly depictions to account for the resurgence of ethnic nationalisms and communal identities around the globe. Thus, within sociology and psychology, as well as in more popular genres, considerable attention has been given to the idea that virtual spaces allow for fundamentally new constructions of identity: Interactive chat rooms and online spaces were often seen to be gender-neutral, egalitarian spaces.

At this juncture, the Indian state in the post-colonial period too has assumed the role of an interventionist to bring about social transformation. Contemporary debates on development thus involve complex processes and procedures of institutional changes and the redistribution of economic and political power for a better egalitarian society. Keeping in view the onslaught of globalisation, many social scientists have argued that marginalised groups (especially the SCs (scheduled castes)/STs and OBCs) will be adversely affected. In particular, they have emphasised problems such as uneven regional development, wage disparities and increased levels of inequality. Keeping in mind these remarks, the point of focus of this chapter is: What are the implications of this paradigm change for those who are weak, poor, 'marginalised' and downtrodden? Can the nation-state tackle the 'social concern' (welfare goals) for 'marginals' in the globalisation era? To put it differently, what would be the effect of globalisation on the principle of universalism and multiculturalism vis-à-vis 'marginal' groups, at regional, national and global levels? In a radical sense, one can identify how against the state incompetence, the 'Dalit'[1] population is strategically mobilising themselves through online ethnography and multimedia. Relevantly, Spivak's (2003) insistence that we transform the site of cross-cultural knowledge into an open field of new 'self-other' relations is of particular significance for the so-called 'Dalits'. Speaking on the mobilising strategy adopted by the voluntary organisations or the activists of globalisation, it is either in the form of 'transnational advocacy networking' or 'coalition formation'.

Indian *Dalits* in the Era of Globalisation

It is needless to mention that the challenges posed by globalisation to existing non-global forms of civic rights and collective action vary fundamentally along two axes with regard to position in social structure and with location in the geography of globalisation i.e. 'context' and the 'space'. Following the proponents of 'critical globalism' who take a neutral-view of the process of globalisation, it is presumed here that globalisation has dual implications on the 'marginal' group and categories – both negative and positive. According to Scholte (1996: 53), 'globalisation has often perpetuated poverty, widened material inequalities, increased ecological degradation, fragmented communities, marginalised subordinated groups, intolerance and deepened crisis of democracy; they also see that it has had a positive effect...various subordinated groups have of grasped opportunities for global organisation'.

---

1 The word 'Dalit' was a popular connotation of the 1960s in public discourse. The word gained currency in public spheres during the SCs-Caste Hindus riots in Bombay in the early 1970s. The Dalit Panthers, an organisation of the SCs in Maharashtra, used the term to assert their identity for rights and self-respect. Later, the term was used with a wider connotation. It includes all the oppressed sections of society – STs, landless and poor peasants, women and others. It does not confine itself merely to economic exploitation; it also relates to suppression of culture and more importantly, the denial of dignity. For some, it connotes an ideology for fundamental change in the social structure and relationship. Gangadhar Pantawane rightly points out that 'Dalit is not a caste; it is a symbol of change and revolution'. To Gopal Guru Dalit the category is 'historically arrived at, sociologically presented and discursively constituted'. It is secular in nature, not confined to any particular caste or religious community.

No doubt globalisation depicts both manifest and latent functions on the Dalits (see, for details, Saxena 2010). In positive terms, the process involves tremendous exposure of these local entities to a new orientation and enhances their consciousness. It orients them to the forces of market and finance on one hand, and on the other side access to revolutionary means of communication and media. Dalits have had mixed fortunes in contemporary globalisation. On the negative side they have been marginalised in multinational corporations, international NGOs, global governance institutions, and the globally oriented information technology industry. Dalits have generally lacked the educational foundations and international exposure to gain access to these global arenas. Dalits have also lost jobs in the 1990s when neoliberal global restructuring in India brought a withdrawal of the state, their largest employer. Thus, the important aspect to be noted is the nature of utilisation of globalisation by the Dalits in the form of how and why the Dalit anti-discrimination struggle is made into a struggle for human rights (internationalisation), or how human rights are made into Dalit rights (glocalisation).

Simultaneously, globalisation has had an adverse impact on all social groups, which have already been pushed down by centuries of oppression. It is a fact that in the last decade the livelihood of Dalit communities became miserable. Under the old economic policies of Indian Government, Dalits were given minimum protection and support in the fields of education, land, capital and employment. Until the 1980s there was visible growth and development among Dalits in these fields. One can observe a decrease in unemployment, increase in wages and fall in poverty mainly due to high expenditure of government on the welfare sector, particularly in the rural areas. However, in the present era of privatisation, the State's indirect withdrawal ('disinvestment' heavily in public sector and imposed huge cuts in the welfare part of the budget and privatisation of all the sources of services and workplaces) of 'welfare' from the service sector meant that people, particularly Dalits, became vulnerable. Further, the shift of decision-making power into the hands of transnational institutions like the World Trade Organisation, International Monetary Fund, World Banks and others has severely reduced the sovereignty of national government and resulted in a very serious drift. In this context the struggle for dignity and social equity has to be the principal issue among Dalits, so that they are well equipped to contribute from their perspective and experience a struggle against satanic globalisation. The civil society groups working among the Dalits are so much under pressure from local issues that they hardly get to link their pressing issues of identity and dignity with the larger issues of globalisation. This can be understood in terms of a 'new social movement' at a global level. Throughout this process, many Dalits on one hand lose their jobs from public sector industries and factories, but on the other hand they are not able to find any new jobs in the 'open' market which is highly privatised and requires capital and specialised skills. Lack of reservations owing to the profit motive of capitalists in the private sector debars Dalits' entry into the competitive world. In this regard we find that the Dalits are at the lowest end of the economic and social ladder and are quite obviously at the receiving end of the elitist culture promoted by globalisation. Economically, the earlier small gains made through reservations have been, in essence, reversed; socially, the elitist culture (Hindutva), which marginalises the poor generally, will have a double impact on Dalits.

On the other hand, the process of globalisation ultimately leads towards homogenisation of world-culture in some significant aspects. To quote Hannerz (1996: 17): 'In the most general sense, globalisation is a matter of increasing long-distance interconnectedness, at least across national boundaries, preferably between continents as well'. We can say that these processes of linkages across borders include a restructuration of spaces for 'marginals', leading to the disappearance of fixed links to villages, towns and national frontiers. In this regard, Waters (1995: 136) points out that the process of globalisation specifies greater connectedness and de-territorialisation simultaneously. If we try to look at it in positive terms then it tries to break the barriers i.e. de-capsulation of communities and identities. In the long run this may lead to the disappearance of inequalities, because it is not possible for ethnic identity to survive without a specific territory or place. This situation will have a positive impact on the people who were marginalised as against the dominating categories in specific territories. In this framework it may be perceived as a welcoming process for the 'marginals'; it will not only put them out of the hands of high castes but they will also get fair scope for economic empowerment and social mobility, which they are unable to get in earlier stratified systems. Further, globalisation policies will increase their free flow in the international market in terms of labour, goods, ideas and capital. Quoting Deliege (1999), one can say that 'today in this global world "marginals" aspire to more comfortable material circumstances and demand more dignity'. This global/international mobilisation will provide an opportunity for global solidarity and for upholding human rights. In this regard, Jogdand (2000) has rightly argued that much-cherished principle of growth with justice; social responsibilities and accountability; equity and self-reliance have been rendered obsolete with the new slogan of liberalisation and globalisation. Here, Buell's (1994) argument stands valid that 'Tighter integration (due to globalisation) has thus paradoxically meant, and continues to mean, proliferation of asserted differences'. In addition, Mendelsohn and Vicziany (1998: 1) emphasise that 'marginals' will almost everywhere become much more assertive about their human and political rights. An example to support this argument is the establishment of organisations like World Social Forum (WSF) and specifically Asia Social Forum (ASF), which provide advocacy on issues regarding neoliberal globalisation and its impact on discriminated communities. To quote Vivek Kumar (2007: 326) on the issue of Dalit diaspora and social solidarity: 'Dalits settled abroad did not remain aloof from each other...They created their own organisations to develop social solidarity with different Dalit communities....The Federation of Ambedkarite Buddhist Organisations (FABO) and Voice of Dalit International (VODI) are also working in UK to uplift Dalits back in India....A more organised effort came in the US from literate NRI Dalits when they formed "Volunteers in Service to India's Oppressed and Neglected" (VISION) in 1975'. In addition, the National Campaign for Dalit Human Rights has, thanks to Durban, become a 'globally mobile' organisation, with (one assumes) tongue-in-cheek reference to upward mobility.

Aspects of globalisation have brought more visibility to Dalit struggles. Through the International Dalit Solidarity Network, established in 2000, NGOs have highlighted the plight of Dalits at global forums. Literate Dalit professionals have globally promoted several Dalit icons, including Buddha, Guru Ravi Das, and Dr. B. R. Ambedkar. Ambedkar is now celebrated through named lecture series and busts at Columbia University, the London School of Economics, San Fraser University, Manchester Metropolitan University and the University of Calgary. Dalit movements have also exploited global communications technologies and lower costs of global transportation in order to raise awareness of their issues. Dalit solidarity groups have thus taken their case to global governance institutions like the United Nations Human Rights Council and global civil society gatherings like the World Social Forum (see Kumar, V. 2004).

According to Ram (2001: 53), the phenomenon of Ravidass deras has taken the form of a sort of a new socio-cultural Dalit movement in Punjab – what has also come to be known as the 'Ravidassia movement' or 'Ravidass Deras Dalit movement'. The Sants of Ravidass deras, again, particularly of Dera Sachkhand Ballan, have been quite successful in blending together the bani of Guru Ravidass and the philosophy of neo-Buddhism as propounded by Dr Ambedkar. 194 Dera Sachkhand Ballan has become a paragon of the Ravidass movement in northwest India. It has also been regulating the affairs of various Ravidass Deras overseas through its international trusts. Dera Sachkhand Ballan has established the following international charitable trusts abroad for dissemination of the *Bani* of Ravidass amongst the Dalit Diaspora: Shri 108 Sant Sarwan Dass Charitable Trust [United Kingdom]; Shri 108 Sant Sarwan Dass Charitable Trust [Vancouver Canada]; and Shri 108 Sant Sarwan Dass Charitable Trust [United States]. All these trusts are managed mostly by non-resident Indian Dalits from the Doaba region of Punjab who constitute a large diasporic community (Ravidassia samaj) of the devotees of Guru Ravidass and the followers of the Dera Sachkhand Ballan.

If we try to put the above discourse on the measuring scale, we may arrive at an understanding that globalisation is worse for 'marginals' on many fronts, but one cannot negate the brighter side of the picture showing the positive implications of globalisation. As 'critical' globalists we should welcome the mixed results of the globalisation on Dalits. Further, regarding the question of the condition of 'marginals' in contemporary society, this can be supported by the fact that quantitative and politico-economic changes are observed and implemented rapidly in comparison to qualitative changes, and it takes time for assimilation and adaptation to take place.

Nation-State and the Transnationalism of Dalit Identity in Modern India

The role of 'transnational networks' or 'activists without borders' in advocacy and policy making was first brought to the fore by Keck and Sikkink (1998). They showed that transnational advocacy networks have been able to influence policies, not least in areas such as human rights, the environment and women's rights. Alliances were formed between various Dalit groups to come together and to raise their concerns on an international platform. These alliances were also being supported by lower caste activists in other South Asian countries, such as Nepal and Sri Lanka. They used the 'boomerang theory' to explain this transnational activity. They argue that 'when a government violates or refuses to recognise rights...domestic NGOs bypass their state and directly search out international allies to try to bring pressure on their states from outside'. 'This', they say 'is most obviously the case in human rights campaigns'. Through their activities abroad NGOs frequently utilise a 'mobilisation of shame' to bring visibility to their causes and to re-frame debate at home and make their domestic governments more compliant.

Gail Omvedt traces the start of transnational Dalit activism back to the declaration of Emergency in 1975 when Dalits in solidarity with Black Americans mobilised and protested against a visit to the United States by Indira Gandhi. For the first time Americans were hearing stories of Dalit atrocities from what they knew only as the 'land of Gandhi' (Omvedt 2004: 188). In the UK, an extensive transnational Dalit movement also began to form (Hardtmann 2003). About the same time, in Toronto a Dalit small businessman, Yogesh Warshade, founded the Ambedkar Mission which since has developed into a global NGO, the Ambedkar Centre for Justice and Peace. As the ACJP website notes, the centre 'has been globalising the issues for Dalits...of India for the last 15 years' (http://acjp.sts.winis.net). Since 1991 the ACJP has been appearing in various venues including the Canadian Parliament and at various human rights forums at the United Nations. Prominent among these forums is the UN Committee on Elimination of Racial Discrimination (CERD).

Surprisingly in India, as a failure to the state rule, the statistics provided by the National Crime Records Bureau (NCRB) show that most of the crimes committed against Dalits were rape and murder and a majority of the accused belonged to the higher castes. According to NCRB, 240 rape cases against Dalit women were reported in 2006 and the number increased to 318 in 2007. Further, the Central government may wax lyrical about empowering the downtrodden, but in the last five years it has denied the SCs a whopping Rs.72,500 crore ($15.16 billion) that should have been earmarked for them under a special scheme called the special component plan. Scheduled castes today form 16.2 per cent of India's 1.2 billion population. Therefore, between 2005 and 2009, the Central government should have set aside Rs.129,000 crore for Dalits. But as much as Rs.72,500 crores was not earmarked, as the National Campaign on Dalit Human Rights (NCDHR) has pointed out. 'The figures of allocation are a mute witness to the history of denial of exclusion. It is not only for the last five years; this trend is observed for the last 28 years since the inception of the special component plan in 1979–80', states the NCDHR (for details, see Silicon India 5/7/09 and the NCDHR website). Thus, the most recent phase in *dalit* politics has been driven by a new intellectual *dalit* elite consisting of intellectuals, academics, trade unionists, writers, journalists and social workers mainly from South and Central India. The facts speak about the utilisation and sharing of online technology for mobilising and raising voices against ill-practices.

For these reasons, perhaps, Dalit movements and campaigns including the International Dalit Solidarity Network, the World Council of Churches Dalit Solidarity Program and the National Campaign for Dalit Human Rights (NCDHR) systematically engage international forums and transnational alliances in a boomerang pattern of activism, which aims to bring pressure to bear on the Indian State by activating transnational networks at UN forums and international conferences such as the Global Conference against Racism and Caste-based Discrimination (at New Delhi, 2001) and various World Social Forum (e.g. Mumbai World Social Forum) events.

In relation to the raising of Dalit issues transnationally, the 2001 UN World Conference against Racism, Racial Discrimination, Xenophobia and Related Intolerance (WCAR) in Durban was significant as the new *dalit* movement achieved a real breakthrough at home, while also consolidating its position internationally. Even though the Indian Government delegation blocked inclusion of caste discrimination issues from the WCAR official document, the *dalit* WCAR caucus and its international supporters managed to place caste discrimination in the spotlight of the international media, and on the agenda of the social movements and NGOs present in Durban (Hardtmann 2003).

Back in India, the creation of a new *dalit* movement related to initiatives by non-Indian organisations. In 1997, partly as a result of the UN recognition of caste discrimination, the international human rights NGO Human Rights Watch decided to engage with the *dalit* issue. Funded by the Ford Foundation, in 1999 it published the report 'Broken People: Caste Violence against India's "Untouchables"' (Human Rights Watch 1999). This became a landmark initiative even as the report was still in preparation. A condition set by the Ford Foundation was that the report should serve the Indian *dalit* movements. In 1998, Human Rights Watch organised a meeting of a number of regional Indian *dalit* organisations, to advise on and engage with the report. This helped to initiate the Indian umbrella organisation National Campaign on *Dalit* Human Rights (NCDHR), also in 1998, which quickly became the focal point for most of the new *dalit* political activities.

Contextually, Hardtmann (2003) emphasises that starting in the 1980s, the new *dalit* elite movement was internationalised right from the beginning. Pressure groups belonging to the *dalit* diaspora in North America and Europe such as 'Volunteers in the Service to India's Oppressed and Neglected' (VISION) and the 'Ambedkar Center for Justice and Peace' (ACJP), based in Washington DC and Toronto, respectively, began to lobby other NGOs as well as UN organisations, to make them recognise caste-based discrimination as descent-based discrimination on a par with racial discrimination, and to view caste-based discrimination as a human rights offence (for details, see Bob 2007: 176). The website www.ambedkar.org reveals the presence of another stream of Dalit diaspora in the US, UK and Canada. This 'new' Dalit diaspora migrated as free labourers and professionals. Dalit activists from Punjab put down their migration to the UK to pre-independence, but according to Muman (2000: 71), a Dalit from Punjab, 'I came to Britain in the late 1960s from a remote village in India. During this period mostly semi-literate Dalits migrated as industrial and domestic labourers'. Indian Dalits started migrating to the US in the 1970s. They were first generation literates and professionals. This 'new' stream is politically conscious and has influenced politically subdued 'old' Dalit diaspora as well.

Currently, the UK and the US are becoming the hub of activities of the Dalit diaspora. Dalits here celebrate and commemorate Ambedkar's, Buddha's, and Ravi Das's birth and death anniversaries respectively with lots of fanfare. In the UK, for the last three years Dalits have taken the initiative to organise an Ambedkar memorial lecture at Manchester Metropolitan University with a vision of spreading Ambedkar's thought throughout the world. Another unique effort of the Dalit diaspora in the UK in the cultural realm is that on April 23, 2003, they established an Ambedkar Museum at Wolverhampton. Dalit diaspora has thus used the internet to unite Dalits the world over. There are about 51 sites, which provide information about Dalits in India and abroad. A few important sites are www.ambedkar.org, www.dalitusa.org, www.dalitistan.org, www.dalitawaj. com, www.dalitindia.com, etc. Similarly, Dalits also run e-magazines such as Dalit-International@yahoogroup.com, dalits@ambedkar.org, Buddhistcircle@ yahoogroup.com, and Sakyagroup@yahoo group com. Their numbers are increasing day by day. Through these sites and magazines the Dalit fraternity keeps itself up-to-date with the latest happenings within the Dalit diaspora and Dalit community in India, which helps them to take prompt action based on this information. All this was not possible earlier because they had no links with each other. The whole process of sharing information about themselves has sensitised them and made them conscious that distance is no more a hurdle in the path of unity (Kumar 2004: 114).

To quote Ram (2011: 15), the phenomenon of Ravidass deras/temples/ gurdwaras is not only confined to the state of Punjab, it has also gained equal importance among the rich Dalit diasporas. The recent attack on the Ravidassia sants (spiritual persons) of the Dera Sachkhand Ballan of Punjab during their visit to Guru Ravidass Temple in Vienna on 24 May 2009 has brought the phenomenon of the Ravidass deras to the centre of the world map. The Ravidass Deras in fact have become a critical agency that graphically manifest and articulate the otherwise dormant dimensions of alternative Dalit agenda in Punjab and overseas. Punjabi Dalit diasporas have established their separate Ravidass deras abroad in large numbers. Some of the most prominent Ravidass deras abroad are in the following cities: Vancouver, Calgary, Brampton, Toronto, Montreal (Canada),

New York, Sacramento, Pittsburg, Seattle, Fresno, Fremont, Houston, Selma, and Austin (United States), Wolverhampton, Birmingham, Bradford, Coventry, Derby, Lancaster, Southall, Southampton, Kent and Bedford (UK). In the last few years many Ravidass temples and gurdwaras have also been built in Austria, Italy, France, Germany, Spain, Holland, New Zealand, Greece and the Lebanon (see http://www.tribuneindia.com/2009/20090622/edit.htm). Similarly, Ad Dharm as a political movement petered out in post-partition Punjab, but as a religion of the downtrodden as well as a counter-public Dalit sphere it continues to flourish even today. It is in fact pursued far more vigorously among the Punjabi diasporas in Europe and North America, who have been able to establish a solid system of social networking across the globe. Moreover, Ad Dharm as a religion continues to flourish in the premises of a large number of Ravidass deras in Punjab and abroad.

The National Campaign on Dalit Human Rights (NCDHR), formed in 1998, sought to bring international attention to the issue of atrocities against the Dalits. The First World Dalit Convention that was being held at Kuala Lumpur, Malaysia in October 1998 also urged the UN to appoint at the earliest 'Special Rapporteurs' in order to investigate the human rights violations of the Dalits. The International Dalit Solidarity Network (IDSN) that was established in the year 2000, with its secretariat in Copenhagen, Denmark, also played a significant role in mobilising international support for the Dalit women's cause. Following the setting up of the IDSN, a number of organisations and networks across the globe took up the cause of the Dalits. For instance, in Europe alone, networks working on issues of caste-based discrimination are operating in seven countries, all of which are members of the IDSN.

On the web-page of the NCDHR, phases of the organisation's activities are described: (1) raising visibility, (2) internationalising Dalit rights, (3) holding state accountable and (4) the present state, holding the four movements that were discussed earlier. The present phase is concerned with the following goals: '(1) to hold the state accountable for all human rights violations committed against Dalits; (2) to sensitise civil society by raising visibility of the Dalit problem; and (3) to render justice to Dalit victims of discrimination and violence' (the homepage of the NCDHR, accessed 20 April 2010).

The National Campaign on Dalit Human Rights (NCDHR) thus continues to expand into the transnational sphere where it gains visibility, solidarity, and also increased access to resources. Before the Dalit movement attended the 2001 UN World Conference Against Racism (WCAR), it experienced other successes which are likely attributed to increasing interconnections between regions and movements. In fact, Peter Jay Smith (2008) points all the way back to the immigration of Dalits to Europe as the beginnings of the 'internationalisation of the Dalit issue'. The internationalisation of the Dalit movement is not under contention here. Instead, the year 2001 is cited as the moment of transnationalisation. The NCDHR participated in the World Social Forum (WSF) in Porto Alegre in 2001 as well (see Daily 2009).

Major Contemporary Dalits Transnational Organisations

- *National Campaign on Dalit Human Rights (NCDHR)* – Founding Date: 1998. Founding Place: Bangalore. Website: Ncdhr.org.in. Raises national and international awareness through outreach, transnational networking, policy reform and various other subnational organisations.
- *Navsarjan* – Founding Date: 1988. Founding Place: Gujarat. Website: Narvsarjan.org. Training, awareness, fieldwork and legal intervention. Works with NCDHR, IDSN, Dalit Foundation, Indian Institute on Dalit Studies.
- *Dalit NGO Federation* – Founding Date: 1996. Founding Place: Kathmandu, Nepal. Website: Dfnnepal.org. To eradicate caste-based discrimination through a process of empowerment, networking and alliance building of Dalit and pro-Dalit institutions. Works with smaller organisations in Nepal and larger international organisations, especially throughout Asia.
- *Dalit Solidarity* – Founding Date: 2000. Founding Place: Tamil Nadu. Website: Dalitsolidarity.org. Works with the extremely rural and poor communities. Provides access to education, health care, and economic opportunities. Exclusively subnational, but works with NCDHR.
- *International Dalit Solidarity Network (IDSN)* – Founding Date: 2000. Founding Place: Denmark. Website: Idsn.org. Works with international policy-makers, UN and EU.
- *Dalit Freedom Network* – Founding Date: 2002. Founding Place: Greenwood Village, CO, USA. Website: Dalitnetwork.org. Missionary work and conversion to Christianity.
- *The Dr. Ambedkar Non-Resident Indian Association (DANRIA)* – Small collaborative group of non-resident dalits living in the United States who have incorporated an NGO in Baltimore, MD. Their goals are to provide educational assistance and social uplift to dalits living in India. They are actively seeking funding for a manual scavengers programme in Uttar Pradesh.
- *The International Commission for Dalit Rights (ICDR)* – In order to promote a global movement in support of Dalit Rights, South Asian and international Dalit leaders as well as activists and supporters held a series of consultation meetings in 2005 and 2006 in Nepal, India, the United States, Geneva and London. These meetings led to a decision to establish for the first time an International Commission for Dalit Rights, an independent and impartial global forum on Dalit Rights, which was formally launched on March 21, 2006.

Transnationalism, *Dalit* Women and Invisible Marginality

Dalit solidarity organisations have now begun lobbying foreign private corporations and development agencies operating in South Asia regarding affirmative action (DSN UK 2005a, 2005/06; IDSN 2005, 2006). The final evidence that the international 'alternative' movements are determined to keep the *dalit* issue firmly on the international public agenda came with the award of the 2006 Alternative Nobel Prize to Ruth Manorama, an activist for the rights of *dalit* women, and for *dalit* rights in general. *Dalit* issues are now a staple of the agendas of the international alternative movements.

In a recent work, Manisha Desai emphasised that 'transnational feminist practices have become the dominant modality of feminist movements across the world, since the Fourth Women's World Conference in Beijing'. Desai defined transnationalism as 'both organising across national borders as well as framing local, national, regional, and global activism in "transnational discourses"' (2005: 319). No doubt transnational activism and the appropriation of a discourse of human rights have played a significant role in shaping the activism and organisational formation of the Dalit (formerly untouchables) Women's Movement.

Thus, Beijing served as an important venue for the Dalit Women's Movement. It was the first time they were able to express themselves directly on an international stage. Yet this was not the last time they were to be present at UN forums. In fact, for Dalit women, as well for the Dalit and Women's Movements in general, the UN has offered spaces for affiliated NGOs and a host of transnational advocacy networks active in the area of human rights.

The virtual invisibility of Dalit women led Vimal Thorat to assert in 2001 that 'both the Dalit movement and women's movement have consciously ignored the Dalit women's issue'. Thorat noted that despite two generations of articulate committed Dalit professional women, these 'articulate women are not invited by Dalit forums, especially the political parties. Why?' Thorat's ire was directed not only at the Dalit movement but also at the Indian women's movement. Thorat stated: 'This betrayal of Dalit women's issues is matched by the utter disregard and tokenism with which Dalit women's issues are taken up by the women's movement'. Despite this invisibility, Thorat did acknowledge that 'nevertheless, the Dalit's women's articulations are growing' (see Thorat 2001).

Thus, apart from the UN, another key site for transnational feminist activism since the Beijing Conference of 1995 has been the World Social Forum (WSF) (Desai 2005, p. 325). The Dalit Network Netherlands (DNN), in collaboration with the NCDHR, the NFDW, the All India Dalit Women's Rights Forum, the Feminist Dalit Organisation, Nepal, and the IDSN, organised a conference on human rights and dignity of Dalit women in The Hague, November 20–25, 2006.

Another phase is 'internationalising Dalit rights'. For this phase, NCDHR states that it has made 'major strides in giving visibility to the plight of the Dalit community'. These strides have been made through NCDHR's participation in all World Social Forums (WSF), the World Conference Against Racism (WCAR, the 40-day Dalit Swadhikar Rally throughout India), 'The Situation of the Dalits in India' at the European Parliament in Brussels in 2006, the first International Conference on the Human Rights of Dalit Women at The Hague in 2006, the recognition of the problems of Dalit Human Rights by the United Nations in August 2001, recognition by the European Union in May 2007, and lastly, recognition by the United States Congress in July 2007. NCDHR also won the RAFTO award in 2007 for its work on progressing human rights. The NCDHR website does not make declarative statements about the final accomplishment of this phase as yet.

AIDMAM is the All India Dalit Mahila Adhikar Manch, a forum for Dalit women to work towards altering the double-burden of Dalit females – Dalits and women. It seeks to challenge the structures that enable discrimination, whether patriarchal, caste or class based, or economic. The DAAA is the Dalit Arthik Adhikar Manch, a branch of the NCDHR that focuses on changing the economic and educational practices in India which leave Dalits behind while other castes move forward. The NFDRLM consists of the National Federation of Dalit Land Rights Movements. This organisation focuses on Dalit access to land and an agricultural livelihood. Lastly, the NDMJ is the National Dalit Movement for Justice, a broader movement within the NCDHR. It mostly consists of Dalit survivors of violence or discrimination as well as sympathisers and seeks to enforce justice. It does so by attempting to 'establish [Dalits] as equal citizens in the society under Dalit leadership within our rising consciousness...to promote and protect Civil Political Rights of Dalits for ensuring...fair justice'.

One thus finds that the exclusive nature of many national projects may, in turn, shape those very people who are excluded from an alternative inclusive community – one that then contests its own exclusion from the nation. One possible alternative inclusive community is beyond the local or national level, and may be found at the global level of transnational social movement networks. These networks act as sites of global inclusivity, gathering people from around the world who share grievances.

Conclusion

Globalisation is the intensification of worldwide social relations which link distant localities in such a way that local happenings are shaped by events occurring many miles away and vice-versa. To indigenous and marginal groups, it signifies that they are suddenly catapulted from their traditional ways of life into tension and conflict, both within their own group and in their interaction with other superior groups at a global level. Sociologically, it may be understood as a process of 'universalisation' whereby the parochial elements have to disappear.

The first international result came in 1996, when NGO pressure led the UN Committee on Elimination of Racial Discrimination (CERD) to declare 'that the situation of the Scheduled Castes and Scheduled Tribes falls within the scope of the convention' [see the International Convention on the Elimination of All Forms of

Racial Discrimination (ICERD)]. During the late 1990s, CERD reported critically on the efforts by the Government of India to minimise caste discrimination (Thorat and Umakant 2004: xvii–xx). According to the UN Committee on the Elimination of Racial Discrimination (UN CERD 2007: 3), however, 'there is a strong comfort level in both society and the state that crimes against Dalits do not matter, and need not be punished. This attitude of impunity is rooted in social and cultural values and though the Constitution has made a very conscious change, the mindset in society has not changed...Protecting the rights of marginalised and vulnerable persons is probably the most overlooked and disregarded area of human rights in India'.

Thus, globalisation depicts both manifest and latent functions in society. Economic liberation is observed as manifest consequences but it may lead to several latent consequences like the decline of the nation-state, threat to cultural identity, uniqueness etc. With reference to 'marginals', it may show a different impact. Instead of being a threat to such identities, it may become a means for their identity construction. By appropriating strategies of representation, organisations and social change through access to global systems, local communities and marginal interest groups can both empower themselves and influence that global system. Further, we cannot deny the role of Dalit diaspora, the media, NGOs and civil society which can transform their fate in the globalised world.

References

Bob, C. 2007. Dalit Rights are Human Rights: Caste Discrimination, International Activism, and the Construction of a New Human Rights Issue, *Human Rights Quarterly*, 29 (1), 167–193.

Buell, F. 1994. *National Culture and the New Global system*. Baltimore, MD: Johns Hopkins University Press.

Daily, Lisa A. 2009. Constructing a new nationalism from below: The Dalit movement, politics and transnational networking. *Graduate School Theses and Dissertations*. http://scholarcommons.usf.edu/etd/1920.

Deliege, R.1999. *The Untouchables of Hindu Organisation*. London: Berg.

Desai, M. 2005. Transnationalism: The Face of Feminist Politics Post-Beijing. *International Social Science Journal*, 57 (2), 319–330.

Faist T. 2000. Transnationalization in international migration: implications for the study of citizenship and culture. *Ethnic and Racial Studies*, 23 (2), 189–222.

Hannerz, U. 1996. *Transnational Connection: Cultures, People, Places*. London: Routledge.

Hartmann, E. -M. 2003. *Our Fury is Burning*. Stockholm: Stockholm Studies in Social Anthropology.

International Dalit Solidarity Network. 2003. Statutes of the International Dalit Solidarity Network. http://www.idsn.org/statutes.html (Accessed 18 May 2005).

Jogdand, P. G. 2000. *New Economic Policy and Dalits.* New Delhi: Rawat Publications.

Keck, M. E. and Kathryn, S. 1998. *Activists beyond Borders: Advocacy Networks in International Politics.* Ithaca, NY: Cornell University Press.

Keck, M. E. and Kathryn, S. 1999. Transnational Advocacy Networks in International and Regional Politics. *International Social Science Journal*, 51 (159), 89–101.

Kumar, V. 2004. Understanding Dalit Diaspora. *Economic and Political Weekly*, 39 (1), 114–116.

Mendelsohn, O. and Vicziany, M. 1998. *The Untouchables: Subordinates, Poverty and the State in Modern India.* Cambridge: Cambridge University Press.

Muman, Sat Pal. 2000. 'Caste in Britain' in Report of the Proceedings of International Conference on Dalits' Human Rights.

National Alliance of Women (NAWO). 2007. Final Strategy Paper to take forward the Implementation of the CEDAW Concluding Comments. http://www. unifem.org.in/Strategy%20paperON%20CEDAW%20-%20UNIFEM.pdf (Accessed 3 December 2011).

National Federation of Dalit Women. 2002. How Dalit Women's Lives Mirror Descent Based Discrimination. http://www.dalits.org/CERDStatementRuth. html (Accessed 24 October 2011).

National Federation of Dalit Women. 2001. NGO Declaration on Gender and Racism. In: A. Rao (ed.), *Gender and Caste.* London: Zed Books, 363–367.

Omvedt, G. 2004. The UN, Racism and Caste. In: S. Thorat and Umakant (eds.), *Caste, Race and Discrimination: Discourses in International Context*, New Delhi: Rawat Publications.

Patterson, R. 2006. Transnationalism: Diaspora-Homeland Development. *Social Forces*, 84 (4), 1891–1907.

Ram, R. 2011. Beyond Conversion and Sanskritisation: Articulating an Alternative Dalit Agenda in East Punjab. *Modern Asian Studies*, 46 (3), 639–702.

Saxena, A. 2009. *Shifting Manifestations: Scheduled Castes in Jammu and Kashmir.* Jammu: Saksham Books International.

Saxena, A. 2010. Locating prospects of dalits in the era of globalisation: some critical reflections. In: D. K. Singha Roy (eds.), *Surviving against Odds- The marginalized in a globalizing world.* New Delhi: Manohar Publishers.

Scholte, J. A. 1996. *Beyond the buzzword: towards a critical theory of globalization: Theory and Practice.* London: Pinter Press.

Smith, P. (Jay). 2008. Going Global: The Transnational Politics of the Dalit Movement. *Globalizations*, 5 (1), 13–33.

United Nations. 1996. http://www.unhchr.ch/tbs/doc.nsf/0/30d3c5041b55e561c1 2563e000500d33? [Accessed 12 March 2012].

Waters, M. 1995. *Globalization.* London: R&KP.

Young, I. M. 1999. State, Civil Society and Social justice. In: I. Shapiro and C. H. Cordon (eds.), *Democracy's value.* Cambridge: Cambridge University Press, 141–162.

Conclusion

The Diasporic Web: Reflexive Dialogue and Agentive Awareness

Johannes G. de Kruijf

> In the setting of what I call 'high' or 'late' modernity – our present-day world – the self, like the broader institutional contexts in which it exists, has to be reflexively made. Yet this task has to be accomplished amid a puzzling diversity of options and possibilities.
>
> Anthony Giddens, *Modernity and Self-Identity* (1991)

In the same year in which Tim Berners-Lee posted a message on the alt.hypertext newsgroup about where to download his Web server and browser – thus making the Web a globally available service – Anthony Giddens published his influential book on 'the emergence of new mechanisms of self-identity' (1991: 2). According to Giddens, the late (or high) modern world of the late twentieth century could be considered a 'runaway world': a place defined by an unprecedented and extreme dynamism of social life. This dynamism, he claims, results from a separation or distanciation of time and space and the subsequent disembedding of social institutions. Whereas in pre-modern eras, time and space were connected through 'the situatedness of place', modernity is characterized by 'the "lifting out" of social relations from local contexts and their rearticulation across indefinite tracks of time-space' (1991: 18). Giddens argues that these shifts in time-space, coupled with disembedding tendencies, prove particularly transformative because they 'propel social life away from pre-established precepts and practices' (1991: 20). Modernity as such could be seen as a post-traditional order in which reflexivity determines the organization of social life and fuels its accelerated change.[1]

Giddens explores the issue of (self-)identity for the sake of explaining the linkage between present-day reflexivity and change. He considers the search for self-identity a contemporary 'problem'; a quest for an answer to one of the existential questions that surfaced with the erosion of taken-for-granted tradition. His assessment of this quest revolves around the notion of *lifestyle*, a notion that he defines as 'a more or less integrated set of practices which an individual embraces [...] because they give material form to a particular narrative of self-identity' (Giddens 1991: 81). As far as Giddens is concerned, lifestyle is the inevitable consequence of the condition of high modernity. More specifically, in contexts

---

1 See Beck *et al.* (2003) for another elaborate assessment of this issue. They consider reflexivity a hallmark trait of today's second modernity.

of time-space distanciation and profound disembedding, we have no choice but to (reflexively) choose and adopt lifestyles.[2] And, Giddens says, it is the making and remaking of these lifestyles that concerns the very core of contemporary self-identity.

In the conclusions to this volume, I would like to argue that a focus on these 'virtually prehistoric' ideas of Anthony Giddens about reflexivity and identity allows us to distill important common denominators from its diverse collection of analyses. In fact, I believe that these ideas also help us to unravel the very impact of the World Wide Web on the diasporic experiences and practices of its migrant users in general. Their particular relevance can be explained as a result of the highly post-traditional nature of migrant settings and the incredible potential of the WWW for projects of identity and selection/execution of lifestyle choices. The post-traditional nature of migrant settings relates to that what Giddens – after Peter Berger *et al.* – calls the 'pluralization of lifeworlds'. Diversity and segmentation, as traits of contemporary social life, are obviously particularly prominent in the lives of those who are highly mobile and often reside, as members of a minority group, in contexts marked by high levels of social and cultural diversity. Irrespective of the efforts and ability of individual migrants and migrant groups to preserve their distinctiveness, the presence of alternative ways and beliefs is undeniable. More specifically, if 'choice' is inherent to present-day existence at large, its urgency is especially great among those people whose biographies – and, to an increasing extent, also daily lives – span different places and socio-cultural realities.

Especially within the realm of Cultural Studies, this particular diasporic experience has been explored and debated (e.g. Hall 1990; Gilroy 1993). It is often linked to processes of identity and identification and analyzed as the reason for the emergence of imaginaries and types of consciousness that narrate an awareness of multilocality and eclectic understandings of selves shaped by a multiplicity of histories and associations (Vertovec 2009: 6–7). The various chapters in this book indicate the impact of such experiences of multiplicity in migrant settings. They narrate an urge to contemplate, define and position oneself in plural environs that are experienced as unescapably transformative. Projects of identity, both individual and collective, in the realm of religion are illustrative. The analysis of, for instance, Lal concern intensely reflexive quests for defensive demarcation triggered by the experience of vulnerability under conditions of diversity. Additionally, Lal's exploration shows the awareness of the potential of computer-mediated communication (CMC) for the subsequently acute diasporic projects of identity. This awareness, which is apparent in the other analyses as well, helps to explain how CMC has rapidly become a primary catalyst and agent of migrant transnationalism. It is linked to the activating capacity of the World

---

2   As Giddens himself also indicates, 'to speak of a multiplicity of choice is not to suppose that choices are open to everyone, or that people that all decisions about options in full realization of the range of feasible alternatives' (1991: 82).

Wide Web; the way in which especially today's user-centered Web encourages active involvement in processes of information and self-expression.

Giddens' interpretation of lifestyle seems most appropriate to summarize the gamut of online actions and activities of the Indian migrants described here. Each in their own way, the case studies illustrate how the Web (according to Skop, 'thirdspace') functions as a site of transnational lifestyle practices. Whether you analyze the use of multifunctional *Indernet* in German-speaking Europe, virtual constructions of transnational selves in the blogosphere, the digital witnessing of religious tours by remote *Shankaracharyas*, or Web-based interconnectedness among the scattered following of the *Vallabh Sampraday*, online conduct of Indian migrant users involves the execution of identity projects. The specific shape of these projects is a complex product of reflexive choice-making and creative experimentation that reflects the offline existence of migrants as well as the particular nature of the WWW as a space to be and become. The inseparability of digital and physical realms surfaces in practically all the chapters. The way in which the Web's potential is utilized tends to be structured by the positioning of users in the 'real' world; by their ethnic and religious embeddedness, their socio-economic status in the place of residence, and their feelings of rootedness or alienation. Skop's analysis of the differential use of the internet for ethnic identity formation illustrates this influence of offline conditions and experiences.

The relevance of the constitution of the present-day WWW for the particular manifestation of identity projects relates to its nature as a social medium. Reflexivity online is inevitably a public practice and often a joint endeavor. It entails the making and remaking of the virtual self by means of the publication of ideas and impressions in the form of text, images, symbols and typography and design. This process is inherently communicative and should not be defined as solely a movement towards ultimate creative freedom and individualization. As Parker and Song (2006: 577) argue in their analysis of diasporic internet activity in Great Britain, self-projects cannot be disconnected from the 'collective experiences of large-scale social categories'. Parker and Song employ the concept of 'reflexive racialization' to explain how personhood online remains structured by pre-existing relations and classifications (2006: 590), albeit in ways that reveal the migrants' complex mixtures of loyalties and their grasp of the Web's potential. The latter is quite apparent in cases presented in this volume. Online practices of Indian migrants – indeed clearly shaped by ethnic, religious and class-based categories and affinities – show a distinctively agentive understanding[3] of the internet; a thorough awareness of the various ways in which ICT can be employed to serve the needs that come with the kind of existence that Mitra earlier referred to as 'Trans-Indian'.

---

3   Pacherie and Dokic (2006: 106) define an agentive understanding of action as an understanding of action that involves the awareness of 'the more complex relationships between an agent with a goal, the instrumental means used and the effects produced'.

Such an awareness, or agentive understanding, manifests in individual as well as collaborative quests. Saxena's exploration of Dalit politics, for instance, nicely illustrates how the success of (diasporic) grassroots activism results from a sensible utilization of online technology in strategies for mobilization and representation. As such, it can be argued that the reflexivity that Giddens linked to contemporary self-identity projects – shaped by mediated experiences and experiences of media – concerns more than just the contemplation of lifestyle options. Instead, the practice of reflexivity online includes lifestyle as well as the technology or means of its experience or experimentation and expression. In other words, migrant transnationalism in digital spaces involves a contemplation of self-identity that is inseparable from the assessment of the practical potential of the Web as an (incessantly expanding) system of information and communication which on one hand facilitates the reproduction of social, political, religious and cultural forms and on the other comprises an unprecedented instrumentarium for mixture and innovation.

It is obviously the awareness of this potential, as well as of the centripetal and centrifugal forces that can be generated by computer-mediated communication in diasporic contexts, which inspire the organizational online practices described in the chapters on 'Power'. A good example concerns the *Rashtriya Swayamsevak Sangh* (RSS). As Therwath (2012) notes, 'The RSS was quick to learn and tap the potential of the Web in order to bind together a heterogeneous and geographically spread-out community and transform it into an "imagined community"'. A belief in the economic potential of such an imagined online community shows in Santos' analysis of 'NRI Matters'. This Web portal, owned by a Mumbai-based marketing agency and sponsored by a bank, strategically explores the possibility of online interactions and exchanges to forge a 'powerful' community of non-resident Indians. Quite like Hindu-nationalists, their attempt to realize this community unsurprisingly involves the communication of standardized (and idealized) impressions of transnational Indianness. These appealing impressions relate to the projects of self-identity these conclusions focus on. They are composed to shape individuals' perceptions and practices of identity and delimit disconnecting eclecticism and flexible choice-making of migrant internet users.

The case of cyber-Hindutva suggests that, concerning their focus and ambitions, organized projects of community online closely resemble offline projects. For the *Sangh Parivar*, the World Wide Web serves as a platform for the articulation of these projects; a space that facilitates the broader process of a transnationalization of Hindu nationalism. The particular constitution of this space, however, complicates the effectiveness of such organized attempts of online community formation/fortification. This is not just because of the Web's inherent heterogeneity or its non- or counter-hegemonic propensity. Rather, this is because of its user-centeredness. Empirical examples throughout this volume indicate that today's Web is increasingly well suited to address the idiosyncratic needs of transnationally situated users. They reveal how, more than a space of integration, the diasporic Web functions as a highly versatile space where belonging can be experienced and community is practiced. As noted by Parker and Song, internet use thus helps to redefine 'the intangible moods, tones and embodied dispositions constituting the diasporic habitus' (2006: 577). Yet we have also seen that the diasporic Web is more than mainly a transformative element of pre-reflexive systems. In fact, the work of Anthony Giddens helped to explain the online presence of Indian migrants as often goal-oriented and highly reflexive. Their transnationalism online is inspired by the urge to connect and interact, and can for instance be directed at enhancing social capital[4] and participating in political, cultural or religious circuits. It is invariably marked by high levels of identity awareness, even when the primary objective of online transnationalism does not seem to be the actual negotiation or representation of the (collective) self. Perhaps we can draw from the realm of dialogical science (e.g. Hevern 2004; Hermans 2010) and thus conclude that the diasporic Web that emerged in this book appears to be an inherently dialogical space; a space in which practice inevitably involves social acts of positioning and repositioning through which unusually contemplated self-identities materialize.

References

Beck, U., Bonss, W. and Lau, C. 2003. The Theory of Reflexive Modernization: Problematic, Hypotheses and Research Programme. *Theory, Culture and Society*, 20 (2): 1–33.

Berger, P. L., Berger, B. and Kellner, H. 1973. *The Homeless Mind: Modernization and Consciousness*. Noida: Random House.

Ellison, N. B., Steinfield, C. and Lampe, C. 2007. The Benefits of Facebook 'Friends': Social Capital and College Students' Use of Online Social Network Sites. *Journal of Computer Mediated Communication*, 12 (4):1143–1168.

Giddens, A. 1991. *Modernity and Self-Identity: Self and Society in the Late Modern Age*. Stanford, CA: Stanford University Press.

Gilroy, P. 1993. *The Black Atlantic: Modernity and Double Consciousness*. Cambridge, MA: Harvard University Press.

Hall, S. 1990. 'Cultural Identity and Diaspora'. In: J. Rutherford (ed.), *Identity, Community, Culture, Difference*. London: Lawrence and Wishart: 222–237.

Hermans, H. and Hermans-Konopka, A. 2010. *Dialogical Self Theory: Positioning and Counter-Positioning in a Globalizing Society*. Cambridge: Cambridge University Press.

Hevern, V. W. 2004. Threaded Identity in Cyberspace: Weblogs and Positioning in the Dialogical Self. *Identity*, 4 (4): 321–335.

---

4   Ellison, Steinfield and Lampe (2007) introduce the concept of maintained social capital to explain the internet user's ability to stay connected with members of a previously inhabited community.

Pancherie, E. and Dokic, J. 2006. From Mirror Neurons to Joint Actions. *Cognitive Systems Research*, 7: 101–112.

Parker, D. and Song, M. 2006. New Ethnicities Online: Reflexive Racialization and the Internet. *The Sociological Review*, 54 (3): 575–594.

Therwath, I. 2012. Cyber-Hindutva: Hindu nationalism, the diaspora and the Web. *e-Diasporas Atlas*, April 2012.

Vertovec, S. 2009. *Transnationalism.* London: Routledge.

Index